THE
EQUATORIAL
EFFECT

An Alluring, Precarious Six Years in Indonesia

WM. STEELE TOLLISON

Printed Worldwide
First Printing 2024
First Edition 2024

10 9 8 7 6 5 4 3 2 1

ISBN : 979-8-218-45992-5

THE
EQUATORIAL
EFFECT

DEDICATION

For Raymond, Alby and Aldin

My time in Indonesia represents a significant portion of the story of how you came to be. Each decision, each stumble I made set a course that would bring each one of you into this world. This is our story and part of your history. I want you and any descendants to appreciate your rich, colorful heritage and important legacy. Beyond all national borders, this world, this planet belongs to you. Go forth, live happily, embrace it and it will embrace you.

TABLE OF CONTENTS

FOREWORD

It was early 1993 when I reluctantly accepted an overseas assignment that would transplant me from the comfort and routines of my Midwest American home, to Jakarta and the tropical unknowns of Indonesia.

Indonesia is a fascinating archipelago of more than 13,000 islands north of Australia, spanning 3,200 miles mostly south of the equator. Jakarta is the capital city, located on the island of Java.

This story begins as digital technology was in its infancy and barely available. Air travel was simple. America was inaugurating President Bill Clinton and Indonesia was approaching another important but dangerous crossroad in its turbulent history.

Several extensions transformed this one-year assignment into a then unthinkable six years; six years in a country that would forever change the course of my life.

An inherent interest in writing led me to chronicle the events I either observed or often lived. I share these chronicles, notes, records and recollections in this deeply personal story that tells of adventure, passion, danger and deceit. It unveils my efforts to manage (or at times, mismanage) complex events encountered along my path. That includes the obstacles I placed there myself.

Maintaining ethics and a healthy sense of self became a struggle as I ventured deeper into this alluring, foreign society. I was swept into the darker side of a proud and hopeful nation where at times, I came face to face with my own darkness. Fighting to pull out of the self-destructive tailspin that devours so many expatriates, I toiled against myself to climb to an altitude where self-respect, hope and aspiration for a solid future would surely await.

Along the way I encountered crooks, psychopaths, human traffickers and shameless corruption. This included the plight of one young woman, a pen pal who became ensnared by the modern-day, global trafficking networks that prey on the country's innocent. There were times when my life was preserved by a split-second decision or blind luck.

This story captures one exceptional period of my life along with its often-unintentional turns. It reveals my immersion and ultimate acceptance into Indonesian culture. My love of the country and respect for its people would eventually become apparent.

As Indonesia descended into the economic and political chaos of 1997-99, I worked to assist the American community there as well as protect my unanticipated new family, guiding them through the turmoil to a safer future in America.

This writing speaks of the best and worst of human qualities, mine included. It touches on betrayal, redemption, confrontation and the ultimate rewards of rescue. At times it's serious stuff. Other times it's downright funny.

I like to believe that above all, it's the story of a man who encountered many unknowns and strove to do the right things. In addition, of a father's fortuitous journey to build a life where three brothers would someday grow together.

1

ENTERING THE UNKNOWN

SETTING THIS IN MOTION

Four hours into the southerly flight from Hong Kong, dozens of small, densely forested islands slowly, silently appeared off the port like soft lily pads on the glassy emerald surface miles below. Above the wing, a distant orange flame from an offshore oil well struggled to cast its flickering light; the relentless approaching nighttime draining its brilliance like a vast, thirsty sponge.

Moments later, the tired cabin came alive with familiar indicator lights and electronic tones as a delicate oriental voice announced in three languages our descent and preparation for landing.

It had been a really long trip. Getting here required four planes, two long layovers, 28 hours in the air plus a restless overnight in Hong Kong. With stubborn confidence in my internal body clock and a usual ability to dilute any situation by applying logic, I now sat wearily in submission—humbled behind a seatbelt and disoriented by time zones, datelines, fatigue and a wristwatch that no longer made sense. In an exhausted, mental fog, I relied on the crinkled itinerary in my shirt pocket to confirm my whereabouts. I thought to myself, *if this is Saturday, this must be Jakarta!*

I didn't exactly volunteer for this gig. A few short weeks before, I carefully considered the offer of a one-year assignment based in Jakarta, Indonesia. The projects involved the construction of several massive energy facilities on the island of Java. Our company was part of a joint venture with three other international engineering and construction companies, each having equal but independent responsibilities. The scope of the work drew considerable international scrutiny because the World Bank was contributing funds. I was asked to coordinate the development of more than a dozen complex, multi-million-dollar equipment and service contracts – an administrative logistics role.

Having already logged five years with my own company, most of my assignments had been in support of infrastructure projects in remote areas of the lower 48 states. At this time, domestic business was booming and I was assigned to a satellite division based in Missouri. I lived north of Kansas City in Pleasant Valley, Missouri where I supported projects going on around the world. Other than the occasional domestic business trip, I stayed close to home. I wasn't planning on going anywhere. Perhaps working here wasn't the perfect job, but it was close enough.

The assignment they were proposing would put me in direct contact with governments, lawyers, administrators and technicians from at least nine different countries, some of which involved foreign languages. At the time, I could only speak English, Southern and a little bit of Pig Latin.

Considering this offer reminded me of a decade earlier and a previous engineering company. Back then, I was assigned to a four-year project in desolate, windswept Wyoming. There was a large, Rand-McNally world map on the wall of our remote, dilapidated field office. It was dirty, old and torn—taped back together in places by other personnel seeking shelter at one time or another. Sometimes when the unforgiving wind howled and the weather was dangerous, I'd stay inside and peruse that faded old map, wondering about all those exotic-sounding places around the globe.

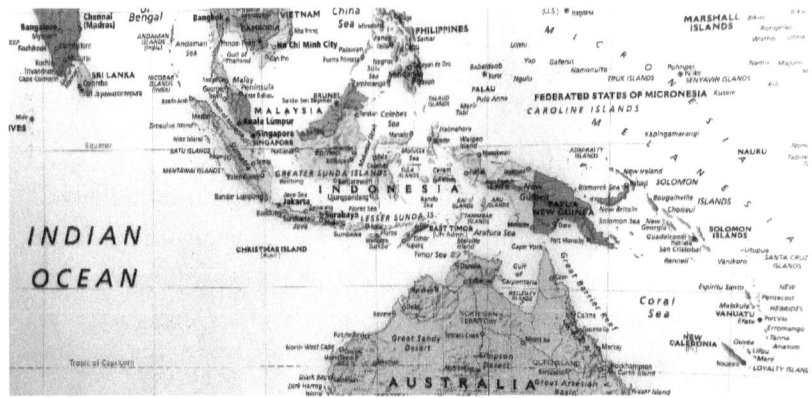

I specifically remember looking at Jakarta on that map. It was one of those curious, out-of-the-way places. *What was there? What was life like in that sleepy little dot on that big map?* It wasn't simply out of this country; it was 12 hours ahead of the Midwest and on the other side of the freakin' planet. Even back then, that impressed me—a guy who never thought for a moment he'd venture far outside the States. It seemed kind of odd to me, that old map, that old pondering returned years later to become a matter I'd have to seriously consider. Consider it, I did. That was a fair request.

I looked at the partner's offer from every angle. This included respect for what was going on in my personal life.

After 23 years in a lonesome, unconventional marriage, I had been single for about a year. I had just turned 42 with no children, no thoughts of ever having any and no other responsibilities except to myself. That took a bit of getting used to. So did dating, especially at my age.

My previous romantic history felt at times as though I had been barely surviving in a vast, barren desert for more than two decades—sadly clawing my way out into a lush, sultry oasis where all of life's fruits were mine to respectfully savor. I reached this new world a bit naïve, knowing little about modern relationships of the time. My intentions were good but at times it seemed that every step was followed by a misstep. I had a lot to learn and it was easy to embarrass myself. Still, it was far better than I had ever known.

Some dating experiences were disappointing. Others were amazing and worthy of nurturing. Alas, I learned about heartache, letting go and yeah, that stung. But a new year was upon me and the only path was forward.

As 1993 arrived, I started to see a tall attractive girl from Tulsa. She was about my age, highly educated, articulate and she turned heads. Leigh was an Administrative Vice President for an international organization in the Kansas City area. Nice as it was, there were sobering strings attached to this new romance. She was devoutly religious and an admitted micro-manager who could at times, be quite controlling. Leigh was surprisingly open-minded and quite forward in lots of areas that mattered to me. When she wasn't evangelizing, she was especially fun to be with.

Early on, she made it inordinately clear that long-term involvement with her required me to find, accept and love Jesus.

Hmm, let me consider that for a minute longer, I thought silently to myself. I possessed a smidgen of spirituality but there was nothing religious in my DNA. Still, we enjoyed one another and that had value.

I was around good friends and aside from that manageable religious pressure, I was experiencing sustainable intimacy for the first time in my adult life.

Personal relationships aside, I was nowhere near equipped with the specific credentials, education or experience to take on anything of these project's magnitude. My previous decades supporting construction, engineering and procurement throughout the U.S. were substantial but it was dwarfed by the size and complexity of this Indonesian venture. Add to that, I didn't consider myself to be nearly as organized as this assignment deserved. Sure, I could execute a complex task from Point A to Point B but I might wander off to Points C and D somewhere during the process. This precarious assignment could easily turn into career suicide, especially as a first international gig on the other side of the world. Everything in me signaled this was a scary proposition.

I carefully evaluated my accomplishments, trying to understand what made these folks believe I was the guy for this significant assignment. Was it simply because I was available and had a pulse? I had a strong background in operations, electro-mechanical installations and was often a hands-on, go-to guy when one of our projects hit a snag. I had also worked closely with attorneys, applying comprehension, people skills, research, preparing briefs and position papers. However, every detail I was learning about this assignment told me it required an experienced legal background along with supporting paralegals. That wasn't me.

~ ~ ~

Here in the Midwest, we generally worked five days a week and life was comfortable. I had a newly built home in Pleasant Valley, Missouri and an upward career path with a future so bright, I had to wear shades!

I concluded that this Indonesian opportunity was simply not right for me. Not now. After practicing my explanation, I presented my decision to the project team. Sure, I was apprehensive about their potential reaction but I respectfully declined the assignment. I breathed a little easier, knowing I had put this issue to bed.

After all, why on earth would I want to give up any of this for even a moment, much less a year? I proudly reasoned with myself.

On a cold afternoon in late January 1993, I was called to Jim Martin's office suite to hear his simple answer to this question.

Jim was 65, plus or minus. He was a tall, handsome man with a full head of white hair and a ruddy face that whispered secrets of too much good whiskey. I had been a guest at his home once and knew he enjoyed quality Scotch.

Jim was one of only four managing partners in a business that employed hundreds of contract and full-time professionals. He was smart with a long, deep knowledge of the industry. Jim suffered no fools and was notorious for being direct. Today would be no exception. For a moment we shared pleasantries and talked about a couple of projects I was working on. Then he got to the point.

"The project team tells me you decided against going to Indonesia," he tipped back in his chair and folded his arms. "The attorney we had there just quit and took a job in Manila. We showed your resume and experience history to our partners and they like you. We've committed to having someone in place before the end of February. So let me put this to you another way. Your job is there now. You need to hand off your current work, get your affairs in order and be on a plane in 22 days."

I was tempted to ask, *or else...?* But I had always enjoyed a good relationship with Jim and was wise enough to recognize this was not a request.

When I came to grips with the gravity of this development, I called Leigh to discuss options. I was considering leaving and finding another job. But oddly, Leigh was thrilled with this news, enthusiastically encouraging me to go. I wasn't nearly as thrilled.

"Seriously", she exclaimed. "There's no alternative?" I could hear her tapping her pen on her desk.

"Well, you wouldn't want anything else anyway. You'll always regret it if you don't take them up on their offer."

Offer? I thought. This may have once been an offer, but it was now a demand.

"It sounds like an awesome opportunity, an exotic location and challenging work," she reasoned.

Leigh was pulling out all the stops to convince me. "God is calling you, Steele. Just let go and let God." During that time, this was a common phrase adopted by evangelicals. I didn't respond. It wasn't what I needed to hear.

"This will make us stronger; we can make this work together," she said, applying her soft, compassionate voice. "I'll come visit you and umm...," she purred seductively. That made more of a dent in my armor.

I mulled it over on the drive home after work. I respected the team's predicament but knew it was ultimately my choice. Leigh's unanticipated reaction toward the assignment had jarred me into considering it from other perspectives. Becoming single a year ago had unlocked all sorts of positive changes in my world. And apprehensive as I was, I couldn't deny that this might be the key to still more. *But was I stepping off a curb, or stepping off a cliff?*

My resistance boiled down to just two honest concerns: can I really be effective in this unfamiliar role and more personally, how am I going to feel doing without—stepping backwards into another vast, barren desert, so to speak?

It seemed that many remarkably knowledgeable people were convinced I really was the right guy for the job. Who was I to argue with those learned observations? That vast, barren desert thing; well, there would be opportunities for visits. It was only for a year and at the time, I had plenty of years to spare.

The next morning, I accepted the assignment, albeit reluctantly. It was January 29.

The primary project team welcomed me aboard, including me in their meetings. I needed to learn as much as possible about this distant place where I would be living, and quickly. I had lived in 12 different states, worked in that many others and understood what was involved in moving around from state to state. But this would be different.

Much of the information about Indonesia and this assignment would come from communications with employees who were already there. They were people just like me who at one time or another had struggled with this same transition. They understood and were happy to share. I faxed questions to them in the evening and had their response the next morning. A lot of their personal and favorite things were not easy to find in Jakarta so they asked if I could bring small things when I came over; things like eyeglasses, a thermometer, a gardening hat, medications and baked goods from families. I found myself agreeing, which helped them build trust in me.

In the early 1990s, new digital technology was just that: new. In our office, we had begun to install our first desktop computers onto everyone's workstation. They were mostly a curiosity at this point. Classes on computer usage had started but the machines themselves would not become networked in-house or externally for months.

Cumbersome portable bag phones started to appear across the U.S., but were not widely used and certainly not dependable. We were talking about pagers and cell phones, but tower network systems were primitive and rare. For all practical purposes the Internet was nothing more than a vague, political campaign promise. Fax machines, desk phones, landlines and long banks of pay phones were the most established, dependable ways to communicate.

From my association with the Linda Hall Library in Kansas City, I learned that Jakarta was actually an enormous city and one of the major business hubs for all of Southeast Asia. Expatriates from many countries were there supporting various fields including banking, international relations, infrastructure, technology, agriculture, medicine, mining, energy and more. There was clearly more to this destination than that sleepy little dot on that big Wyoming map.

Preparing to leave—completing tasks at work, home and around town was all-consuming. I had to seamlessly transfer responsibilities to other staff. My external clients were not happy that I was leaving their projects because this can be disruptive. I didn't say it, but they'd have to take that up with the boss.

I spent the coming weeks scrambling to get my affairs in order, including finding a suitable tenant for my house. Most of my possessions had to be categorized, packaged and moved to long-term storage. I was allowed another 100-pounds of personal items for shipment. What to carry on the plane and what to check required careful consideration. This venture also needed new luggage and clothing suitable for the tropics.

Then, there was the matter of the brand-new Nissan I had bought just three weeks before. It had less than 1,000 miles on it but I had no affordable place to store it.

Before departing, I needed to assign a Power of Attorney, prepare my Last Will and Testament and sort through all my finances and personal obligations. There was a series of 12 vaccinations over an eight-day period to complete. Somewhere in all of this, I made a short trip to South Carolina to visit my aging father and establish an automatic bank transfer to help my family with his care.

Overwhelmed would be an understatement. Getting all this right was critical. It would be a long way home if I forgot something. It was a lot to accomplish in a short time but Leigh stepped up and applied her Franklin Planner and exemplary organizational skills to the task. She remained exceptionally encouraging and supportive of me taking the assignment as we worked tirelessly, side-by-side to pull all this together.

Leigh enjoyed difficult projects, approaching them with bulldog determination. She committed to managing my personal affairs and taking care of my Nissan at her home in Kansas City. Although our relationship was new, she promised to continue with those commitments as long as needed. We advertised and found a tenant for my house, leasing it just two days before my departure.

I flew out of Kansas City early the morning of February 19, crossing 12 time zones and landing in Jakarta as evening fell on February 20, 1993.

2

WELCOME TO JAKARTA, BAPAK

Into Another World

It was an eerie awareness being 12 hours ahead of the folks back home. The 747 bounced and lumbered along the concrete to the terminal where we would sit for far too long.

Departing the comfortable Cathay Pacific jet I thought, *this is far more surreal than I expected.* I felt like a groggy lamb in a field of a thousand wolves, moving into still another strange airport, lugging a year's worth of clothing, consumables, assorted personal papers and an unmistakable sense of denial. One at a time, I shook out my feet in front of me to get my land legs back to operational status.

As I walked, I wondered how I must appear to the people here. With a full head of dark hair, 5' 9" and no destructive habits, I was fit for my age. I dressed and carried myself well. Wearing my New Balance shoes, beige Dockers and a white Arrow button-down shirt, no one was going to mistake me for anything other than an American. The first Indonesians I saw were my height or smaller. *We'll get along fine!*

So here I was, a stranger in a strange land wondering, *am I really going to adjust here or will I fall flat on my face?* I reminded myself, *don't overthink this.* Borrowing a quote from Mark Twain, I thought, *I have been through some terrible things in my life, some of which actually happened.*

This was going to be my home for a while, so I needed to adjust my somewhat salty attitude. A hot shower and sleeping on something not moving would surely help.

I joined other worn-out passengers headed toward the banks of immigration counters where I would take my place in the long queue. I held my packs closely. When my turn to pass the yellow line on the floor finally came, I was relieved to find that the agent spoke English reasonably well.

He took my passport and asked, "Where you are coming from? Where you will stay in Jakarta? Business or pleasure?"

I answered his questions factually until he asked, "Anything for me, 'Pak?" ('*pok*, short for *Bapak*), (*bah-pok, a usually friendly term for sir*).

I thought he was just kidding around, making small talk. I didn't realize he was asking for money. He didn't seem to be doing anything, just looking at me for a response. After an awkward moment, he realized I didn't understand what he was hinting at.

"If you have something for me, just put it in here and close it." He handed me an empty manila folder. People in line behind me could easily see what was going on.

OK, I got it this time. I didn't have any Indonesian currency yet, so I put a U.S. $20 in his folder and slid it back across the counter.

His stamp promptly went to work on my passport and I was cleared through with a big smile and a, "Welcome to Jakarta, Bapak."

I had not expected an immigration agent anywhere in the world to so openly ask for a 'consideration' to do their job. But this was the way people did things, not just on this island, but throughout the country. It would take me several such events before accepting that in Indonesia, cash talks.

Waiting by the luggage conveyor, I pondered how I was going to handle all my stuff. Within minutes, there was a fully loaded backpack, a front pack and two large heavy suitcases to deal with. All the luggage carts had been checked out except... Ahah! There was one lone cart over along the south wall all by itself! I made a bee-line for it and in a flash, it was mine. I was ecstatic until realizing that one of its wheels was broken. *Of course it's broken*, I grumbled. As best I could, I situated the luggage onto the opposite corner from the broken wheel. Then off we went, kerthump, kerthump; pretending not to notice the hillbilly spectacle I was creating. Now, it was on to customs where they examined my bags but passed me on without incident; another perk from tipping the immigration guy earlier.

Along the high concrete walls leading out of the airport were six colorful money changing booths. They were little phone booth-sized enclosures decked out with posters and flashing lights resembling fortune-tellers rather than financial kiosks. Inside the booths, small fans pushed barely enough air to compensate for all the hot lightbulbs. I picked one that looked the safest and offered two brand new $100 bills to receive the attendant's advertised 'Rupiah' rate of Rp.2,600 to $1 USD. The attendant appeared to be maybe 25, unkempt, in a blue uniform that hadn't seen a washing machine in a while. Cramped in that small kiosk, he inspected each bill, using a magnifying glass while searching for any reason to devalue them. His shifty behavior previewed his next move.

"I give you Rp.2,200 because damaged."

"What damage?" I asked surprised. "These are brand new bills that just came from the bank. I've never even folded them. There's not even a wrinkle."

The attendant pointed to what he claimed was a dog-eared bend on one corner of one of the bills. The bill was pristine. But I understood immediately what he was doing. Still, I doubted I'd get a better shake at any of the other airport changers.

The evening was quickly progressing so I begrudgingly accepted his Rp.2,200,000, but only for one of my hundreds. I took the other one back. I'd learn that this damaged-money game was repeated by every money changer throughout the country, trying to stretch their earnings. I eventually got pretty good at playing it.

I struggled to keep my bags on the rickety luggage cart, pushing along with hundreds of weary travelers and their belongings. We were funneled through four exit doors into a sea of humanity waiting outside. Jakarta's early evening heat took my breath as I left the air-conditioned terminal, walking into the stifling humidity. Within moments, my shirt was wet.

Hundreds of unfamiliar faces formed a gauntlet as they waited on friends, family and customers. Scores of hands grasped for my bags, pulling me in one direction or another. I was right about the wolves!

"Taxi Meester?"

"Where you go, Meester?"

"Woman, Meester?"

"Hotel, hotel?"

In this roiling crowd, I again checked my zippers, pockets, wallet and luggage. I was desperate to keep track so nothing would be separated. Ahead I saw a clean-cut, uniformed man holding a professional-looking sign that read, *Bluebird*. To me, that looked like a voice of reason in an otherwise chaotic jungle so I steered in his direction and asked, "Hotel?"

"Oh yes, Meester, Jalan Sudirman (*su-deer-man street*)." His English was choppy but actually pretty good. "Meter or no meter, he asked?"

What's the difference? I wondered

"Meter please," I responded, handing him the hotel instructions provided by my employer. Later, I'd come to know that taxi drivers get a larger share of the fare if their passenger selects 'no meter'.

The driver flashed a perpetual happy grin, taking charge of my crippled cart. We hobbled further through the noisy mob as it continued to encroach on the steady flow of arriving passengers. Among the yelling and shoving, people continued putting their hands all over me. Other drivers were still grabbing at my bags, attempting to steal away the fare. Vendors were in my face, trying to sell all sorts of petty things I'd never seen before.

As we made our way out and beyond the hot, frustrating fiasco, I blurted, "This is fucking insane." No one even heard, much less understood what I'd just said. I couldn't even hear me.

The driver had a helper waiting by our Bluebird taxi. Dozens of other taxi/helper setups waited curbside. The two men were quickly loading my large bags into the trunk when the thought occurred that with all this chaos, they could easily drive off before I got in. As they reached for my two packs, I told them I'd like to keep those with me inside.

"OK, Meester," the driver said, as I quickly hustled into the welcoming back seat of the cool, quiet taxi.

After the chaos of the last 40 minutes, that taxi felt like an oasis. Anxiety gradually gave way to the kind of trust one develops when realizing you're not in control. Right or wrong, I began to accept that this driver had my back and knew what he was doing.

He wasted no time pulling away from the chaotic curbside, into the broad circle lanes that exit the airport's international terminal. We entered a straight four-lane highway; two directions separated by a 50-foot wide, shallow mote. The road was well lighted, smooth and resembled a nice section of an American interstate. On either side of the jungle-lined boulevard, the saltwater marshes and open water was just a couple of inches below the road's surface. This highway was built on reclaimed land. Further away from the highway, dozens of monstrous, lighted billboards grew out of occasional clearings in the tall tropical vegetation. Most billboards advertised foreign products and services from companies outside of Indonesia. These structures were easily four times the size of a typical American billboard.

At the road's edge, older men and women carved out enough space to hang their small kerosene lanterns so they could fish comfortably into the night. At a couple of points about a mile apart, I recognized heavy gates capable of closing off the entire road and all airport access. We must have traveled for another five minutes at high speed before passing under the large, ornate airport entrance monument. It was beautifully constructed, colorful and artistic with the theme of Indonesia's mythical, Ramayana characters.

We had travelled fast for about 10 full minutes without stopping or going through any towns.

"Good road," I leaned forward and told the driver.

"Is best road in Jakarta" he responded. "Yes, is new. Airport new."

I'd soon find out he was right. It really was the best road in Jakarta.

~ ~ ~

"You look Kevin Costner, you know him? He is friend?" asked the driver.

"I only know who he is. I do not know him," I replied.

I would later understand that Indonesians often compare Westerners with celebrities they've seen in films and other media. But Costner? That was a stretch.

I found myself respectfully mimicking the driver's use of language and it seemed to be working. He asked if I knew Bill Clinton and gave me a 'thumbs up' when I answered, "Yes." I would come to understand that Clinton, whether he knew it or not was a superstar in Indonesia, second only to John F. Kennedy.

In a few more minutes we entered the outskirts of the city—the reality of Jakarta. Once we were off the nice road, we encountered seriously congested traffic. Serious to me. Not to my driver.

I've never been able to find just the right adjectives to effectively convey the traffic, driving practices and that taxi ride over bumpy, often narrow roads to my hotel. At the time, Jakarta had more than ten million people packed into an area roughly the size of metropolitan Kansas City, which had around two million. Apparently, half of Jakarta's population comes from around the country for work. I had seen cities like this on television or in a film but to be in the midst of it—the smell, the taste of traffic pollution, the poverty, the tiny outstretched hands pressing against the taxi's freshly wiped windows. It reminded me of a scene from the film, *The Year of Living Dangerously*. It was a hot, harsh reality I had never imagined: far more impressive than that little dot on a map I used to wonder about.

Next to our taxi and as far as I could see, crowded, filthy buses belched thick black clouds of diesel exhaust. Reckless trucks with cargo hanging off the sides squeezed between lanes, their drivers forcing the rickety machines into space that simply wasn't there. Women in skirts rode side-saddle on small motorcycles that mixed and rapidly merged with taxis, three-wheelers, limousines and bicycles. Horns blared, engines revved and brakes squealed into an inescapable collage of relentless, deafening noise. Then there were folks dodging and pushing cumbersome, overloaded two-wheeled carts right through the middle of it all.

Drivers treated the white painted lane and directional markers and the green, yellow and red stoplights posted at intersections like mere recommendations. They didn't seem to be seriously associated with the control of traffic.

Jakarta seemed to have been decorated with colorful, modern road art to make its downtown resemble other world capitals. Tonight, this strange, tangled city was lit like the Las Vegas strip.

After a one-hour ride with speeds that ranged from turtle to 110-kph, we arrived at my hotel. I was so glad my driver knew my destination; I would have never made it if I had to navigate in this gigantic city.

The hotel crowd that greeted our arriving taxi was refreshingly smaller and certainly less intimidating than the mass of humanity at the airport. As we stopped under the huge welcoming canopy, six young men in crisp, matching uniforms politely surrounded the car. I was still holding tightly to my packs as I stepped once again into the stifling heat and unpleasant odors that defied identification. Perhaps it was better I couldn't identify them.

While the driver carried my other luggage to the curb, I counted out my fresh rupiah. The fare was the equivalent of about 18 dollars. I shook his hand and gave him about half that much again for a tip. That seemed to make him really happy.

"Oh, thank you, Meester." He handed me a napkin with his name and phone number scrawled across it.

"You need taxi, you call; you ask for me, OK Meester?"

"Puwanto, your name is Puwanto?"

"Yes, Meester, you call for me, OK?"

"Yes Sir," I responded.

"Aduh, Meester," then he was gone, looking for his next fare.

Before I could grab the first suitcase, two of the hotel's bellmen were there and spirited them onto an immaculate, shiny brass cart. I turned and walked into a clean, spacious five-star lobby a world away from the noise, heat and foulness just outside its doors.

With around 1,000 rooms, the recently completed hotel offered world-class accommodations. Like several other hotels in the city, it was built to accommodate the country's athletes and visitors from other nations during major sporting events in the capital city. When there were no major games going on, the hotel would accommodate business guests to maintain occupancy. The system seemed to work well, as the place seemed to be full.

Without realizing it, I had arrived in Indonesia just as Ramadan was about to begin. I didn't know what that was, but it was clearly a big deal to the Indonesians. I asked the concierge who explained it was a particularly important, month-long religious worship and celebration, "A time for peace, prayer, fasting and sharing."

The hotel was draped in fresh floral arrangements and colored electric lighting, quite like Christmas in the States. That helped explain all the banners and colorful road art.

The receptionist was a beautiful, slender girl with long black hair cascading to her thin waist. She wore a vivid green form-fitting, formal costume with gold trim around the neck and sleeves. Her costume was identical to that of other counter staff.

With English better than mine, she said, "Mister Tollison, welcome to Jakarta. We have your reservation. May I please see your passport?"

It was surprising how many people spoke English. My concerns about language were instantly dispelled.

I presented my passport and credit card and she completed the reservation.

"Mister Tollison, we will be keeping your passport for the duration of your stay with us."

"Excuse me," I said. "My passport must remain with me. I will need it for other agencies." After some friendly arguing and a consultation with the hotel manager, she agreed to make a copy and returned my passport.

This whole time, the bellman had quietly stayed right by my side. Obviously, he'd seen all this before. I received my key and started for the elevator that would serve the eighth floor.

Right away, the bellman took the key. "This way, Sir."

OK, so he was the guide and I was apparently just along for the ride.

Inside the elevator, he pushed the button for my floor and when the door closed, he offered still another, "Welcome to Jakarta, Bapak. You have girlfriend here?"

"No, just myself," I responded.

"Shall I bring someone for you," he confidently asked.

Surprised at this boldness, I just shook my head and grinned. "No, no thank you."

The bellman went into the room, turning on the lights and air conditioner, then unloading my bags from the cart. I gave him a Rp.10,000 note and away he went in search of his next arrival. It was 8:45 p.m. I took a moment to look around the room and get my bearings. Right away, I noticed the double shower was set-up for two athletes to share.

I was tired and hungry but there was no way in hell I was going to leave this room tonight. Airline cookies! Somewhere in one of my packs, there were a couple of packages of leftover airline cookies, pretzels or peanuts! Leftovers, along with a complimentary bottled water and I had dinner covered. *Welcome to Jakarta, Bapak*, I thought to myself.

I lay across that cool unfamiliar bed, taking a moment to reflect. This had all come about really fast. A month ago, I was content. I had my routines, my own bed, my new car, a stable career and all the other trappings of a productive, comfortable life. I felt good about my friends as well as my budding romance. Tonight, looking around this hotel room, stunned after traveling for well over 40 hours, I couldn't be any further away from that world.

I hadn't felt this far out of my comfort zone since being drafted back in 1970. But hey, I survived that, too. Enough looking back, sleep was not far behind.

3

STUDIES IN CONTRAST

The Logistics of Becoming an Expatriate

It was my first Sunday in this new world and the hotel was an especially busy place. This would be my quarters until I found a permanent place to live. Sports teams, tourists and business guests from around the world came and went at all hours like honeybees around a hive. The majority appeared to be Japanese and Australians. There was a lot of oil and manufacturing money in the region.

In the main and smaller lobbies on each floor, it was common to encounter solicitors: assertive, well-dressed men in fitted suits or bellmen covertly offering to arrange personal services in the form of female companionship. It created a constant risqué undertone, especially when my phone rang in the middle of the night. Talking with associates, I learned this goes on at all major hotels in Indonesia's larger cities. I filed that in my memory bank under dangerous, unofficial business.

On this morning, I enjoyed the hotel's international buffet breakfast, even though it lacked recognizable coffee. I spent most of my day walking several blocks in one direction, then the same in the others while getting a feel for my locale. Heading south two blocks, I came upon a mall-like shopping center called Ratu Plaza. I was looking forward to my first venture into an Indonesian store. Climbing the marbled steps and through the large, glass doors, I was surprised to see an American A&W restaurant!

That morning, less than a dozen of the mall's stores were open. This wasn't because of any particular religious observance, but because the place was still under construction. More stores would open as spaces were completed. Workers who lived on the site toiled behind plywood partitions, hammering, drilling and pouring concrete, 24/7. The local craftsmen slept and worked in shifts. Unless it was a national or religious holiday, work of this nature never stopped.

I walked through each of the open stores, looking at children's clothes, wire rat traps, table radios, high-end watches, jewelry and a hoard of other things displayed together on the same tables. I took my time, ambling aimlessly. I truly had nothing more important to do.

That said, I did know what I'd be doing for an early dinner and this time it wouldn't be pretzels and peanuts. I left Ratu Plaza with my A&W burger, fries and packets of strange-colored ketchup that turned out to be *sambal*, a particularly spicy hot sauce. Familiar foods would get me by until I could learn about local cuisine.

Walking back to the hotel, a soft warm rain began to fall. Steam danced from the hot streets and sidewalks like mysterious, translucent genies escaping a bottle.

Being just south of the equator, Indonesia has two primary seasons. I arrived in the middle of Jakarta's wet season; October through May, when localized, sometimes serious flooding was common. The dry season is generally June through September. The change from one to the other occurs within a couple of days. The temperature fluctuated very little, usually between 78 and 88-degrees Fahrenheit. The muggy, high humidity was constant.

Early mornings at my hotel presented a laughable picture if I sort of squinted as I looked. Heading off to their morning's business, the Japanese left in limos, the Italians in B'mers, the Australians in taxis followed by us Americans on foot.

In line at Monday's breakfast buffet, I met another American who had business with our primary project. He knew the way to our office so when my sandwich was ready, off we went. Above eight smoky lanes of traffic, through a labyrinth of makeshift little villages along our hot, humid walk, we carried our briefcases and later, our white plastic bags of dirty laundry for housekeepers in our neighborhood to wash. Times had changed for this new kid in town.

My first day at the office was also the first day of Ramadan. Building on what I had learned from the hotel concierge, Ramadan lasts a month and its start date varies from year to year. It's marked by spiritual growth, kindness, patience and fasting. Ramadan is one of the five Pillars of Islam which includes declaring one's faith, sacrificing worldly comforts in order to help others, daily prayer, fasting and an eventual pilgrimage to Mecca. During fasting, healthy Muslims should abstain from eating, drinking and having sexual relations from dawn to sunset. After sunset, all bets are off! Folks with health considerations are encouraged to first, take care of themselves.

I was too new and awkward to realize our Indonesian colleagues had begun their fast at dawn. Here I was, enjoying a breakfast sandwich with my warm tea, paying no attention to my Indonesian friends who were fasting.

"Would you like some of this sandwich," I asked our receptionist.

"No thank you, Mr. Steele," she politely responded.

A moment passed before I realized what I had done. My new friends were especially gracious in helping me understand what they were doing.

"We will abstain from eating until nighttime, then we will eat a lot," she explained.

Jamitri chimed in, "Yes, Mr. Steele, and we will get very grumpy and sleepy by afternoon."

Jamitri was one of our self-titled 'Office Boys.' Regardless of his own fasting, he would have warm, morning tea on our desks, six days a week. Jam, as he became known, was in his early 20's. He came from a distant village where he had finished high school then headed to Jakarta to find work. Like other Indonesians in our office, he supported our team but under the jurisdiction of our Indonesian engineering associate. Jam had been working there more than a year by the time I arrived. Eager to learn and with a great personality, he turned out to be helpful, honest and knowledgeable of the country and its culture. I leaned on him for information and he practiced his English with me.

I didn't like referring to our staff as 'boys', so I asked Jamitri, "How about I give you the new official title of *Office Liaison*?"

Jam was proud to have it.

~ ~ ~

Before long, I was getting into the swing of the work while learning about my American and Indonesian coworkers. I hadn't met most of the Americans before. Some I knew from the Missouri office. I had worked with our engineering manager on three projects back in the States. He took me around to the individual offices and workstations, introducing me to our combined staff. It was a warm welcome at every stop.

Some of the American staff were career expatriates, moving from country to country in support of international work. These professionals along with their families, seldom returned to the States, and that was just fine with them. Other staff members were short-term specialists, flying in for a specific task before returning home a month or so later. Most were like me, here on a one-year assignment. Most solo expats and families assigned to these projects enjoyed being there. A few only saw the negative and complained a lot. So far, I was excited to be in Jakarta.

~ ~ ~

Throughout my early days, our team often met with our partners at their headquarters. Their conference rooms were on the eighth floor of an older, open-air building. There was no air conditioning but a wide, covered deck just outside protected the rooms from direct sunlight. The slow, Indian Ocean winds at that height made the rooms reasonably comfortable.

During this period, the meetings were usually less than three hours. Rick Wilder, our Jakarta Project Manager said that would change next month when Ramadan is over.

Wilder was a savvy, salty character who had crossed paths with many of the people I had worked with on projects back in the States. His primary background was in metallurgy, non-destructive testing, military-grade welding and inspections at the government level. He taught and often gave talks regarding these specialties. The engineering industry considered him an honorary professor.

Wilder and I stood on that deck one afternoon looking west, counting 52 tower cranes in that one, narrow direction. Jakarta was in the midst of an unbelievable building boom.

~ ~ ~

Although new to this foreign assignment, I had a good idea how the projects were structured. The Indonesian government required all foreign contractors doing business in-country to have a fully autonomous Indonesian engineering associate. A good relationship with this associate could help achieve legitimate business goals that may not fully comply with Western laws. Therefore, our associate was important. If something such as a personnel matter or request for a gratuity needed attention, our autonomous associate could take care of it under Indonesian law. That might well include any number of discreet matters occurring outside of project business. I'd learn that working with our associate wasn't always above board, but ultimately, it was a win-win.

Our Missouri office and Jakarta project team were providing engineering and design services. Additionally, we would prepare all the procurement contract documents that when ready, would be awarded directly by our partners to suppliers, manufacturers and service organizations from around the world.

Our primary partners and Indonesian engineering associate were closely involved every step of the way. They controlled what went in to each contract, any modifications, the timing of milestones and which suppliers were allowed to bid.

With varying complexity, each contract package would have hundreds of pages of technical text, records of all discussions and agreements, price breakdowns for every component, start and completion schedules along with detailed engineering drawings for everything being provided by a supplier.

Our team did not award the contracts, our partners did. Our job was to create every contract, explain them, then re-write them until our partners were in their best position to award them. It was common to re-write a contract more than a dozen times, often reverting to its original form just before being awarded. Each one would take months and require hundreds of man-hours to complete.

My role was to catalog those works in progress, monitor the status of each page, each change, then expedite our work toward readiness. The structure worked, but had its frustrations.

Around the hotel, unique landmarks made it easy to stay oriented. But our office was located in a residential area where many of the homes and streets looked alike. I found out the hard way that even for Indonesians, it was easy to get lost walking around Jakarta. I quickly learned to pay more attention.

Walking to and from work became a choice that provided exercise, saved considerable time and a little bit of money. For example, a taxi from the hotel to our office was only about four dollars. But, because of poor traffic planning, complex directional routing and lack of exit points, taking a taxi could often take us 45 minutes to an hour each way. A taxi from the hotel required a ride through incredible congestion a kilometer north into the city just to reach the nearest turn-around point. From there, the drive took us two kilometers back south, past our office. Then we turned around once more, heading back north before accessing the proper lane to reach the actual exit to our office. It was laughable and only practical during heavy rain.

I enjoyed walking the mile or so because if I didn't stop to talk, it was easily 30 minutes less than taking a taxi. But I always stopped to talk.

~ ~ ~

The muggy, morning walk through the city's perpetual construction areas held an array of serious challenges. Our established morning route seemed at times a bit like a video game. The object was to maneuver around chunks of jagged concrete and nail-filled boards, into and out of the chaotic street. We moved quickly to get around open manholes and deep pits in what might seem to be a sidewalk. The rules were simple and few. If you were hit by oncoming traffic, fell into a pit, got nabbed by a thief or otherwise injured yourself: Game Over!

There was an added dimension to the game when the morning rains were heavy. While taking this route during severe street flooding, a coworker was unable to see that someone had removed a submerged manhole cover. He stepped into a deep, concealed manhole leading to a filthy street sewer. Despite the jagged concrete and rebar, he crawled out of the dirty, neck-deep hole with only a handful of cuts and abrasions.

Limping back to the hotel, his only consolation was a long hot shower with his nasty clothes still on. Then he self-administered first aid consisting of cotton balls and Listerine, living to tell the story.

From my hotel, walking to the office required crossing a long, curious pedestrian footbridge spanning eight lanes of unpredictable traffic. The dangerous roadway, *Jalan Sudirman*, was a major artery leading from downtown south to a dozen smaller communities. Throughout its history, the metal footbridge had clearly been an inviting canvas for graffiti artists and others leaving initials or disgruntled messages. On the wide stairway leading up, someone had long ago added the black spray-painted letters, 'Funky Street.' That stood out and seemed to inadvertently, yet appropriately represent this socioeconomic crossroad. To most people, the large bridge was already a landmark and well-known point of reference. Being the observant expat I was, I started calling it the *Funky Street Bridge*. That quickly caught on among other Americans along with our Indonesian friends.

Up the iron stairway, hundreds per hour of the 'haves' and the 'aspiring' on their way to and from work stepped around a dozen or more grossly disfigured beggars too crippled to have gotten there by themselves. At dawn, opportunists deposited these people on the landing where all day, they displayed their anatomical atrophies as the only advertisement for badly needed rupiah. Captive crossroads like this were the one time the public had no choice but to come this close to so many seriously unfortunate souls. It was sad and awkward for me. I'm sure it was for everyone crossing this bridge. But we crossed, careful to show respect.

Indonesians and expatriates routinely carried a little extra money to share with those in need. Coins landing in the wide-mouth metal cans sounded like hail on a tin roof. Rain, shine or blistering heat, this ritual went on every day. Each time I crossed, I knew that whatever I shared would never mask that painful image, or the sorrow I felt walking so closely among these folks.

Further across the bridge, one of many haggard vendors unfolded an aged canvas, displaying his life's inventory of lighters, locks, flashlights, belt buckles and the inevitable selection of cheap, plastic wristwatches.

I sometimes felt there might be a lesson hidden somewhere on the Funky Street Bridge. I didn't expect it would ever reveal itself.

~ ~ ~

At the end of my second week, our office received a bulletin from the U.S. Embassy in Jakarta advising Americans to remain cautious. There had been a serious, terrorist bombing in the basement of New York's World Trade Center. Not so long ago, I had coffee at a Starbucks in one of those basements. Oddly, I seemed to be the only one concerned about the embassy's message.

Another bulletin reached us a couple of days later, alerting to a developing situation near Waco, Texas. Time would show these types of alert bulletins were routine. In the years ahead, they would become even more serious to expats in Indonesia, but I didn't know that yet.

~ ~ ~

Aside from work, my other priority was finding a place to live. My initial hotel expenses were covered but the goal was to find more permanent housing as soon as I could. Once out of the hotel, I would receive a generous monthly allowance to apply against the total cost of living.

Jakarta offered several levels of accommodation. Because of the extreme traffic and limited, dilapidated roads it was wise to live close to the workplace. Most of our expats lived within three or four miles. They had knowledgeable drivers but it still took them 45 minutes to get to work. A drive of 10 or so miles in either direction might easily have cost them two hours.

Small, so-called luxury apartments within secure complexes ran an average of $3,500 a month. During that time, the same apartment back in Kansas City would have been about $800. Single-family homes were about the same as luxury apartments, but I'd also need to cover costs for household staff and essential security. Many of our expats, especially those with families simply bit the bullet and spent their entire allowance as well as a significant portion of their salary to live well. I wasn't a cheapskate, but the pricing seemed extravagant.

Jakarta had no secrets. Those people who controlled the expat housing market were well aware of these housing allowances and priced their offerings accordingly.

During my second week, a friend introduced me to an Indonesian lady who represented numerous owners throughout the local housing community. Ibu Fani (Ms. Fah-ne) contracted with foreign businesses to help expats find accommodations. She showed me eight offerings but for some suspicious reason, and regardless of location or condition, they were priced about the same as my allowance. I quickly realized the landlords had locked up the local accommodation industry for expatriates. Unless I wanted to spend everything I was making, I'd have to search exclusive of this sewn-up industry.

I thanked Ibu Fani, telling her, "I'll call you if I need your help."

She responded with a polite but snarky, "I am sure you will, Bapak."

I never did.

I spent nearly three weeks at the hotel, mixing 11-hour workdays with late nights combing this jumbled, capitol city for affordable housing. Living out of suitcases was getting old but I was not about to cave into the expensive housing trap.

Night after night, the televisions in the hotel lobby were obsessed with grim news about the ongoing siege in Waco, Texas. I wasn't particularly concerned with news from the States. My focus was on getting out of the hotel.

~   ~   ~

Out of the blue, one of our office drivers told me about a small, nearby apartment being renovated. He had been talking with a worker across the street who mentioned it to him. I thanked the driver and provided a customary 'envelope' for favors shared between friends.

The apartment was in an old, once-elegant three-story structure from the 1960s. The complex was maybe 200 feet long and 60 feet front to back.

Much of the entire building seemed to be slowly undergoing different levels of renovation. Because of its age, peeling paint and street appearance it was mostly ignored by Western expatriates. I had seen this building every day for two weeks but hadn't realized it was an apartment building. There were 18 very small apartments at ground level and around 20 larger, substantially more expensive apartments on the two upper floors. Most of the ground-level units had been out of service for a long time and were gradually being refurbished. Construction took place during the workweek, but not at night or weekends.

The small studio I viewed had a bedroom, bathroom and kitchen. The bathroom had a single shower, vanity and important to me, a Western-style toilet. It had a standard front door and oddly, a smaller, secret-like servant's door that led to a service area somewhere out front. A big selling point was its rotary telephone with direct international access. To say the little apartment was tight would be an understatement, but it would suffice.

Worn down as it was, the building's exterior silently spoke of a bygone era where Dutch architectural influence gave way to modern, international designs. Facing the street, large white columns framed a series of elaborate, half-round balconies with potted palm trees on the two upper floors. Stately Asian Elm trees flanked the circular drive and supported a rusty barricade-type gate which I would have to operate manually. The building's interior was aged, but attractive and welcoming.

From the receiving area at the center, the entrance led to a beautifully preserved sunken lobby lined from floor to ceiling with gorgeous, ceramic tile and accenting marbled fixtures. Large ceramic pots held colorful plants filling the open air with exotic, seductive fragrances of honeysuckle, frangipani and orchid. Covered chairs, sofas, benches and slow overhead fans provided plenty of opportunity to hang out and enjoy this quiet break from the world outside.

Around Jakarta, other similar structures as well as large elegant homes built through the 1960s were majestic but lacked modern utilities and were significantly more costly to maintain. At the time I arrived, the exterior of this once-stately complex was showing its age but the common interior areas were clearly exceptional. Also exceptional was its location. It was very close to my office and certainly convenient.

When I first looked at the little-bitty apartment, the electricity was not on. It was dark, musty and still filled with debris from renovations. It awaited window coverings, lighting, hot water and other key appliances most Westerners would expect. But when those were installed, it was cleaned out and the air conditioner was operating, it became my place. The owners provided a full-size bed with bedding, a kitchen table with chairs and a two-burner, gas cook stove. Also included was a mirrored desk/dresser with a drawer that regardless of generous applications of WD-40, squeaked loudly every time I closed it.

Having observed Jakartan landlords taking advantage of expatriates, I was now bypassing them and negotiating directly. Still, this 400 square foot efficiency would cost me as much as a decent studio in New York City. But that was OK. I could still save two-thirds of my housing allowance. An added bonus was being able to walk to work in two minutes and save on transportation. I would not have to rent an expensive car or hire a driver like most expatriates. Nor would I have to spend hours each week coming and going in snarled, smoky traffic. With the Indonesian vice-president's compound six blocks away and the Russian embassy staff next door, it was a quiet and stable neighborhood.

~ ~ ~

Over the next few weekends, Jamitri and other Indonesian staff offered to help me find essential furnishings and household necessities to make my stay more comfortable.

My new friends took me around the communities to little shops, small restaurants and places they enjoyed. We shared meals, practiced languages and formed what I felt would become lasting bonds.

They taught me how to haggle over prices. "Shopkeepers and merchants expect you to negotiate. Half off is easy. Keep haggling, be persistent and you can get even more discount."

A toaster, hi-wattage power converters, electrical cords, lamps, kitchenware, rattan nightstands; my friends knew where to get the best deals. At this point, they understood what I needed much better than I did.

Soon, I had moved in. A week later, my 100-pound shipment from the U.S. arrived at one of the air courier terminals downtown. Rather than waiting for them to schedule delivery, a driver and I took a light truck and picked it up, saving a week or more. It was good to have everything in one place.

~ ~ ~

From the lobby in the center of my unique apartment building, a wide artistic marbled staircase lined with fragrant blooming plants curved upward to service the larger, upper apartments. From there, it wound onward toward the rooftop and gradually fanned out to unveil a secluded pool that was open to the vast nighttime sky. It was pleasingly quiet. On all sides of the dimly lit pool, potted palms, tropical plants, a manmade waterfall and subtle, blue lighting enhanced the alluring décor. Left of the pool was an old wooden bar standing silent and abandoned—its empty shelves, cabinets and tattered stools a testimony to the patrons who decades before had shared drinks, stories and the scandalous secrets of this seductive rooftop oasis.

Despite its plastic pool chairs, chaise lounges and plastic tables, it still created an interesting, mysterious place as night fell. I imagined a forgotten romantic era when it might have hosted foreign journalists, sneaky spies, deal makers, exotic cocktails and ladies in long evening dresses: an edgy ambience not unlike that of Bogart's *Casablanca*.

Two housekeeping families lived, did laundry and serviced the entire building from three small, un-air-conditioned rooms in the rooftop's fourth quarter. I seldom saw them but they cleaned my apartment and laundry for an equivalent of about eight dollars a week, paid to the management. A daily, 1,000-rupiah (*50 cent*) tip left on the kitchen table meant a 25 percent increase in my housekeepers' daily salary. They took good care of me.

The high rooftop was available all hours. Moments spent there provided a brief sanctuary from the troubling noise, sights and smells on the streets below. Three floors above my new home, I sat alone by that calm blue pool, taking in a fading orange sunset. An epic, white cockatoo watched me watching him against a continuously evolving skyline. This rooftop was unusually comfortable and serene; an environment as good as it gets in Jakarta.

Behind this building and out of view, the contrasts were stark. Just 30 feet below the lush plants and decorative masonry wall, a thin row of makeshift shanties with rusty tin roofs teetered over a foul open sewer. In a narrow space wedged between the backs of these two tall buildings, dozens of little makeshift homes backed against high walls topped with menacing, embedded glass shards all along its top edge. The walls shielded the elegant, ground-level mansions and the two vastly different cultures from one another. From the shanties below, thick blue smoke from burning garbage rose and dissipated like streaming tentacles weaving between skyscraping sculptures, northward out into the modern Jakarta skyline.

Children played, dreamed and grew along the sewer's edge below. Good people lived and died, sandwiched in a long, narrow contaminated world-between-worlds no more than 25 feet Wide.

As the end of my first month concluded, Eid Al-Fitr, which celebrates the end of Ramadan, was approaching. Businesses began closing or limiting hours. The city was slowing down. People with luggage, cloth bags and cardboard boxes secured with tape and string boarded overloaded buses and trains. In a mass exodus, they made their way back to remote villages to spend time and share this important holiday with family. As Jakarta's population was escaping the city for the holiday, I began to enjoy being there on my own. Each day, I gained a better sense of the culture, the language, my work and my new friends.

Indonesia was approaching 250 million people and growing rapidly. It hosted the world's fifth-largest population, including people of amazingly different cultures. The country rightfully boasted of beautiful mountains, endless beaches, clean air and unspoiled solitude. But not in Jakarta. Jakarta was a busy, dirty city where services, public safety and infrastructure had to wait for other priorities. It was clearly a city of extreme contrasts. Nonetheless, it was fascinating to experience.

With more than 50 years of independence, this ancient country had just begun to tap its vast, natural resources, including its people as it rapidly moved forward. I could see that with careful planning, stability and lots of luck, the less favorable contrasts throughout this city would diminish over time. I didn't know then, that I would eventually become immune to them, like most other expatriates.

4

ESSENTIAL ADJUSTMENTS

BECOMING A BETTER LISTENER

I had been in-country a few weeks when it hit me. No, not some bright idea, a severe stomach bug. My system was fighting against Jakarta's food-borne bacteria, and it was a painful transition. I was one sick expat for three days, unable to keep anything on board. The Indonesians kept recommending charcoal tablets to get my nausea under control. I wasn't going for that.

"Charcoal, you mean like burned ashes?" "C'mon, guys, really?"

Instead, I eventually rode miserably in the back floorboard of a Kijang to see an international doctor. She administered intravenous fluids and sent me home with an over-the-counter prescription for what else? Charcoal tablets!

Like others, I'd learn by trial and error that in Indonesia, I had to be prepared to take care of myself. If I got hurt or sick, I'd likely be on my own for a while. During the following months, that would happen several more times. My system gradually acclimated and I got better at selecting safe foods. I also collected a decent supply of Imodium, Pepto Bismol, Neosporin, bandages, antiseptics and yep, charcoal. Don't leave home without it.

~ ~ ~

Before long, I realized that expats often socialized together during and after work. In fact, they seemed to cluster together, not reaching out to the Indonesian communities. It was that birds-of-a-feather syndrome. During the week and especially on weekends, it seemed someone was always hosting an expat get-together at his or her home. The hosts generously extended invitations and declining was perfectly acceptable.

If a bajaj showed up bringing someone, they knew right away who it was. The bajaj had become my trademark ride. These little orange and black, three-wheeled go-carts were powered by a two-stroke, one-cylinder engine that made a distinct metal-on-metal clanking sound. They held a driver and two passengers. If need be, the Indonesians could squeeze in four passengers. Allowed only on back roads and side streets, they were cheaply made and cheap to hire.

Kind of like me, I often joked.

I sincerely appreciated the invitations offered by my fellow expats and over the years, attended many, but I was more likely to hang out with the Indonesians. Although being with the locals was sometimes awkward, most times it was fun. They knew their way around the city. They showed me places and things many expats failed to experience. They looked out for me and I for them. I knew living here was a once-in-a-lifetime opportunity so I made the most of it.

By now, finding good food was no longer a problem. Deciding where to go was. Depending on work priorities, many of the expats would go to lunch together. Most often, I would go across the street to my apartment and nap for a half hour. When I ate out, one of many favorite lunch places was the American Club. It was an official Embassy facility that served Jakarta's American expatriate community. Behind its compound gates was a nice restaurant, large swimming pools, tennis courts and other sporting opportunities.

To utilize the club's full services required an expensive membership. Since I seldom patronized the place, I was not a member. Plenty of our American expats were members, so tagging along as a guest was perfectly acceptable. They served quality American and Indonesian cuisine. Lunch and dinner were open to Americans and their guests.

~ ~ ~

The colossal Blok M area was the main southern depot and hub for the city's buses to terminate or transfer onto other routes. Its entire area included around nine city blocks or around 36 acres. The area was also home to hundreds of kiosks and services, a dozen malls, numerous international banks and probably 100 restaurants of one size or another.

The Pasaraya at Blok-M was Indonesia's most prestigious department store. It was owned by President Suharto's oldest daughter. It was an unusually large six-story building, not including the basement level that housed its immense food courts. Occupying a quarter of a city block, it contained countless square feet of food, services and retail space.

Among other convenient food spots in the Blok M area was Bakmi Gagamada, famous for its nasi and bakmi goerengs. These fried rice and noodle dishes coupled with chicken, pork or shrimp became a mainstay for me.

Blok M was a 15-minute walk from my place, making it a great option for getting a quick dinner. It provided an exceptional variety: dozens of affordable local foods along with well-known Western options. With an open mind and curious pallet, I quickly became a fan of most Indonesian foods. Of course, there were exceptions like durian, a heavy fermented spiny fruit notorious for a bad smell that kept it banned from close quarters such as airplanes. Then there was *ikan jengko*l (stinky fish), an especially odiferous, fermented fish that was popular among older Indonesians. It lived up to its name.

In the downtown city center, Jakarta's large, international hotels served wonderful foods for those wanting more upscale dining. Their Sunday brunch buffets were world-class and quite popular. Downtown also hosted the newly-built Hard Rock Café staffed by cool, savvy Indonesians. Inside, it was easy to forget where you were.

Another restaurant popular with global expatriates was famous for its stone steak. The delicious Australian steak arrived at the table on a 600-degree flat stone, allowing the patrons to cook it themselves to their liking. With dark, cramped tables and drunken expats dealing with dozens of 600-degree stones, what could possibly go wrong? Occasionally, it did.

Back in Kansas City, Leigh had worked out a communication schedule where we'd talk a week for about an hour. I happily assumed responsibility for the cost. There were still no affordable cell phones, so this was all by long-distance land lines. Because of her position, Leigh received a 35 percent discount on all her local, long-distance and international calls. The discounted charges went to her then I reimbursed accordingly.

Even with her discount, that four hours a month still cost $600. Usually, we'd talk on my Saturday night which was her Saturday morning. I'd send her one ring to let her know I was ready. Then she'd call me back. After our call, I'd usually take time to go outside, walk around the community or enjoy the lobby's peaceful solitude while having my dinner.

In early 1993, credit cards were not widely accepted outside the large hotels. We relied on cumbersome American Express traveler's checks. It was a good idea to keep at least Rp.100,000 (*about $39*) in small bills on you when you were out and about. That would get me a haircut, a good meal, a beer or two and a taxi ride downtown and back.

I was safely and comfortably living alone with much smaller expenses yet receiving a similar allowance to our expats with families. Including an already-lucrative salary back home, I was now making an exceptional amount of money: more than I had ever made before. I was saving most of it. By year's end, I opened overseas accounts with BCA and Citibank in Indonesia, and the Isle of Man in the U.K. This was in addition to funding my accounts back in the States.

All around the city, including the prestigious Pasaraya, men's haircuts included the 'full treatment.' Getting a haircut began with a wash, rinse, conditioning and a second rinse. This was followed by a slow scalp, face, shoulder, arm and hand massage. The full treatment took about 45 minutes. If for any reason I didn't want full treatment, I needed to say so or else I was going to get it. It was always a pleasurable experience and cost about $4. My tip usually doubled that.

Massage and bath salons were respectable establishments located all over the city. Patrons included Indonesians and expatriates, male and female. Salons offered a standard one-hour massage for about five dollars. The massage ladies would giggle and ask, "*Sehat atau bahagia?*" (Happy or healthy?) Happy was a couple of dollars more.

5

THE GOOD, THE BAD and THE GRITS

Always Carry Cash

In mid-April 1993, my former project team asked if I could arrange to come back to Kansas City for meetings and help clarify transition issues with our project clients. With some rearranging of responsibilities in Jakarta, I was soon on another 40-hour trans-Pacific journey. Along the way, I had a long lay-over in Hong Kong. But this time, there were no overnight stays like those I experienced on my maiden trip in February.

This short trip allowed me to take care of a few things at the office, check in with the new tenant renting my house and spend time with Leigh. She seemed to enjoy the colorful fabrics I had brought her from Jakarta.

April in the Midwest was warming up nicely. I helped Leigh with her yardwork, removing overgrown brush and spreading topsoil. We enjoyed one another's companionship as well as the romantic intimacy. But she never missed the chance to somehow remind me that I should be growing religiously. For example, she mentioned the first *Jakarta Chronicle* I had sent to her. While other friends and family enjoyed it, she was embarrassed to share it because it contained no reference to spirituality, especially mine.

"It's nothing more than a shallow travelogue that lacks personality and could have been written by anyone." Her usually pleasant face contorted into a frown. "Where's God in your writing?" she complained.

"Ouch!" Once again, I felt her message.

Leigh was born into a large, devout community where her religion was lovingly, but aggressively taught from birth, then substantiated throughout her life. I was not. She considered religion in everything she did. I did not. She was chastised, laden with guilt and even punished for questioning her religious teachings. I found that cruel and archaic.

I wondered, *would any of this have changed had I immersed myself in her religion? Would she be content with me pretending, like she saw so many in her circle of friends doing? Would it not be hypocritical to feign acceptance when that's not who I am?*

After expressing such profound disappointment, in the same conversation she softened and told me, "I get really lonely and regret having encouraged you to take the assignment."

I sensed cracks widening in our relationship. She did, too. But the fruits we were both enjoying were simply too fulfilling to ignore.

~   ~   ~

While back in the States, I picked up a few more personal things requested by my American colleagues in Jakarta. For myself, I bought two large jars of Jiffy peanut butter and six boxes of Quaker instant grits.

The day before my return flight, our HR Administrator asked me to transport a small shipment of 'Hepatitis A vaccine' for our resident expat families in Jakarta. Several families were due for boosters and additional doses. Without the vaccine, they would become vulnerable to this common but dangerous disease.

"This vaccine is not readily available in Jakarta and is regulated by the Indonesian Health Ministry. It can only be imported or obtained through their bureaucratic government channels, which take forever to act," she explained

"You mean that bringing this vaccine into Indonesia is illegal?" I asked, uncomfortable with the idea.

She replied, "Technically, yes. Singapore, too. We'll provide you with descriptions and a letter explaining where it comes from. You'll just need to keep it refrigerated and keep it on your person. You'll be fine."

That didn't make me feel any better, but I agreed.

On our way to the airport, Leigh and I stopped by a Walmart and bought a small insulated lunch cooler. Nothing conspicuous about that! We drove to the Baptist Hospital near Kansas City's Brookside community where the nurse met us, placed the vaccine in the cooler and packed it with ice.

She reminded me, "These ice packs need to be refreshed about every four hours."

~ ~ ~

By noon, I was airborne once more. The three-plane flight was Kansas City to Denver then Denver to Los Angeles. I'd leave L.A. at 11:00 p.m., spending the next 17 hours on a Singapore Airlines (*Sing-Air*) 747. Along the way, flight attendants were happy to replenish the ice.

Descending into Singapore, I was tired, sleepy and irritable, regardless of my comfortable business-class seat. I had travelled a long way babysitting those vials in my carry-on.

During the final landing approach the flight crew announced, "In Singapore, possession or trafficking in unauthorized drugs is punishable by imprisonment or death."

I wasn't sure that getting busted with five vials of Hep-A vaccine would have gotten me hanged, but this announcement was enough to cause anxiety. I was rightly concerned about the real possibility of spending time in a Singapore jail while the authorities studied the situation and looked at their options.

The landing in Singapore was mostly for refueling. A handful of passengers deplaned while a few new ones boarded. I stayed on board.

So far, so good but during the stop, inspection agents boarded and told everyone to remain seated. A moment later, additional agents boarded with drug-sniffing dogs. I immediately cringed with a dread I didn't know how to process. Exhaustion was quickly replaced with fear. I sat really still. The beagles came right by me as I sat on the aisle with the contraband on the floor between my feet. A minute later, they came by again in the opposite direction. No barks or sniffs, no stopping and onward to exit the plane. Good doggies!

I wasn't sure when I resumed normal breathing but it felt as though I had been holding my breath for hours. *Clearly, someone was watching over me, right?* I wondered how Leigh would respond when I told her about that thought.

Singapore had been the scariest stop, even though it turned out to be no big deal. But approaching Jakarta on my final leg of this journey, I was once again one nervous traveler.

~ ~ ~

Returning through Indonesian Immigration at Jakarta's airport, I was hoping this would all go smoothly. I had the 20 dollars already in my passport and laid it on the counter. But this time, the gate officer found a questionable glitch in my visa and asked me to step out of line.

"I see you were just here and now back so soon, Meester," he said in broken English.

"Yes, I had to make a quick trip to Kansas City and now I am returning," I responded.

My sweaty fingers gripped the straps of the carry-on. Surely, they must have seen my white knuckles.

"Come with me," another officer directed as he took my passport.

Other passengers looked away as I was taken out of the line. I sensed their concern. I was led out of the main lobby, through a series of dark hallways to a small, interrogation room. It was dingy and smelled of smoke.

A single light hung from a cord in the ceiling. I was sure I had seen this setup somewhere in a movie but I was actually in this scene.

I repeatedly explained my travel situation to three different officials who rotated in and out of the cramped, little room. Meanwhile, the incriminating carry-on sat unnoticed beside me on the floor. I could hear myself talking to them while the other side of my brain focused on the illegal vaccine, the six jars of likely illegal peanut butter and packets of white, granular grits stashed in my other luggage. *How can I ever explain 'grits' to these people?*

The next hour felt like a week. The officials seemed as frustrated as I was scared. In their broken English, they were not getting their point across very well.

Finally, one of them returned, cigarette smoke coming from his nose and mouth.

"How much you want to pay me to let you in?" he asked.

"Ah, OK!" I finally understood what they wanted.

There was a bit of friendly bargaining where we exchanged fake smiles.

Knowing this was likely more serious than a $20 gratuity, I asked, "$100 U.S.?"

"$100 for me, $100 for my friend," he responded.

"OK," I nodded in agreement.

He checked the hallway for anyone that might be nearby then took the $200 and my passport, telling me to wait right there.

Yeah, like I'm going to get up and run.

He returned about 10 minutes later, handing me the fully-stamped passport minus my initial $20. He then personally escorted me all the way through customs without any further threat of inspection. My concerns had been misplaced. This was all about money.

He walked me toward the airport exit gates and toward the hordes of people before one last wave and an enthusiastic, "Welcome to Jakarta, Bapak!"

Where had I heard that before?

By the middle of May 1993, I had been in-country three months. It was past time for me to get my Semi-Permanent Resident's visa. This required me to again leave Indonesia and complete that application at the Indonesian Consulate in Singapore. This was usually a one-day process. Our Indonesian staff arranged all the tedious paperwork and made the required appointment. My job was to simply show up at the Indonesian Consulate, hand them the paperwork, my passport and $100 U.S. *Easy enough*, I thought.

As an unofficial perk, we were allowed to travel to Singapore on a Thursday afternoon, stay overnight, complete our visa requirements on Friday then be back in the Jakarta office by the following Monday morning. The travel, meals and lodging were covered within reason. It was like a foreign weekend get-away where everything was pristine, clean and English was the predominant language.

I arrived in Singapore just after 3:00 p.m. on Thursday, May 20. From the airport to downtown, I was wowed by this clean, pleasant city. Rows of colorful flowers, orchids and other succulent plants lined the well-marked boulevards. Unlike Jakarta, traffic here flowed smoothly and the taxi actually smelled nice.

Having been so fascinated with Indonesia and everything I was experiencing, I wanted to buy a camcorder to capture my time and share videos with friends and family back home. Camcorders were available in Jakarta, but others had told me that throughout Indonesia, even the best name brands used lesser quality parts and were not well-warranted. They advised that Singapore had higher standards and was the better place to find what I wanted, so buying a camcorder was my first order of business.

After perusing several shops, learning about these video machines and an unsuccessful attempt at haggling, I settled on a Sony Hi-8 unit. At $1,300, it was their top of the line for the time. To go with it, I bought a stash of blank Hi-8 tapes, a tripod and an aluminum hard shell case. I didn't think much about it at the time, but that small camcorder stayed near my side for years to come.

That evening, I found my way to the shaded courtyard of the historic Raffles Hotel. I used my own money to dine on Kobe beef, enjoy my first Singapore Sling and listen to a young Singaporean lady playing classical piano from the central gazebo. I could easily get used to this alluring, hospitable place. Walking back to my cheap hotel, I turned on the news and watched the massive flooding taking place all around the upper Midwest. Kansas and Missouri were right in the heart of it. *Stay safe, friends.*

Early the next morning, I took a taxi to the Indonesian Consulate. I was not alone. It seemed like hundreds of people were there early, waiting in the muggy morning heat for the 8:00 a.m. opening. Speaking Indonesian, the officials announced over loudspeakers that for free resident visa documents, people needed to pay the equivalent of $100 U.S. cash in order to get same-day service. Otherwise, it would take four days. Free documents for $100? That's Indonesia!

One angry, defiant guy from Western Europe paid for four family members and loudly insisted he would not leave until he got a receipt! Guess he's still there.

Our Jakarta staff had prepared me for this game of fees, so I was not surprised. I now understood why they told me it would take a full day. It didn't have to, but it did.

There were no appointments honored, no organized queues, just frantic people from many countries selfishly wedging their shoes in front of others to gain an edge: pushing and elbowing their way to the counters in the hot, overcrowded room. The wobbly, overhead fans in the high ceiling provided no relief.

After losing ground for too long and not getting any closer to the counter, I knew I had to adopt the same aggressive tactics. I felt bad about it, but I did it and it finally worked.

Singapore is often referred to as an autonomous city-state. Just south of the Malay Peninsula, it is a small island of around five million citizens. There are four distinctive communities including the predominant Chinese, Indian, Malay and Eurasian.

I spent the remainder of that weekend as a tourist. I rode the pristine rail system to every place it went, dined at the open-air food courts and walked around the island's many sites. Of course there was shopping at Tang's, Singapore's oldest and world-renown department store.

My short visit to Singapore really was a weekend getaway and much appreciated.

6

THE EQUATORIAL EFFECT

Inverted Attempts at Eye-Rolling Humor

We expats often made humorous observations about our situations, concluding there were laws of nature which must surely have been inverted between the Northern and Southern Hemispheres. Things just seemed to work in an opposite manner south of the equator. Among the more obvious was the direction of tropical storms, rotating clockwise north and counterclockwise down south of the equator.

Being the curious, observant types we *thought* we were, we noted other unique conditions and occurrences which, without the benefit of scientific explanation, we simply attributed to a phenomenon we humorously referred to as the *Equatorial Effect*.

For example, in the Northern Hemisphere feeble old ladies gathered and discussed their rheumatism. Down south in the Southern Hemisphere strong men gathered and discussed their diarrhea.

In the North it was cheaper to get drunk than to get laid.

In the North it was difficult for a white man insistent on being a pot-bellied, loudmouth, know-it-all, insensitive, flatulent geek who smokes, blows his nose on his sleeve and treats women like golf clubs, to have a beautiful, intelligent, loving companion less than half his age. Down south in Jakarta, it was common.

In the Northern Hemisphere people drove on the street and walked on the sidewalk. Down south in Jakarta it was often inverted.

In Jakarta, a car's horn was used constantly except during emergencies, when it was not used at all. Its three main functions were as a form of audible graffiti, to say hello and to whistle at women without rolling down the window. Headlights were used during the daytime as warnings and not at night, because the battery must be saved for emergencies. Driving concepts such as right of way, courtesy and public safety were non-existent. The reason you took that defensive driving course in high school finally set in.

Throughout Indonesia, anger was expressed by silence. Not so in the Northern Hemisphere.

'A' is pronounced 'ah.' 'I' is pronounced 'E.' And 'Q' didn't make it across the equator.

In the north, a 400 sq. ft. studio apartment does not include a servant's quarters.

In the Northern Hemisphere, white-collar workers often held better jobs than oilfield workers. In the Southern Hemisphere, oilfield workers made more money than a U.S. Congressman and white-collar workers had to scrape and save.

For expats, even dating was the reverse of back home, with girls pursuing us. As the new kid in town, I had yet to discover that American guys were seen as special by Indonesian women. It seemed that Americans had earned the reputation for being more kind, compassionate and generous than some of the other foreigners, and sometimes, even more so than the local guys. Thus, they were rewarded by the interest and companionship of some nice women, *and some not so nice.*

This kind of attention seemed far less complicated, counter to typical relationship dynamics in the Northern Hemisphere. It was quite noticeable to both American men as well as American women.

Because of a promise and at the encouragement of Leigh, I attended an Indonesian Christian church a couple of times when I first arrived in the country. There were other nationalities in attendance but I seemed to be the only American there. That made me a novelty and I suppose, an interesting person to talk with.

Attending church and signing the register somehow got my name out into the community and I began receiving unsolicited letters from girls throughout the country. They were mailed to our office address in Jakarta, which was the address I gave at the church. Most who wrote were quite open about introducing themselves and expressing their interest in a relationship. Some were seeking employment: others just wanted a pen pal. In all, there were well over 50 letters during the first four months of my arrival. Every one included a photo.

I wasn't certain, but odds were I wasn't the only American getting letters like this. Whenever the office staff brought my mail, they had a good time teasing me.

Leigh and I often laughed about my *postal problem*. Occasionally, I'd read one of the letters to her and she'd giggle, fake disdain and remind me, "Don't expect that kind of attention when you get back here."

When I no longer went to church, the letters eventually tapered off, although they continued to trickle in throughout the coming months. Women pursuing me? Flattering for sure, but how was this even possible? *The Equatorial Effect!*

One of the letters I enjoyed was from a 20-year-old girl who lived in the rural mountains about 50 miles away. Keep in mind that 50 miles there might as well be 500, given the bad roads and primitive transportation in many of the rural areas. Susan was interested in a pen pal and was as open and seemingly honest a person as one could imagine.

Her first letter contained a photo of her standing on an ancient stupa at the Borobudur Temple near the central-Java city of Yogyakarta. She had no clue how I looked or anything about me. She wrote that she had not heard from her dad in nearly 10 years and was helping to support her mother and little sister. She had earned her high school diploma and was working on additional education. She had three months to go until she'd start looking for a full-time job.

In subsequent letters, she wrote colorful, interesting stories about her country, family and life. The margins were often decorated with little etchings and smiley faces, attesting to her consistently positive nature. In contrast to her situation, her letters were always optimistic. I admired her seemingly hard work, her attitude and her ability to connect through the stories she wrote. Reading between the lines, I saw hurdles ahead for her that she couldn't even imagine.

She seemed to be a mature, responsible and determined kid, yet innocent, naïve and clearly vulnerable. She was also rather cute. Yeah, the thought crossed my mind. But being much older, many miles away and in a romantic relationship, I never considered anything other than occasional correspondence. I did however, come to enjoy that correspondence. It felt honest and interesting, written with surprising depth from an Indonesian's perspective. I knew we'd never meet but corresponding with her on such a simple and innocent level seemed to offer a balance to Jakarta's social chaos while providing more insight into the culture.

I hadn't anticipated making so many business and personal connections. I met a lot of expats who were interested in connecting with others from different parts of the world. It was enlightening.

At the rooftop pool, a Canadian lady who lived on the top floor of my apartment building came over to introduce herself. Mature, poised and attractive, she and I sat and talked for a while in between refreshing dips into the cool water. She had worked in Jakarta for nearly three years, promoting business on behalf of Canada's Chamber of Commerce. She enjoyed casual friends, cooking, various wines and late-night swims. Sometimes she'd leave a phone message or a note taped to my door inviting me to dinner, drinks or both on a Sunday afternoon.

She had a casual boyfriend in Canada; I had a casual girlfriend in the States. They both knew she and I were acquainted. Sometimes additional expats accepted her invitations. Other times, it was just the two of us. We enjoyed the visits, the conversation and companionship; nothing significant beyond that. But you can see the Equatorial Effect at work here, right?

Another example came one evening after work. I was playing tennis with friends on the lighted courts at the hotel. While sitting one out, I talked with a pleasant Indonesian gentleman and his wife who were also playing there. These folks seemed to be a bit further up the local food chain as evidenced by their skilled English, attractive attire and the black Mercedes parked outside the fence. They were happy to talk with Americans and I was equally pleased to talk with them. They asked about the nature of our business, mentioning that they both worked in textile management.

As the conversation continued, the lady told me she would like to have two authentic Chicago Bulls T-shirts for her two young sons.

"Is there any way you can bring some, perhaps when you travel to the U.S. again?" She asked. "I can pay you in advance."

"No promises but let me have your contact information and the boys' sizes. I'll see what I can do."

That night, I sent a message to friends in Missouri. The shirts arrived about three weeks later. The lady was surprised when I called to tell her.

The next evening, she showed up at my apartment to pick up the shirts and pay me.

"These are a gift and I hope your boys enjoy them."

She was humbled and grateful. The next evening, she knocked on my door again. This time, she brought with her, two well-dressed Indonesian girls in their late 20s. I learned that these girls had been educated in Singapore and were both administrative professionals in the textile conglomerate owned by the lady and her husband.

"You have done a nice thing for our family," she said. "I want to introduce you to these girls as friends who are happy to show you around the city. They are like family to us. It is good for everyone. You can practice your Indonesian and they can practice their English."

These girls speak better English than I do, I thought to myself.

We all walked out to the lobby to sit and talk for a while. We exchanged contact information including my newly-acquired email address. The girls had been using the new, world-wide internet for months now and shared their addresses with me.

Together and individually, I had friendly, fun outings with each of these ladies and their friends. But over a couple of months, our connections simply faded. That seemed all right, but it left me convinced there really was something to this Equatorial Effect.

For an American guy who hadn't exactly been sought after by the women in his home country, having anyone bring two wonderful girls to my door had been highly unusual. In my lifetime, would that have ever happened in the Northern Hemisphere? I knew the answer to that.

Good, bad or indifferent, the hemispheric inversion of nature and human behavior was quite noticeable throughout Indonesia. Had we accidently stumbled onto something profound with this equatorial thing? I didn't live by it or pay it much attention at the time. But it was there, and constant. By going with the flow, I often benefited. I had no idea how much it would influence my future, slowly contouring my own way of reasoning, decision making and behavior until I, myself, was turned somewhat upside down.

~ ~ ~

My weekly routine gradually evolved toward working into the early evening then home to my apartment across the street to watch yesterday's news, kick back and skim through my new batch of letters from Indonesian girls. I was kinda' spoiled.

There were times when I felt a tinge of guilt because there were more letters than I could effectively read, much less respond to. Still, I kept them, sharing a few with Leigh now and then. Aside from validating the Equatorial Effect, they were good examples of differences between relationships in Indonesia and those back in the States.

7

JAKARTA CHRONICLES

IT TRULY IS THE LITTLE THINGS!

In Indonesia it felt as though something interesting occurred every day, something worthy of journaling. One night in late June seemed ordinary enough. The dry season had just started but regardless, the dark air was heavy with moisture and bristled with an eerie, dry lightning in the distant mountains to the south.

I wrapped things up and left the office about 7:30 p.m. As I routinely crossed the street to my apartment, there was a blinding flash and an immediate loud, stunning crack of thunder in the wires right above my head. In an instant, everything stopped. As if in slow motion, I turned to see sparks spilling from the top of an ancient, 80-foot elm tree next to the apartment's driveway. Steam and glowing splinters flew from its trunk as dirt and gravel exploded from the ground and broken asphalt around its base.

In a second, I realized the tree had succumbed to the lightning as it groaned, twisted and searched for its direction to fall. I stood still, not because I was stunned but because I couldn't tell which way to run. The next moment, my feet got the message ahead of my brain when they determined it was coming toward me. With energy and speed stolen from a concurrently whispered micro-prayer, I placed enough distance between us that the highest branches slapped the ground no more than a couple of feet behind my smoking heels.

I immediately shook off the dust, composed my disheveled clothing and pretended, *Hey, no big deal.* Having lived in Jakarta for four months, I'd gotten pretty good at dodging moving objects.

For the next six days, the street was blocked and the electricity at our office was out. The fallen tree had taken out key power lines on its way down. The local electric company was in no hurry to remove the tree or reconnect the electricity. Half-day outages from wind and thunderstorms were frequent, but this was a whole new challenge.

Luckily, my apartment was on a different feeder circuit and still had electricity. To keep our business functioning, I arranged a deal with my apartment management to set up two workstations in their building. Jamitri and I moved computers and printers over, allowing our secretaries to continue producing key documents. In Indonesia, if you can conceive an alternative solution, you can execute it; no committees required.

Writing had become a more important hobby and sharing these kinds of experiences felt good. Perhaps more so, it was another tool helping me to stay close to people who mattered. My writings started out as letters to friends and family as well as regional pen pals. Over the years, it morphed into more than a dozen chronicles. Some were serious, others clearly not.

With these chronicles, my loosely planned goal was to make people laugh and record these experiences for posterity. Usually, the feedback was positive. Serious humor was all around me. I first had to sense it then blend it with the truth, tweak it a little and write what I saw.

The paragraphs below are an example of these short-story chronicles along with an attempt at sharing my sometimes-comical observations. This one entitled, *It's the Little Things* was sent to my friends and family back in the States:

Chris and Rita are lizards. Not some slime-ball human couple you wouldn't want to be around, but real life, tongue-flicking little reptiles living in my poorly lit Jakarta kitchen. In a half-hearted attempt to respect both our life forms, I've regressed to communicating with reptiles and proposed an arrangement with these two. Since I pay the rent, I get full run of the place. They are requested to stay in the kitchen, not bite and take care of their personal business outside. There's growing evidence that they're not really interested in all aspects of my arrangement. At least they're not biting.

No, I haven't completely lost it. Not yet. Anyone who has lived in the tropics has lived with these entertaining critters. I'm just trying to get them to earn their keep. I've decided that Chris is the smaller of the two and just a bit younger. He's about four inches long; Rita maybe four-and-a-half. For room and board, they're to keep the insect infestation minimized. They do a pretty good job, unless the insect is bigger than them.

My primary complaint is that they're always startling me. I hate it when I wander into the dark kitchen and my hand touches Rita, who's sitting on the light switch. I yell, she runs and Chris laughs so hard, he falls into the toaster!

There are other varmints that would also like to be roomies, including some sizeable rats. They peacefully coexist with an abundance of tired, old kitty cats throughout the neighborhood. Several families have told of uninvited guests who would chew through Tupperware or through steel cookie tins to cop a cheap meal. They're in the streets at night and once, I thought I saw a pack of babies playing in the low, yellow light of a late-night street vendor's lantern. They looked to be three or so inches long; dozens of them scurrying in and out of the shadows on the dark, broken asphalt a few steps ahead. Getting closer, I realized it was just cockroaches. I felt so much better.

A Java roach is the second-most unwelcome guest. And the bastards can fly! Twice now, these crispy crawlers have intimidated Chris and Rita, inviting themselves to snooze upside-down on my bathroom floor.

I turn on the light, they yawn and stretch those spiny legs upward, twitch their wings a bit and look at me with those beady, red eyes as if to say, "Where's the coffee, Man?"

On my first encounter, 'John Wayne' here, grabs a tennis shoe and rides in there to send Mr. Whiskers to Mecca. That was a big mistake. He was far more plump than crispy, and I spent the next 10 minutes cleaning gunky bug parts off the bathroom walls.

As April gives way to May, Indonesia eases into its dry season. I think that means it rains only once a day. Now the mosquitoes arrive.

Along with some coworkers, I've had an opportunity to see some of the mountains and outlying towns. A 12-hour bus tour travels through miles of tea and rubber plantations to steamy volcanoes and back through some lush and beautiful, but crowded countryside. Rice paddies seem to fill every flat spot and into the elevated terraces up onto the hillsides.   Remnants of ghostly, elegant Dutch architecture are common throughout the mountainous regions south and east of Jakarta. Large, dilapidated villas are tucked into distant, wooded settings in what used to be a rich man's world.

Crowded roadways are dirty and badly potted. Even inside the clean, air-conditioned bus the pollution from the leaded and diesel fuels used without controls coat your clothing and skin with a distinct black film.

Wherever we traveled, there were people walking the roads, in the forests, on rooftops, on top of moving trains and buses and throughout the rice fields. The most densely populated island on earth, Java is literally crawling with people.

At each bus stop, local marketers besieged us with colorful Indonesian crafts, art and handiwork. There were children offering to rent big umbrellas to shelter people from the rain. Snakes, animals and exotic birds were being sold from cloth bags. There were beautiful wood and bone carvings made by artists in Irian Jaya. Most prices could be reduced by continually walking away. The problem was, they followed and pestered you by keeping their wares in your face. One Jakarta vendor followed a group of us for more than six blocks through heavy traffic, trying to sell a blow gun. These things were crude but ornately carved from bone and worked quite well. Non-poisonous darts were included. His price steadily declined from $35 to $8 before he finally gave up. I later wished I'd bought it.

A lot of the merchandise and souvenirs were worthwhile bargains, if you negotiated well. Locally produced leather goods were good quality and surprisingly affordable. You wanted to avoid trading in live animals. It was often inhumane and could contribute to the extinction of a species. And most expats learned the hard way: it was wise to be cautious of street food vendors for obvious reasons.

Indonesians in the domestic service industry, such as housekeepers, cooks and drivers were usually loyal and efficient. They could also be wonderfully innocent. One of the expat families told their cook they wanted fresh fish for dinner. Upon their return late that afternoon, the fresh fish were swimming in the kitchen sink.

The housekeeper who took care of my apartment was full of surprises. My tennis shoes were dirty and wet from walking in the rain, so I left them to dry on the tiled bathroom floor. I didn't realize they were gone until they reappeared two days later, cleaned with the laces ironed and rolled neatly beside them right where they'd been left. After that, I was careful not to leave pieces of dental floss lying around.

Clothes were washed, ironed and placed immaculately in the wardrobe each day. Dishes were washed, put away and the place was cleaned six days a week by a lady I never saw. Now, I could make some chauvinistic joke about the 'perfect woman', but I'd be kidding, right? Truthfully, I could quickly become accustomed to having a maid.

Indeed, Indonesia is a vast and fascinating country. But you could never overlook the little things!

Sundays were usually our only full day off but occasionally our partners would have a retreat or meetings in another province. That allowed us to take a couple of concurrent days off. During one such occurrence in late May 1993, I went with coworkers to, a small, isolated island north of Jakarta in a region called *Pulau Seribu* (*Thousand Islands*). Other island trips in the northern Pulau Seribu region would eventually include Kotok, Putri and Pramuka.

Each of these small islands had its own characteristics, often including endemic flora and fauna. For example, Kotok had an abundance of large monitor lizards that grow to six feet. They weren't the least bit shy when it came to tourists' mealtime. The staff served the three daily meals while continuously dragging these hungry lizards by their tail away from the tables. They were ominous, but they didn't attack. That was little comfort when I would look down from my table, between my knees and there was this huge crocodile-looking creature following every move I made with the food in my hand. Whenever they showed up, the resident cats kept their distance.

Later in early June, I made my first trip to the exotic island of Bali. Over the years, I returned to these amazing places many times, writing about everything I experienced.

8

THE ROAD TO MERAK

PROFOUND LESSONS CARRIED FORWARD

As with most foreign companies working in Indonesia, our office was staffed with Indonesians and a mixture of mostly Caucasian from a variety of Western countries. The locals often referred to us as *Bule* (bu-lay), which translated to *white people*. It was usually said with friendship and affection. None of us were offended.

Our teams were collections of engineers, construction, business and operations managers who were there to assist the Indonesian energy provider in building and upgrading their facilities across the country. Our design and business offices were in Jakarta while the primary project and construction offices were just over three hours away on the western-most tip of Java. There, the massive construction site employed more than 2,500 workers as well as our on-site construction management teams. Our site team was housed there in a large temporary man-camp. These man-camps were specifically built to accommodate the workers, engineers, and management teams from the beginning, until the completion of the project.

In our Jakarta office, there were a number of full-time Western expatriates who rotated in for typical one-year assignments. Like me, many would eventually stay longer. Most of us were American. At times, we'd be joined by a Brit, a Canadian or perhaps someone from another European country. Our office employed at least as many Indonesian professionals including abundantly sharp engineers, managers and secretaries. We also had a staff of local drivers, housekeepers and security guards.

There were two types of security guys working for us. The 'satpam' wore a blue uniform with a small knife belt. They actually had a little bit of training. The other security guys or 'Penjaga' (*jah-gah*), were often a bit of a wild card. They were usually not uniformed. Most expat families and many Indonesians hired a jaga to sit in their driveway from sunset until sun-up as a deterrent to robbery. The jagas working for us were polite, capable and loyal. But they'd be the first to tell you that across the city, a jaga provides security when he's employed. When he's not employed, he provides the need for security.

The road leading from Jakarta out to West Java was narrow and treacherous. It detoured through many small towns and villages where roadside fruit stands and makeshift shops took advantage of the traffic bottlenecks. The road out to the town of Merak carried all the traffic including heavy trucks and overflowing buses to and from the ferries that traversed across the Sunda Strait between Java and Sumatra, Indonesia's largest island. It was a dreadful, lawless highway. Horrific traffic deaths along that 75-mile stretch were a daily occurrence.

June of 1993 had quickly given way to July and for a change, we had a two-day weekend coming for the Fourth of July. All of us had put in a lot of time. The nearly five months I had been in-country already felt like a year. It was time for a break. A group of about 15 employees and family members put together an informal boating/diving trip. We were heading to Sangiang, a small, mostly uninhabited channel island at the halfway point in the Sunda Strait.

We arranged four vehicles to carry the crew and equipment, giving us a little insurance in case one of the jalopies broke down. I'm not a diver but I wanted to go along for the sailing adventure and to photograph more of the country. When it came to photography, my senses were always on: notepad and cameras ready to record observations that other people might completely miss. Plus, it was simply good to get away from work for a little while.

When Saturday morning came, we gathered at our office parking area, lugging our cameras and diving gear, ready to head out. Well, most of us were ready.

Our drivers were local guys hired from our office pool. They were our best drivers and were far more experienced with that dangerous road than the rest of us put together.

We planned to drive out to the jobsite where we'd stay overnight in the camp's unassigned rooms until catching the two chartered boats the next morning. We were traveling in a caravan of well-used Toyota Kijangs, a boxy, utilitarian vehicle with cheap, tinted glass. In my ride, there was only one seatbelt in the whole vehicle and it was not functioning. But at least we had semi-working air conditioning to shield us from the notorious heat. The ride was somewhat softened by a combination of basic suspension and thin, barely-cushioned seating material. I wished I'd brought a pillow.

As we got underway and moved out of the city, I tried not to look as buses, cars and trucks came at us head on while passing other vehicles on the narrow, two-lane road. There was no law enforcement. And if there were any maximum speed limits, no one paid any attention to them. The heavy traffic was truly a free-for-all. There were times when our driver would be forced to take the grassy shoulder, sliding sideways to get out of the way. My achy arm went to sleep clinging to the flimsy grab bar above the windows.

Along the way, we told tall tales, noisily roasting one another and anyone else we could laugh about.

Around three-quarters of the way to the camp, we stopped for lunch at the *Cobra* restaurant, so called by expats because among their other entrees they served fresh, live cobra. The proprietor explained that when ordering, a customer selects their meal from a sand-filled aquarium where live cobras await their fate. I could see two of them behind the glass. And they could see me. The snake, who like me didn't volunteer for this gig was then beheaded and its blood drained into a small glass right there in front of the customer. While the meat was being cooked, hearty souls would be offered the blood as a macho health drink. I always thought it was for showing off.

There were customers from many cultures in the restaurant that afternoon. None of them ordered cobra during our lunch break. All of us were glad.

About two hours into our journey, the rains came. We couldn't even see the oncoming traffic. After a brief but drenching downpour, the sun returned and our road trip turned into a steaming hot afternoon excursion that made the already insufficient air conditioner strain even more. Traveling further along the road toward Merak, our progress slowed and we became snarled in traffic that seemed to go on forever.

Nearing the ferry ports, the stop-and-go traffic was predictably more stop than go. We inched closer and could see the enormous ferries being loaded and unloaded—discharging cars, buses and large, heavily laden trucks onto the grossly insufficient roadway. Our driver took the opportunity to ease just far enough to the side of the road so we could all get out and stretch.

"Break time," he informed us.

He had pulled off near a bustling, make-shift market that had sprung up along a junction leading from the villages in northwest Java. It was a perfect location for these kinds of micro-businesses: the merchants displaying their wares mere inches from the nearly-stopped traffic that held their potential patrons as virtual captives.

The dusty crossroads also served as a makeshift depot for buses, their conductors hawking and collecting fares as people jumped on and off moving buses heading back into Jakarta.

I slowly opened the car door into a sea of busy humanity. My fellow travelers and I got out and walked through the markets. Finding a bottle of cold water was my top priority.

Dirty brown and blue tarps were draped over poles tied together with nylon string to form shaded, little kiosks. There, merchants had stacked colorful pyramids of fresh rambutan, mango, oranges and bananas alongside hand-woven fabrics, clothing and housewares.

The sugary scent of the ripened fruit was too often mixed with the pungent, soured smell rising from nearby trenches, pushed along by a thin stream of putrid, gray water. I buried my nose in my elbow hoping for some relief. The graceless little waterway was laden with trash, rotting debris and whatever else held no redeemable value to the local population. Storekeepers were friendly enough but could turn aggressive if it looked like you were going to leave without buying something.

All around me were dozens of thin, ragged young children: little boys and girls who looked like orphans. They ran barefoot through the markets, between the stalls and into the road, cleaning windshields and begging for coins between the hot, dirty vehicles jammed in the roadway. While some were hustling, others were sleeping on the ground under filthy, burlap tarps strung between bushes on the surrounding hillsides.

A sick feeling rose from my stomach. Some of these children appeared as young as six but no one appeared over 15. Unkempt, likely unloved little ragamuffins; their soiled, determined faces were predominately a blend of Chinese and Javanese. The children with blue eyes, blond hair, light complexions and Western facial features brought forth an epiphany.

I couldn't help but wonder about these children left behind here and around the planet by visiting fathers who didn't know, didn't care or were in no position to care. It jerked at my emotions, making me angry at people I didn't even know. How could anyone leave a little kid alone, fending for themselves in this horrid environment? The dreamer inside me wanted to round them up and take them somewhere beautiful where they would be loved and cared for; where they could have a happy childhood. Alas, I knew that was not an option.

I grew up in poverty but I always had my parents and a roof over my head. These children had nothing. In my heart I knew this was one of our world's most cruel yet preventable tragedies. To see these destitute, hungry little faces in real time was powerful. This was not a television advertisement for some relief agency. These children were face-to-face with me, brushing against me there along the side of that dirty, chaotic roadway. It was a profound, sobering image that would forever remain with me—branding my observations along the road to Merak into my memory.

I made my way through the hordes of noisy vendors and customers, just inches from the road. The heat and smoke coming from the exhaust pipes, reflecting off the static traffic assaulted my sweaty face.

An arm's length away, I noticed a rusty little white van stuck in the congested traffic next to the crowded market where I was walking. Packed inside was a group of veiled girls who looked to be 16 to 20. Clearly, they were being transported to someplace they didn't want to be. The burning sun bore down without mercy on the little van as it sat like all the other vehicles, unable to move in any direction. It had no air conditioning, no ventilation. Its dirty rear windows were closed to keep out the thick, orange dust stirred up by motorcycles, waves of pedestrians and the congested roadway traffic creeping slowly from the opposite direction.

The girls sat in the steamy, drenching heat; handkerchiefs over their mouths. Their expressionless faces concealed from most, what looked to me like fear, confusion and perhaps an acceptance of sorts. They clutched tightly to dingy cloth bags in their laps, containing their few belongings. The grungy driver sat with his arm out the front window, tossing his cigarette butts into the dirt along the roadside. Another man sat in the front passenger seat: 10 people in a micro-van that shouldn't hold more than five. For a short moment, I stopped as one of the girls looked over aimlessly and made eye contact; the dirty glass between our two different worlds distorting whatever observations she or I made.

From within the crowd behind me, a hand rested on my shoulder as I heard our driver's voice saying, "TKW, Bapak" (*tenaga kerja wanita*).

This was the Indonesian term for *worker girls* coming out of the villages. He went on to tell me that these girls were being taken to agencies that find them work so they can help support their families.

"Too bad, they'll never be seen again."

I didn't know what he meant, although it seemed a melodramatic thing to say. Since coming to this country five months ago, every day was filled with things I heard or things going on around me that I didn't fully grasp. I couldn't stop to understand or have compassion for everything I encountered. There was too much of it. Too often, whatever *it* was quickly faded into *no big deal*. But along that important dirty road, the faces of those indentured young girls, those small children, their futures stolen by neglect, indifference and profit, were indeed a big deal to this expatriate.

"Let's go, 'Pak," said our driver.

The traffic was finally beginning to move as we headed back to our vehicle. There was a big sailing weekend ahead of us and at that moment, that's where I needed to focus. As our vehicle pulled forward, I looked back at that little van and the children who worked this stop seven days a week. It was a tough image to shake off.

~ ~ ~

Within the next half hour, we slowly rolled through the outskirts of Merak and entered the road leading us out to the jobsite. The man-camp was on the project property and a long way from the nearest village. Because of the two-day weekend, the workers had left so there were numerous small, mosquito-ridden rooms where we could crash for the night. There was no bedding, not even a pillow; just a thin cloth cover over a four-inch mattress on a basic, wooden bed frame.

It was becoming alarmingly obvious that we had not planned well, a realization that was only going to get worse. Because of the holiday, the camp's housekeepers had the weekend off so there was no one to ask for help. The mess hall was unexpectedly closed so there was no place to get food that night or in the morning. We had taken for granted having access to these normally available services. Uh-oh!

With nothing else to do before turning in, I walked down the short pathway to the coastline. The equatorial sun was just beyond the horizon, taking with it, the remaining light and blistering heat as it silently vanished below a red, dusty sky. Across the darkening water, I could see the ghostly silhouette of Sumatra in the distance.

Strong currents pushed northward from the Indian Ocean making the water lap hard against the concrete riprap surrounding the project's long peninsula. I sat on a large rock at the water's edge, taking time to reflect, taking a photo or two and feeling hungry. It would be an uncomfortable Saturday night sleeping in my clothes; that lone, thin cloth employed in vain to defend against insects that regardless of the holiday were going to get their meal. Little bastards!

I woke three or four times during the night and finally decided to just get up. It was Sunday. First light would arrive before long. Other travelers, also weary from trying to sleep were beginning to stir. I walked around the compound for a while then down to the coastline again. Two hundred yards to my left, I saw a couple of Indonesian women in a small paddle boat approaching the shore. They were dressed in colorful, traditional Indonesian clothing and head scarves. I headed in their direction, thinking I might catch a photo.

As I got closer, I saw they were unloading long strings of fresh bananas. Using my developing Indonesian language, I asked one of the women, "*Bisa saya beli beberapa pisang?*" (May I buy some bananas?)

"*Betul*" (yes), she replied energetically, while carrying armfuls of the precious fruit across the jagged riprap stones.

I bought all I could carry, more than 30 bananas for the equivalent of about four dollars. She was happy, I was ecstatic! Taking a couple for myself, I passed out the remainder to our drivers and fellow travelers. A couple of the guys went down to the water and bought even more. For us, breakfast was served and the boat ladies delivering the much-needed fruit had scored a windfall.

~ ~ ~

Early morning along the coast was beautiful. Before the next hour had passed, we traveled to the nearby dock, organized our belongings and got acquainted with our two boats. We divided into two groups, staking out a place to sit and secure our gear.

The Strata was a 35-foot catamaran owned and operated by Captain Strata. The Heinz & Caroline (H&C) was a 36-foot sloop owned and operated by Captain Brent and his wife. Each vessel was equipped with one dinghy. I joined the group aboard the Strata for the roughly two-hour trip out.

Moments after boarding, I sat cross-legged on the deck with the others as we cast off. This whole trip would be on the deck because there were no other accommodations below. We were trailing the H&C by about a half mile. The Strada was using her engine rather than her sails. It sounded more like a clunky, one-cylinder air compressor than an engine as the H&C continued widening the distance between us. But gradually, the shoreline of Java faded into the blue distance as the boats moved further out into the glassy strait. The thin line between blue sky and blue ocean was at times indistinguishable.

The sun was well up into a perfectly clear sky. It was late morning; the sea and the winds were exceptionally calm. That explained why we were not under sail. At times across the miles of open water, I could see little islands: some forested, others, not much more than a permanent sandbar.

About an hour into our trip, Sangiang appeared on the horizon. In another hour, we expected to be there. This yet-to-be developed, forested island was roughly three miles north to south and about one and a half miles at its widest point. A couple of small native families lived there part time—caring for goats, a couple of dogs and themselves.

Nearing our destination, the faster H&C was already anchored in a wide, shallow cove on the northeast side of the island. Captain Brent and his wife, Caroline, had made it ashore and were unloading the basic equipment to make and serve lunch. Captain Strada brought the catamaran in about 100 yards north of the H&C, then dropped two anchors. Once the anchors were taut, the captain wasted no time bringing the dinghy around to the port side of the vessel. The first three of six divers loaded their gear and headed out to deeper areas away from the island's slope. Captain Brent began ferrying his divers out as well. On our boat, another group began diving off the ship's deck, swimming and snorkeling in the amazingly clear, blue water.

From my vantage point on deck, the sun illuminated the rocky, sandy bottom about eight or so feet below. In addition to the rocks, I saw lots of beautiful coral structures reaching up from the bottom. In about 15 minutes, the dinghy returned for our other three divers. When all divers had been dispatched, both dinghies returned and took the rest of us, along with camera equipment and other supplies to the sandy shore.

Once ashore, I helped myself to one more banana. I didn't want to see another banana for the next week or so. They were a lifesaver, but I'd had my fill. I helped others gather dry driftwood and put it in a circular rock pit that had been used for previous beach fires. That's where lunch would be made.

All plans abruptly changed when one of the girls snorkeling in the cove stepped onto a coral reef that crumbled. Her leg went deep into the coral structure, delivering a severe cut. Both captains, her parents and others helped her out of the water and onto towels waiting on the beach. Captain Brent quickly scrambled onto a dinghy and raced out to the H&C to get a well-stocked first aid kit. His wife and the girl's parents held pressure on the injury until he returned.

The rest of us on shore kept our distance but stood by in case we were needed or had to quickly re-board. For a time, it looked as though we'd need to leave and get her to a hospital. However, within half an hour, they were able to fully stabilize the wound. The accident had not severed any large veins or arteries. Tough kid, and lucky. She took it well and was happy to be there. But she was done with the water for the duration of the trip.

Back to cooking! Captain Brent and Caroline resumed setting up, making barbecue pulled pork and chicken served with large hoagie buns. We stood around or sat on rocks, eating delicious hefty sandwiches, drinking cold soft drinks and beer, making up for our lack of dinner the night before. There were no leftovers.

After lunch, Captain Strata went around to everyone, making sure we understood we only had about an hour and a half remaining on shore. The comfort and safety of the injured girl was one concern. He was also watching a deep cloud build-up beginning to take shape out of the southeast. If we didn't get out well ahead of it, we'd have to wait until it cleared. That could keep us there overnight. Overnight, no food left? We heard him loud and clear.

"Oh, keep in mind there are cobras on this island."

Well, that was good to know.

~ ~ ~

I took off walking, camera in hand on neat little goat paths that led into the tropical forest. High grass on either side of the narrow path looked like a perfect hiding place for snakes. I kept going further along the trails, trying to make as much noise as I could.

A quarter mile or so in, the trail widened and the spooky grass fell away. I came across remnants of eerie Japanese *pill boxes* and bunkers from WWII. The metal doors were long- gone, likely sold off for scrap but the dilapidated, concrete structures were still there; ghostly, abandoned sentinels that once menaced allied ships passing through the strait.

Continuing along the trail, I came across a large, thatched hut sitting about four feet off the ground. On a rope attached to the hut and to a nearby tree, pieces of sun-dried clothing looked as though they had been hanging there for a week or more.

Under the hut, a mother dog attended to her puppies. Her convincing growl and aggressive barking made it clear that getting closer would be a bad decision. I kept walking as two small goats fell in behind. I wasn't sure when they turned back but apparently, they did. I took another trail to my left that led toward the water. Nearing the beach, there was a long, cumbersome collection of washed-up debris that seemed to ring the entire island. Most of it was driftwood but there was a lot of beautiful, fragile powder-white pieces of coral that had been shaped and reshaped by generations of currents and shifting, submerged sands.

To the north a mile or so, I could see our two boats in the bay.

I came across another small hut that sat near the rocky beach. I stopped, placed my camera on a rock, tripped the timer and lifted myself into the doorway of the hut for a photograph.

I didn't want to walk back through that snaky trail so I took the longer, slower route, making my way along the rocky beach back to our site.

Back at the landing, the wind was picking up as everyone pitched in to reload equipment into the dinghies and accompany them out to the waiting vessels. The clouds were already darkening.

With everyone on board, Captain Strada told us there was no way to get around the approaching storm. We would have to push through it and hope we could break into a clearing. The water was getting rough as the dinghy was pulled onboard and lashed down. A moment later, we were underway. With no option, everyone was still on deck, holding onto whatever we could find.

We yelled back and forth, holding onto our cameras, equipment and sturdy railings along the deck. Again, we cracked jokes about our situation and about one another, but the serious looks on everyone's faces told something more realistic.

Captain Strada raised the sail and the vessel increased speed. The H&C stayed much closer this time. After about 40 minutes of true anxiety, we sailed out of the storm and as we traveled east, it turned more to the north. Nighttime was fast approaching but the rest of the return to Merak was smooth sailing. It seemed boring in comparison. No one minded.

Faster than the trip out, we arrived back at the dock in about an hour and a half. Our drivers and vehicles were waiting. The boats docked together and we unloaded our gear; everyone alive and mostly well. We said goodbye to our nautical hosts and organized ourselves in the Kijangs for the long trip back to Jakarta. With a couple of exceptions, the excursion had been fun and we were all happy we had done it.

Thankfully, our drivers were rested and alert, because most of us couldn't keep our eyes open. The dark ride back was much quieter than the ride out. With the perils of the road, sleep was a good option. Our caravan arrived back at our office departure point just before midnight. Other folks still had a way to go before getting home. I simply had to walk across the street, jump the barricade and I was in for the night.

The words from an old song came to mind, something like…*sure is good to be back home again.* Somewhere, sometime in the months leading up to tonight, Jakarta had become home; as much like home as anywhere I had ever lived. I was content with that.

9

SMALL WORLD CONNECTIONS

LANGUAGE LESSONS AND WHO YOU KNOW

As months crawled forward, I became further involved with my work. Still, each day brought something different, something interesting in one form or another. For me, the latest thing was two-way pager technology. It was awesome. My little Motorola pager cost around $250 plus a monthly fee. It would connect with other pagers as well as signal telephones to message me. At the time, this was groundbreaking and the beginning of affordable wireless communication, even if it would only handle 60 characters per message.

Between the continuous long workweeks, I kept an ear open for any opportunity to slip in a short recreational trip. But mostly it was nose to the grindstone for each expat. Although it wasn't in writing, we all knew the long hours were mandatory. We were expected to put in the same hours as our Indonesian counterparts and they were held to a much tougher work requirement than Americans in the States. There were no 40-hour protections here. The schedule was relentless. I generally worked 11 hours Monday through Friday and six to eight hours on Saturday. That said, we learned to pace ourselves.

My Saturday afternoons with the local staff still consisted of up to 10 of us. I was flattered that they invited me to hang out, grab lunch or see a movie. The latest Western films, particularly action movies, were popular at Jakarta's many modern theatres. Most of the films my friends enjoyed were in English with Indonesian subtitles.

A lot of my local friends learned their English through schools but more learned through their association with expats, listening to Western pop music and watching Western TV and films. Movies turned out to be a good tool for both them and me. I was actually able to see the Bahasa Indonesian language being instantly translated to English. I was actively trying to learn the language. The more I hung out, the more language I thought I knew. I would have ample opportunities to embarrass myself.

Early on, our group was in a theater lobby waiting for a film to start. We walked around looking at dozens of framed movie posters, including those for Indonesian films.

I casually commented, "This actor, Akan Datang, sure is in a lot of Indonesian films. He must be well-connected."

I was being serious. Those who heard me looked puzzled, whispering among themselves. A moment later, the whole gang was giggling. One of the girls politely explained, "Akan Datang is not an actor. It means, 'Coming Soon!'"

Another slip-up occurred at the office. I asked around to see if anyone had any aspirin.

Practicing my Indonesian, I intended to tell our receptionist, "I have a headache." So I said, "Saya ada pisang."

The Indonesian word for headache is 'pusing,' not 'pisang.' Pisang means banana.

I had just told the receptionist in front of a bunch of other locals that, "I have a banana." It was quite a while before I lived that one down.

The local and expat staff would sometimes ask me for assistance: personal favors with this and that. I had inadvertently fallen into the role of a peacemaker, a calming problem-solver who could bring differing sides together toward a win-win agreement. Indonesians and expats saw me as a dependable, confidential resource. And yeah, I could get things done, even if sometimes it meant bending the rules to do it.

I was often the liaison for issues between the Indonesians and the Bule, a role that opened me up to getting occasional calls at night and on weekends. Most such calls involved sensitive issues. With Indonesians, it might be related to disrespect or a disagreement. With expats, it sometimes involved finding confidential medical help relating to careless partying or one-night stands. Whenever my phone rang early Sunday morning, it usually meant I would be discreetly arranging for someone to get to a clinic.

Other calls might involve financial issues such as no-interest, short-term loans and other confidential matters. I was able to quickly arrange no-tell bank transfers and could overnight money to and from my bank in the States. I had done some 'essential' favors for people, which earned me their trust. In that foreign environment, whenever someone owed you or you owed someone else a favor, you honored it. That seemed to work well for me.

Dealing with complex contracts, letters of credit and government agencies had put me in contact with lots of administrative operatives inside and outside of our project community. I kept an unofficial network of local bank personnel, doctors, freight forwarders, specialized suppliers and embassy contacts who trusted me enough to go out of their way to help me help someone in need. They knew I'd do the same for them, and I often did. I did not break any laws but don't ask me about bending them.

~ ~ ~

Somewhere during this time, I was assigned additional responsibilities involving support for our invoices to our partners. They were notorious for taking up to 10 months to pay our monthly invoices. We would eventually be paid, but a seven-month delay was normal. Depending on the work milestones we completed, these invoices ranged from $20,000, often as high as $4 million. Therefore, a seven-month delay at four percent could cost our business hundreds of thousands. Even though we were supposed to be on the same side, our partners would have their engineers argue, haggle, hold friendly, exhaustive discussions and use a number of other delay tactics to keep that money drawing interest in their accounts rather than ours.

Project contractors from other countries would *grease the wheels*, providing tangible favors or substantial cash incentives to our partner's key people in the approval process. As a result, their invoices were paid quite promptly. Americans, however, were prohibited from directly paying business-related gratuities by the U.S. Foreign Corruption Act of 1977. American companies were at a self-imposed disadvantage since we were one of only a few international signatories to that Act.

Our partners knew about our restrictions but that didn't matter. They were usually under pressure from several upper layers of management to obtain some form of perk from us in order to pay us on time.

The additional role I had been assigned included doing whatever I could to shorten that payment period. Our *gatekeeper* contact with our partner's accounts group was an Indonesian lady named Ibu Niniek (*Ms. Nin-ek*) Back in the early 1980s, Niniek had worked years as a secretary on an earlier project. That was a time when she would travel eight miles by becak, over unpaved roads and trails to get to and from her office. Over the last 12 years, she had advanced to a mid-level management position, working directly for our partners. She was not directly responsible for approving our invoices but she did have a degree of influence over the folks causing the delays.

Knowing I would be taking on this new responsibility and interfacing with Ibu Niniek at the partner's office, our office liaison, Jamitri came to me and asked, "Mr. Steele, you know Ibu Niniek has daughter that works here?"

"No, I didn't."

I knew Arlita (*ar-lee-tah*) was the secretary to our Civil Engineering team. But I did not know she was Niniek's daughter. Not until now. She was a young girl, perhaps around 20, maybe 22 years old. I recalled briefly talking with Arlita here and there. She was one member of the group that sometimes hung out with the other locals and me on Saturday afternoons.

Small world, I thought.

"Yah, Ita (Arlita) takes three buses, hour and a half each way to get here and home to Muara Karang," Jamitri said.

That's three hours travelling on top of a long workday. Her engineering team and I were impressed with her work, dedication and her exceptional English, just like her mother's.

I met with Niniek around every four weeks at the partner's North Jakarta office. We discussed upcoming invoices, payments and any expected delays. She was a reasonable straight-shooter and did not ask for *considerations*, like many of her associates did.

She always asked how her daughter was doing. "Let me know if I need to straighten her out," she joked.

Having met Niniek a few times by then, I was confident she would.

10

ACCEPTING REALITIES

GRAFT, CORRUPTION AND BEYOND THE BENDING OF RULES

Every week we sent what we referred to as a *pouch* back and forth between our Missouri and Jakarta offices. The pouch was actually nothing more than a cardboard box, taped and secured. At the time, the most reliable air courier was DHL. Therefore, the pouch became known as our *DHL pouch*. It always contained project documents, inter-office correspondence and other business-related materials.

Within reason, we were allowed to include a few small, personal items such as mail to forward or things we wanted to send back to friends and family in the States. Likewise, friends and family could either mail or drop off small packaged items including mail, personal items or labeled medications. The team would put it in Monday's outgoing pouch, usually arriving in Jakarta on Wednesday or Thursday.

The DHL pouch system was especially important because sending or receiving regular letters between the countries averaged 26 days. Packages, if they made it at all, often took 3 months.

The weekly arrival of the DHL pouch in Jakarta was like *mail call*. We all appreciated what we knew was a perk. It likely cost around $200 to send the pouch but it was tremendously important to us all. Leigh usually sent something for me; cookies, a video or an occasional recorded cassette tape telling me about her activities. I would send letters, souvenirs and cassette tapes to her, showing off my developing Indonesian language skills.

The DHL pouch system worked well but had its risks. Some of our expats learned the hard way not to put anything valuable or irreplaceable into the pouch. The outbound pouches leaving Jakarta usually arrived in Missouri on time and in good condition. The inbound pouches were a different story. Indonesian customs always opened our incoming pouches. Their inspectors had unchecked authority and often damaged our incoming mail, documents and personal items. At times, they recklessly sliced envelopes and packages with razor knives, taking anything they wanted and emptying the remainder back into the box. They scattered the contents like garbage, leaving us to reassemble documents and items sent by families. There was no recourse.

Most times, the cuts were only to the surface of an envelope or package, indicating they had not actually viewed the contents. Perhaps that was only to remind us they had been there. Customs personnel didn't seem to be the best trained, the most subtle or most observant. For example, they sometimes completely destroyed a plain, ordinary item while letting something prohibited come through unscathed.

To retrieve our incoming pouch from Indonesian customs each week, our associate dispatched their office manager, along with some cash in an envelope. We learned that if we gradually increased the amount of cash in that envelope, our DHL pouch would reach us more complete and in better condition. Rupiah well spent. That's just how things worked, and no one rocked the boat.

Before taking this assignment, I had a subscription to Playboy magazine that was delivered to my home in Missouri—just for the articles, of course. Once a month, the magazine arrived in a black, nondescript plastic envelope with blank paper on both sides of the magazine itself. Before leaving the States, I had all my mail readdressed to our Missouri project team, who tagged it for me and put it in the Jakarta-bound DHL pouch. Yes, Playboy magazine was prohibited in Indonesia but surprisingly, most times it came through with just a cut or two. If customs approved it, it must be OK! I used that fact as my justification to keep it coming.

In the few instances an inspector actually realized what he had found, I would never see that edition. Nothing was ever said; no reports or complaints were made by customs. The magazine was most likely taken by an individual for himself. His gain, my loss. I knew how and where to request a replacement.

Early on, our local staff figured out that I was sneaking in the magazine. They had heard about Playboy for decades but had never actually seen one. They asked nicely. I accommodated. Whenever the last DHL pouch of the month arrived, my local coworkers were the first to come for the magazine. Even the most religious among them were interested. The girls first, then the guys would share it around the office for a day or two. They always returned it to me in excellent condition, inside a manila folder.

Word of the existence of this magazine eventually reached my invoicing counterparts: the guys who consistently *found* reasons to delay paying our invoices. Taking a chance, I tiptoed around the issue with them, learning just how much they'd like to peruse those pages. My plan was to discreetly route it to them after the office staff returned it to me. That turned out to be a good plan. The average payment time for our invoices gradually went from seven months to three. Even Ibu Niniek was surprised. She understood what was going on among her associates but had kept a warm place in her heart for our people, especially those she worked with decades before. She was cool with the arrangement and we were finally getting some invoice relief without having to violate American law! Indonesian law maybe, but not American.

Let me jump ahead a little bit here. Back in Missouri, toward the end of the following year, a new guy was assigned to a position as a logistics and transportation manager. Jack was smart and regimented but he behaved like an obsessive, by-the-book character determined to make a name for himself.

Although he had plenty of serious logistics work on his plate, Jack decided he should look into our DHL pouch system to assure we were in full compliance, not only with all U.S. and Indonesian laws, but with his personal ethics. He wanted to closely regulate everything that went into the pouch. His plan cut the shipments from once a week to only once a month. He took it upon himself to ban the shipment of personal medications, personal mail and certain business correspondence. He issued a memo saying, "Employees on foreign assignment will be responsible for making their own arrangements for any items needed to fulfill their assignments. There will be no exceptions."

He dug into and tore apart important, informal processes that had worked well for decades. One of the first things he focused on was that Playboy magazine. According to him, it most certainly had to stop immediately. That evening, I phoned him, attempting to explain how the business was benefitting from this *magazine arrangement.*

"I appreciate what you're doing, Jack. But these processes are well-established and working in our business's favor. Changing this will have significant consequences." I explained. He wouldn't listen.

"I don't give a damn," he snarled. "You'll have to figure out another way around it. This stops now!"

And so it stopped. The consequences of his short-sighted directive began almost immediately.

Without better access to many essentials they needed, some of our medication-dependent expats were particularly affected. Within the next month, two of our engineers in Jakarta turned in notices that they planned to leave the project and return with their families to the States. This was a direct result of Jack's demands.

A month after that, I received a call from our Missouri office manager asking for status on the late invoice payments. Seems there had been no monies received for two months. Of course, we knew that this was all concurrent to the changes the logistics manager had forced onto the project. His actions had cost us over $45,000 interest in less than two months.

Our Missouri managers conveyed this fact upstairs to their executive counterparts. A week or so later, I received a surprise call from my old buddy, Jim Martin. I reiterated what Jack had done. Jim was pissed.

"Hold tight. I've got a meeting with Jack this afternoon. This will go back to the way it was, including the weekly schedule."

Jim had the clout to make that happen. The next DHL pouch that arrived in Jakarta contained personal mail, all business correspondence, prescription medications for expats and even some requested by Indonesians. And yes, that magazine was there along with two back copies wrapped in brown paper with a smiley face drawn on it. Nothing had been restricted. Before long, our invoices were again being paid more promptly.

Shortly thereafter, we received a formal *thank you* letter from Jim to every expat in Jakarta.

My pleasure, I thought.

~ ~ ~

During my years in Indonesia, corruption was rampant. Sorry to say, but in the 1990s that was common in businesses throughout the country. Lots of companies and officials sought some sort of concession or perk for awarding contracts, paying their consultants and contractors or anything else that required an *approval.* The expected perk was dependent on the value of the contract. Those fringe benefits we heard about (but didn't see) included trips and vacations for executives, often to Amsterdam to *ride the white horse, (an Indonesian reference to Caucasian prostitutes in the Netherlands).* Sometimes benefits might be tuition and expenses for their kids to attend prestigious universities, such as Oxford or the University of

Amsterdam. The tangible benefits we did see included cars for executives and family members, exclusive offices and golf club memberships.

Another example of the corruption involved *store-front* companies. Business leaders often strategically allowed relatives and privileged people to set up *store-front* companies as local representatives for the global manufacturers. These store-front companies usually had no employees, only a telephone and someone slightly familiar with the equipment. A supplier wanting to sell to a project was required to go through one of these store-front companies to get the contract. Therefore, a portion of a contract's value flowed back to those relatives and privileged people, making everyone up the chain quite wealthy. This caused the final price to skyrocket but with generous money coming in from the World Bank, there was often no incentive to stop the corruption or control the costs.

In Jakarta, we had been working on a contract for Electrical Cabinetry (ECs) for months. Our partners kept stalling, repeatedly running the contract back through their internal committees. Each person in the committee felt they needed to change something in the document or their superior would think they weren't doing their job. Each time there was a change, the contract had to be started back through committee again: the ultimate Catch-22.

Each time, we'd have to produce clean copies for review as well as show them where changes had been made by the last pass through the committee. Often, this consumed months. In the meantime, our team was responsible for maintaining the original schedule.

At that point, the deadline for procurement of the ECs had passed and the delay was jeopardizing other installation interfaces.

For weeks on end, we were caught in the stall strategy, changing the contract back and forth while the real negotiations took place behind closed doors, between the partner's director and one or two of the supplier's executives. A German company was vying to supply the ECs directly to the jobsite, without going through one of their store-front companies. Our partners were putting pressure on the German supplier to use the more expensive store-front. The tug-of-war went on for months. The entire construction schedule was about to collapse if decisions were not made soon.

I was at the partner's headquarters one morning going over some changes their electrical committee wanted. From the room where I was working, I saw a small delegation of Germans who had come directly from the airport. There were four men dressed to a T in nice suits. One of them carried an exquisite brown leather briefcase. I had a good view as they stood in the hallway just outside my glassed-in conference area. I could also see part of the stairway leading to the next floor.

Two of the partner's representatives talked with the Germans as they waited to be taken up one floor into the director's office. As the guy with the briefcase shuffled, a flash caught my eye just above the case's handle. His sleeve shifted just enough for me to see that the briefcase was handcuffed to the man's wrist. The men were escorted to the director's office where two of them went inside with the briefcase while the other two waited like sentinels outside the closed door. Less than 10 minutes later, the two men emerged from the office, joined their two associates and headed back to the airport. The nice briefcase stayed behind.

I kept my head down and pretended not to observe anything, but it was clear to me what had just happened. After lunch, we were told to bring the latest cleaned up version of the EC contract to our partner's office where it was promptly awarded directly to the Germans that same afternoon. Whatever serious problems there were with this contract had been instantly, magically reconciled by whatever was in that briefcase.

Corporations and developing countries are not democratic. Therefore, speaking critically of them can be risky. In writing this history, I have tried to be careful not to offend anyone, including the Indonesian government. I believe discretion is necessary. That said, Indonesian business during the 1990s was for lack of a better term, *less than transparent*.

No country is immune to corruption. The United States certainly has its share, however, I had never seen it this close on this scale. In Indonesia, it touched people in everyday life. In addition to the EC contract, I have been in many other meetings where government officials delayed business matters until *concessions* are made.

I watched police openly collecting pay-offs to allow vendors to sell in their own stores. I saw close business associates deported for expressing their views. I personally paid immigration officials to cooperate in doing what they should have done for free. The message for the business community was always clear: if you don't pay, whatever you're trying to accomplish will be unacceptably delayed or rendered impossible. Your business and ultimately your career will suffer.

I can't vouch for all the stories I heard but I was told there was no end to the things that can be bought in Indonesia. They include votes, permits, contracts, copies of your competitor's contracts, copies of expensive products like Rolex watches, knock-off perfumes and people, (at least rented).

Looking at it humorously, a managing associate from another project told of wanting to entertain some visiting business executives so he sent his local rep out to charter a boat for a day's touring around Pulau Seribu, around 20 miles north of Jakarta. The rep returned empty-handed.

The now-desperate associate sent him back out with a lot more money, saying, "Surely there's something you can find!"

Two hours later, the rep met the executives at the Ancol dock with an 80-foot Indonesian Coast Guard gunboat, complete with uniformed crew, live ammo, girls and beer. I can't vouch for his story, but knowing what I know, I don't doubt it.

Once again, Indonesia is a beautiful and fascinating country where tourists can easily obtain a two-month visa upon arrival at any port. However, in the 1990s those coming there to do business were seen as *deep pockets* and there were many hands trying to get in your pants. It affected productivity, operating costs and profitability.

In spite of the corruption, I always enjoyed living in Indonesia. Every day brought a new adventure. But the unbridled corruption was hard to accept. Writing this chapter has allowed me to vent some of my frustration. Should I ever forget what it was like working in Indonesia during that time, this will remind me.

11

EPIPHANY

A Parting of Ways

It was a Saturday evening in August 1993. Six of us expats hired one of our office drivers to take us around the city for some food, fun and entertainment. That was easier and safer than dealing with taxis and it was a way for our drivers to make good money on the side.

We started our evening at the Hard Rock Café where the Australian beef burgers were an expensive but welcome treat. Adding some beer and dessert made it easy to drop more money in one evening than I'd spend in a week on local food.

A couple of hours later, we made the usual expat stop at the Tavern, a ground-level bar inside the Aryaduta Hotel. The Tavern reminded me of the bar scene in Star Wars. There were characters from all over the planet, each with their own personal reason for being there.

Late on a Saturday night, The Tavern was an interesting place to have a drink or two. Entertainment included watching the eternal hustles, negotiations, cigarette girls, short-skirted barmaids and 300-pound Western expats with their glazed eyes and slack jaws, looking as though they had been welded to their drunken barstool for months. As midnight approached, someone suggested we head for Tanamur. I didn't know what that was but I was willing to find out.

Established in 1970, Tanamur was the oldest and certainly the most renowned of the country's discotheques. It had long earned the reputation of being the wildest. Parked outside was every vehicle imaginable from Lamborghinis and Maseratis to mopeds, becaks, bajajs, bicycles, trucks, sedans, vans and buses. Dozens of drivers stood by their employers' vehicles, guarding them, moving them back and forth to accommodate others leaving or arriving.

By its outward appearance, Tanamur was old and rugged. It was in a large, free-standing building resembling an airplane hangar with a storefront attached as its entrance.

I learned that Tanamur was notorious for its highly egalitarian mix of patrons, an assortment of people from the lowest to the highest levels of social status. This might include wealthy CEOs, government ministers' sons, flight attendants, sons of military generals and expats from all over the world. There were teenage girls and boys from Europe, girls on the prowl, farm girls in borrowed dresses, girls from surrounding islands, girls that weren't girls, bad girls, bad guys, gays, gangsters and wannabees.

Anyone who could pay the roughly $10 equivalent entry fee was welcome. Everyone was encouraged to blend in, dance tightly with anyone and everyone and join others thirsting for the long, wild night ahead. In 1993, Tanamur still reigned as the hottest nightspot in all of Southeast Asia. One British expat described his experience, "It felt like Caligula's Rome in there, without the grapes."

Our group arrived around midnight. Those who had been there before gave the rest of us the lowdown on the place. Everyone agreed that we'd stay for one hour. Anyone not out front by 1:00 a.m. would need to find their own way home.

Getting inside was beyond intimidating. It was scary. What little I could see was alluring, but I could tell that my time in this den of inequity was going to be short. The entire building seemed to groan and bend from the mass of humanity pulsating to the beat of deafening house music. It took 15 minutes to get barely 10 feet inside the door. I was done. It took me another 10 minutes to get back outside. We all left for home well ahead of our 1:00 a.m. agreement. *Perhaps another time.*

Earlier in July, I had received an unscheduled call from Leigh. "I've got a lot of vacation time coming and I'd like to come see you near the end of August." That was especially good news. That said, I was a bit taken back when she told me she only had six days, including her travel time. That meant she would have less than four days with me. There was a slight chance I could fly to Kansas City and see her around the end of the year, so I let it slide. I was happy she was coming.

Leigh was a seasoned international traveler but coming to Indonesia would be the longest flight she had ever made. She was pretty tired when I met her at Jakarta's airport, hired a taxi and showed her the downtown area on the way to my apartment. We toured my office and drove by the church she encouraged me to attend. Surprisingly, she didn't want to go inside.

We enjoyed a cozy evening and the next morning, flew to Bali for two days. I hired a driver and we tooled around, showing her some of my favorite sights. She was excited about the large, colorful quilts made by local people. We stopped at several roadside displays before she found just the one she wanted.

Our last night back in Jakarta was strangely melancholy.

During dinner, out of nowhere she said, "I'm really happy that you go out with the groups. I wouldn't be mad if you're romantic with a girl sometimes, as long as you're careful."

There was a joke-like, big sister tone to her voice but she was serious. At the time, it sounded like a random but generous thing for her to say.

Responding to this surprising declaration of permission, I told her, "There have been opportunities but our relationship is more important. I value this connection we share. It's fun and it brings me happiness."

There was a long pause as she thought about my words.

I continued, "Don't get me wrong, I certainly miss being with you, too; so much that at times, it burns."

Another pause…

"But we're worth the wait, *especially when we do get together*," I teased.

Leigh casually responded, "Well, you never know. We're only human and people get lonely."

Why I didn't ask right then if she wanted to see other guys, I'll never know. But I didn't, and we left it at that.

At dawn the next morning I accompanied her to the airport and on to her departure gate. We talked for a half-hour or so as we perused the tourist gift shops. As boarding was announced and she gathered her things, she hurriedly mentioned, "I'll be spending the remainder of my vacation time with friends."

She didn't identify these *friends*. Normally, she would have. If she had wanted me to know who they were, she'd have told me, and much sooner. Her calculated message seemed to imply that this part of her life may have become none of my business. She went on to recommend that we not communicate between mid-November and mid-December because she would be traveling, at times overseas. Again, she offered no details. We had always been open and communicative, so that was an unusual red flag.

Leigh was great at planning ahead. Even her trips to the grocery store, dry cleaners or other minor arrangements were pre-scheduled in her Franklin planner. I knew she never made big decisions on the spur of the moment. She had previously schooled me on her process and her dedication to that planner. Therefore, I could extrapolate that a month-long international trip with friends (or friend) would have been penciled in at least as far back as May. This was late August. Leigh wasn't being transparent but I didn't confront her. I chose to let it go. It didn't feel like rejection, more like a veiled message softly letting me know that our once-solid relationship was dissolving into something less. The realization wasn't pleasant. But it wasn't devastating. Our time together in Indonesia had been fun, a blurry and nearly sleepless three days. It felt like a moment rather than a visit; one that left many un-asked, unanswered questions. That was Leigh's style.

After her visit, I gradually came to understand that her generous permission for me to date others had not been random at all. In her often-passive way, Leigh had delivered a slowly-developing message. She was skilled at seeding conversations with *trickle-down truths;* allowing a message delivered one day to germinate and bloom into the whole truth long after the seed had been planted. I had been a bit naïve, taking a while to let her crafted messages sink in. But three quick days with me, the better part of a month traveling with *friends?* Yeah, that was rather telling. Our closeness and her commitment were diminishing but neither of us were calling things off. I wouldn't stand in her way. Nor would I remain exclusive.

By late December, I had been in Indonesia for 10 months. Our staff was constantly bogged down by contract award delays as our partner's negotiated for better terms and better *considerations* from the dozens of vendors providing equipment and services. We could not escape the long, fruitless meetings at the partner's headquarters. Often, our entire staff wasted hours in a conference room doing practically nothing while waiting for one important official to arrive from the floor above. Progress was painfully slow.

Every few months, I received a letter from my pen pal buddy, Susan. Her writings were filled with that same, youthful pride and ambition, telling me of her efforts to find real work in the mostly rural region where she lived. Jobs that paid a decent salary were scarce throughout the country, especially in rural areas and small towns away from the larger cities. Even so, that same optimism was always there. She never dwelled on problems.

But by now, I was always busy and hardly noticed when her writing stopped. Rarely, it crossed my mind that she had likely found work and was growing into her own life. I tucked her letters away with the others, figuring no news likely meant good news.

~ ~ ~

I was still hanging out with the Indonesian group on Saturday afternoons. After all, I now had permission, right? But our afternoon group was gradually getting smaller. It seemed that we all had other things going on and I was starting to go out more by myself.

On weekend evenings, I went out with other expats to restaurants and bars that catered to Westerners. Most were located downtown where getting a late-night taxi home was convenient. The Hard Rock Cafe was always a safe place where we could listen to music and count on great food and drink.

Wherever we went, it seemed there were intoxicated expats at tables and barstools right alongside Western expat families with young children. Everyone was peaceful.

"Cigarette, Meester?" Often, there were teams of young Indonesian *cigarette girls* wearing colorful, skimpy outfits, offering free samples and flirty come-ons as they made the rounds between Jakarta's bars, restaurants and hotel lobbies. Most were sponsored by American tobacco brands licensed in Indonesia. A throw-back to America's early 20th-century, there were no age restrictions or protections to keep people from getting hooked on tobacco.

~ ~ ~

Although it had limited hours, the American Embassy Club served exceptionally good food. One evening in mid-December, I had dinner there with Rick Wilder, our Jakarta project manager and his wife.

"You ready to sign on for another six months?" Wilder asked. He was leaning on me to extend my assignment beyond February, 1994, which was coming up in less than two months.

He told me that Jim Martin had OK'd an uptick in my salary. Still, I was doing my best not to commit just yet.

As we finished our meal and started to leave, I noticed a stack of flyers pinned to the framed corkboard by the exit. The flyer was an invitation from U.S. Ambassador Barry's wife. The Barrys were hosting a Christmas get-together and tree lighting event on December 22. All Americans were invited. Lots of expats were returning to their countries over the upcoming holidays. Not me, I had no plans for Thursday the 22. I stuck a flyer in my pocket.

When Wednesday evening arrived, I took a taxi to the Ambassador's home in Jakarta's Menteng community. I was greeted by his friendly, Indonesian housekeeper. Properly dressed for the occasion, I went into their home not recognizing a single person in the crowd. It wasn't long before Mrs. Barry picked up on my awkward, wallflower stance. She came over and we introduced ourselves.

Right away she asked, "Could you give us a hand in the kitchen? It has really gotten busy!"

"Of course I can," I responded.

I spent the next 20 minutes being introduced to other guests while helping the Ambassador's wife dispense fresh-baked cookies to strangers who would become new acquaintances. Socially, that was exceptionally skillful and truly nice of her.

Surprisingly, Indonesia is religiously tolerant. Even though it is predominately Islamic, Indonesia still recognizes Christmas and many other religion's holidays. And, people from other religions celebrate Christmas right along with the 10 percent of Indonesia's Christian population. Regardless of my location, the Christmas season had always been a special time of the year. But dampened by chaos, commerce and cost, to me it had lost much of its sparkle.

Christmas was still a couple of days away. Around Jakarta, many of the businesses including our partner's offices were slowing down for the holidays. Most of our expat staff was gone and there wasn't much going on. I hadn't really planned on it, but I kind of wanted to take a quick trip back to the States. It was nearly impossible to get time away on short notice. But if you don't ask, you don't get! I persuaded Wilder to call in a favor from one of the partner's representatives. This guy was in a position to approve some time off for me. I knew he owed Wilder some favors and by this time, Wilder owed a couple to me. It worked. I made arrangements with other people to cover the minimal work. I messaged Leigh, who had by now returned from her long vacation. I planned to go out on the town with the Indonesians that night, then fly out of Jakarta on Christmas Day.

En route, there was a nine-hour layover in Hong Kong—more than enough time to go into town. Hong Kong was a massive, fascinating city. I spent most of my layover around the waterfront stores and street-side restaurants, wandering through its alluring shops and taking photos and videos. But I could barely scratch the surface of the city's offerings.

In a gorgeous window display at one of the electronic shops, I found a really cool multi-band, shortwave radio that I wanted. I discovered that the bargaining skills I had honed in Indonesia were not effective there—not the least bit. The Chinese shopkeeper operated on fixed prices and although I applied every bargaining tactic I could, nothing worked. But hey, Jakarta had taught me not to give up. So I persisted. In fact, I persisted until the shopkeeper grabbed a broom and chased me out of his store!

Recovering my wounded pride, I quickly and politely relocated to another street and a different electronics store. This time without haggling, I bought that nice Sony Multiband IFC-SW30 Radio at a reasonable price. Decades later, I still had that radio.

I found a couple of small gifts for Leigh then made my way back to the airport. From Hong Kong, it was 13 boring hours to Los Angeles and another equally boring four to Kansas City.

On December 27, 1993, Leigh picked me up at the airport. I travelled light so there was no waiting for luggage. We pulled away from the curb and headed directly to her home in Kansas City. Our drive started out cheerful enough.

"The traveling was worth being here with you." I took her hand.

Leigh kept her eyes on the road. Her jaw tightened and her grip was stiff. I watched a tear form, inching down her face.

"What's going on, Leigh?" I asked, responding to the sudden change in her mood. She pulled her hand away and wiped her eye. "We're still good friends and I still want to do things with you, but I'm really disappointed that you haven't grown religiously."

The awkward conversation continued into her home. Obviously, Leigh was carrying a burden of some kind and her fresh comment about religion sort of laid it at my feet. We'd had these kinds of conversations before so I was pretty sure this was about something other than religion.

I pulled out a dining table chair for her, then sat across from her with my hands folded on the table. In a moment, I reached across placing one hand on hers. "Tell me what's going on, Leigh." I hoped a calm voice would make it easier for her.

"I've really struggled to get the nerve to tell you...," she started; her voice faint and trembling.

I waited.

She took a deep breath then confessed, "I've dated others."

I wasn't especially surprised, but it was still a gut punch to hear her actually say those words.

"Ah, OK." I needed a few seconds to compose. She continued to fidget.

"When did you begin seeing others?" I asked, sounding stronger than I felt. But I thought I was owed that.

"Months, I suppose", she revealed. "Maybe six."

I had a hunch her six months was closer to nine. She probably resumed dating right after I took the assignment and left the States. She had provided plenty of veiled clues during her brief visit to Jakarta. I just didn't want to acknowledge them.

"Anyone special?" I queried, trying to sound unaffected despite the ache in my gut.

She looked at her hands on the table, shook her head while softly responding, "No, just good friends. There's some romance here and there."

Knowing the intensity of romance with her, I didn't ask for further details. That would only add needless embarrassment to the guilt she was feeling. Although she hadn't been transparent over the past months, Leigh had been good to me. I didn't want her to suffer or be hurt. The best approach I could take now was to lighten the mood and try to bring forth some understanding, caring and happiness.

"Thanks for telling me." I placed my hands over hers and felt her fingers stop wriggling. "But I thought we had covered this when you were in Jakarta last August." I looked at her troubled face, waiting for her to lift her eyes to mine. "Your long vacation with *friends*?" I had already put two and two together." I smiled as she shrugged one shoulder.

"It's OK, I'm OK and we're OK." I said, then paused.

"Are you OK?" I asked, smiling and squeezing her hands.

We both chuckled. Her tension began to subside.

"Leigh, I'm really thankful for you and all you've done for me. I totally get it. You need an active social life."

"Thank God." Her sigh caught in her throat and came out a sob. "I wasn't sure you'd understand."

Yeah, I did understand. It hurt but I didn't let it show. I felt a tinge of humiliation, mostly from the unnecessary deception, the secrecy and her little passive-aggressive traps I kept disregarding before stumbling into. By ignoring clues and not asking tough questions at the right time, I played a part in my own indignity. From our beginning, I hadn't wanted to rock the boat. But with transparency and a little bit of trust from Leigh, all of this unpleasantness could have been avoided. In our own ways, we were both culpable.

During my visit, I stayed at Leigh's home while she went about her routines. I took care of some business and visited other friends in the area while she was at her office. She never spoke of that long vacation nor the friends (or friend) who accompanied her. I didn't ask because it no longer mattered. We came together in the evenings, exchanged gifts and enjoyed prodigious, intimate time together. She and I agreed we had a bruised but respectful friendship.

"With benefits here and there," she playfully added.

It was cool to hear her say that. If our intimate paths crossed in the future, I'd certainly enjoy it. But right then, something deeper inside mourned the passing of closeness than in all likelihood, was gone forever.

I left Kansas City and returned to Indonesia just after New Year's, 1994. Going forward there were no more efforts to be exclusive. There was no more veiled pretending, no more pressure to join her religion.

Naturally, the coming months realized dramatic changes in our friendship. The emotional distance between us widened. We no longer called on a regular schedule and our email exchanges faded away. Rarely, she would send a note or a Star Trek episode she had recorded off her TV onto VHS. That said, Leigh continued to honor every logistical responsibility she had initially made to support my assignment. She continued watching after my car and kept my important papers safely at her home. I deeply appreciated her for that.

~   ~   ~

Workwise, Wilder had already asked me to extend my assignment in Indonesia. It took a little while to grasp the idea that there was now nothing or no one else to consider when making decisions. It was me alone and I had good options. I could return to the States and work for my company or a number of others, or I could remain in Indonesia indefinitely.

New opportunities in other countries were becoming available. In Indonesia, I had become acquainted with other expat professionals who worked all over the planet. Most were American. They had lived a lucrative, expatriate life for decades and had no intention of returning to the States, even to retire. As a result of my association with some of these folks, I received serious job offers from professional contracting firms around the world. If I were interested, I could practically name my ticket. I considered the real possibility that I may never again live in the U.S. That felt OK. In fact, it felt good. I could visualize a lifetime of adventure and prosperity ahead.

With one less tie to the States and a vision of a global future, I agreed to stay with my team in Indonesia until the end of August 1994.

~   ~   ~

Since first arriving in Indonesia, whenever I had gone into the modern shopping centers such as Pasaraya or Selina, the salesgirls, office managers or salon girls who cut my hair would smile and slip me a name card with their phone number. It was not unusual for local girls to invite me out for lunch or just to hang out. Before, I had politely said, *no thank you*. But that was then.

With no responsibilities other than work, I now found time to date several beautiful, educated girls. OK, so it became a lot of beautiful, educated girls and a lot of nice girls in between. I admit that I thoroughly enjoyed being the hunted rather than the hunter. The Equatorial Effect was doing its thing! But I was also wise enough to know it wasn't something that would last. I was a novelty. I was as careful and respectful as I could be. I took care with issues that could affect my health and did my best never to abuse this sweet gift of feminine affection so unexpectedly bestowed upon me.

I tried to find meaningful ways to help the girls I dated. I helped write resumes and coached people on interviewing. I paid for optometrist visits, eyeglasses, cataract surgery, dentists and pagers. I bought clothing and helped families, including little siblings who needed medical care or school expenses. The things I accomplished for people were done with money the average expatriate spent on a weekend of partying. Helping people made me feel good. I found ways to do it and would have helped even without the tender rewards I so selfishly accepted.

I was making and saving a whole lot of money and on top of that, the $600 a month I had been spending on phone calls now remained in my bank account. Still, I chose to live just above what most expats might have considered street level. Many of my expatriate associates spent their entire monthly allowances in addition to what they earned. I did my best to save. I walked a lot. When necessary, I hired cheap bajajs and taxis rather than having a dedicated driver. I chose much cheaper housing and sincerely enjoyed Indonesian foods. I understood the possibility that this fortunate situation might not last, so I banked as much as I could.

12

THE TRAFFICKERS

THE DARKEST SIDE OF HUMANITY

The first part of this chapter comes from my own personal experiences, observations and conversations with Indonesians. The second part contains unedited articles and publications directly from respectable Southeast Asian and European newspapers. These include *The Singapore Straits Times*, *Kompas* and *The Jakarta Post*. Therein are many case studies from victims and survivors, told to journalists who translated and reported the actual events.

My awareness of human trafficking first began when a group of us expats set out on that boat trip to Sangiang Island last Fourth of July. Along the way we were stalled in the steamy, ferryboat traffic when our driver made a profound comment that really stuck with me. Upon seeing a little white van filled with village girls heading somewhere for employment, he said with a resigned expression, "They will never be seen again."

Eventually I came to understand what he meant and it sickened me. Organized human trafficking is one of Indonesia's horrible, dirty little secrets. It has been going on for centuries. During my time in the country and even beyond, Indonesia had made little progress toward stopping it.

After that boat trip, I asked my Indonesian friends if they had heard about this business of selling children into bondage. Everyone had. This crime against their countrymen was on their minds but like so many of the country's problems, they were powerless to do anything. The subject was never talked about unless I brought it up. Our Indonesian staff learned about my interest in this matter and over time, brought me numerous, related articles.

From my queries I learned that the country's poverty, widespread slavery rings and lack of law enforcement due to corruption, make the innocent especially vulnerable. Indonesians are also inherently trusting. Too often this trust is used against them in cruel ways. It's also not something any government likes to make public. They would not appreciate some outsider rubbing their nose in it, either. That said, it needs to be exposed so I'm going to pull back this curtain of evil.

To reveal even more about traffickers, I should first tell you how I learned the frightening realities and about the person who told me. This came from someone with direct knowledge, someone who was willing to talk. Although portions of this come from a third party named Tanya, I'm confident her testimony had merit and mirrors the truth.

I returned from the States in early January 1994, finding a lull in our Jakarta work. I had a little extra time on my hands. Since my relationship with Leigh had cooled to the friend stage, my outlook and activities shifted. I'd never been a serious drinker but I became more interested in going to restaurants, bars and entertainment venues. One Saturday when I was looking for something a bit more exciting than usual, I decided to go back to Tanamur by myself. Remembering how we could barely get inside the door that night, I decided to beat the crowd. I dressed casually in some of my nicer clothes. I put some folded money in zippered pockets and a bit more in my shoes. The taxi ride was timed to get there around 9:00 p.m., right as Tanamur opened. Tonight, the driver was fast and delivered me a bit ahead of that.

The club was quiet but it was open so I paid the cover charge and went inside. The smell of stale, spilled beer, cigarettes and cleaning supplies assaulted my nostrils. The room was the size of a gymnasium. The bar and main floor were accessed by a short stairway around six feet lower than the entrance. High above, there were empty balconies and suspended walkways awaiting the night's dancers. I could actually get all the way inside and see around the entire interior.

The first of two DJs was on her platform. She had just queued up "All That She Wants" by the Swedish band Ace of Bass. I had never heard that song in such detail and with such power. The DJ bounced around to the music while organizing the setup for the night's show.

This early in the evening, there were maybe 30 people in the whole place. Around the massive room there were about 15 tables, a few were occupied by young women and house dancers who would go to work when the masses arrived. The venue was vacant in comparison to the crowded place I had seen months before. The music was alluring but no one, not even the house dancers were on the floor yet. The girls slouched around the room while laughing and chatting among themselves, seemingly killing time. These girls would come alive when their real reasons for being there came through the door. But at the moment, Tanamur's dragon was still sleeping.

Getting to the large bar and actually finding a barstool was incredibly easy. For the moment, I was the only one at the main, L-shaped bar; 30 stools to my left, another 20 to my right. In this rare solitude, I ordered an orange juice, fresh-squeezed on ice. It cost around 75 cents. At 11:00 p.m., that same, simple OJ with no alcohol would jump to five times the price.

With no crowd, I could see three other entrances to the building but they were all barricaded. The only exit sign was above the single doorway where I had entered. It was one way in, one way out, with that one set of rickety, wooden stairs leading from the main floor up six feet to the single exit door. If a fire broke out when this place was full, no one would stand a chance. It could easily become one of those horrible news stories a sleepy world wakes to some Sunday morning: *Overnight Fire in Remote Country Kills 1,500!* This club, Tanamur was considered the most densely populated place on the most densely populated island in the world.

Soon, the second DJ arrived. The two energetic young women continued spinning singles and extended versions of popular, Western dance tunes by well-known, global artists such as General Public, Madonna and C+C Music Factory. I could see the sound system included powerful analog and digital amplification with feeder cables encased in rigid steel conduit to protect them from the hazards of unpredictable crowds. A series of 12 tremendous, Electro-Voice speakers, each taller than me, ringed the upper interior of the building. A smaller series of speakers was located along the walls around five feet below the upper ring. The system was state of the art. Being a long-time audiophile, I confirm it rocked.

The music was crisp, clear and of course, loud. The concert-hall acoustics were exceptional so for the moment, it was still possible to have a pleasant conversation. The atmosphere was friendly and laid back.

But in just under two hours, the *dragon* that is Tanamur would raise its head and swell beyond capacity. The transformation would be near instantaneous. At 11:00 p.m., the DJs would increase the volume and switch over to relentless, pulsing house music that would go on until the place closed at 3:00 a.m. Patrons would no longer be able to process what they were hearing; absorbing rather than listening to the music. They'd become a part of it. They'd sense it through the pure, electric energy, the synchronized rhythm of laser lighting, the never-ending beat and the savage pressure from hordes of bodies pressed against each other.

Overhead walkways would spill over with sensual silhouettes of slinky house dancers. Elbow room would be lost. Conversation would require yelling inches away from someone's ear, hand gestures or writing notes on napkins. Getting drinks might take an hour. Restrooms would be out of the question.

I was glad to be there early. My plan was to leave just after the dragon raised its head and began breathing fire.

Within 10 minutes of my arrival, an attractive young woman came over and took a stool next to mine. There were now two of us at the long bar. In broken English, she held out her hand and introduced herself as Tanya. We made small talk for a moment.

"You speak Indonesian?" she asked.

"Sedikit saja." (*Yes, a little.*)

She pointed to my orange juice, "You buy one for me?"

As Tanya sipped her orange juice, I studied her, sitting primly next to me on her stool. She was a slender girl, not much over five feet. I guessed she was in her late 20s to early 30s. Her shoulder-length black hair had some body to it, as if she had been to the salon before coming out. She was pleasantly presentable, dressed neatly in a yellow cotton top with epaulettes, rolled, tabbed sleeves, and a brown skirt that ended respectfully above her knees. It was not the finest fabric, but her attire was neatly pressed and far more modest than the short, cheeky party dresses most of the other girls wore. She didn't smoke. Her face was clean and pretty but displayed a history of hardship. Dressed as she was, she looked a bit out of place. But she seemed quite comfortable in these surroundings.

We hadn't talked much before she asked if I were married.

"No," I responded. "I had a girlfriend last year but we are no longer together."

"You like to take me to your home?" she asked.

"Thanks, but no. I am not interested tonight. Just here to have a drink and listen to music," I answered.

Over the coming minutes, she came at me with variations of the same question, wanting to hook up. My answer was always the same.

She looked around the place, seeming to me as though scouting for more lucrative opportunities.

Not finding any, she asked, "Is OK, I just sit with you and we talk, OK?"

"That would be nice."

I knew this was all about commercial affection. She needed money or she wouldn't be here. And if I monopolized her time chatting, I'd provide respectable compensation before I left. But I wasn't going to take her home.

Tanya was definitely talkative. Between her English and my modest Indonesian, we communicated quite well. She asked all about my world and what I was doing here. She told me she was from a rural area outside of Bogor. Tanya's day job was as a seamstress.

"Very good one," she boasted.

Each Monday before dawn, she traveled by bus into Jakarta to find day work at one of the hundreds of tailor shops. If one shop didn't need her that day, she went to others in hopes of finding a shop that did. Many times, there was none. When she did work, she made the equivalent of about two dollars for a 10-hour day. She explained that Ramadan was just three weeks away and like the lead up to Christmas, the shops were busy and she was currently working every day.

During the week, Tanya stayed with some other girls in Jakarta, then usually went home to her village on Sundays.

She said, "*Ma'af, aku malu,*" which meant she was embarrassed that I now knew what she did when she wasn't sewing.

"I come Tanamur to make money for parents and young daughter."

"It's OK, Tanya. I see you as a very good seamstress."

She caught my humor and laughed along with it.

"I understand. You must love your family very much."

In her fragmented English, she continued, "Allah give me permission to do this because I must to feed and protect my daughter from bad thing. She going high school in two months."

Tanya told of how her husband left many years ago and there has never been any word from him. Perhaps not, but I suspected that years back, she had trusted the wrong person and never actually married. But in Indonesia, it is important to save face. Being an unwed mother would have brought shame to her and her family. Regardless, her story provided a shield against such shame. It would be wrong of me to challenge it. She said her dream was to have a real relationship, perhaps someday marry. But that most men will not accept her.

"I even OK to be a contract wife, if it is with good man who is kind to me," she added.

Throughout Indonesia, women sometimes pair with foreign men in an informal agreement, or *contract*. The contract might be for a set period of time or until the man finishes his job and leaves the country. It is usually quite casual and mutually beneficial, not unlike casually *shacking up* back in the states.

Tanya's stories were interesting, and I was enjoying myself. It was easy to take her at her word, putting together my own observations with the things she had said.

It took me a while to finally recognize that she had in fact made the clothes she was wearing. She actually was a very good seamstress.

I pointed to her yellow top and asked, "You make?"

"Yah, Meester, Tanya make baju semua (*all clothes*) for my family."

Taking breaks between her stories, Tanya never stopped trying to get me to hire her that night.

~ ~ ~

What a difference a year makes! That night I was sitting in a bar on the other side of the planet, drinking orange juice while fending off come-ons from a lady of the evening who wants a real relationship. *Equatorial Effect?* Discounting the humor in this circumstance, I felt a tinge of concern for this woman's future and that of her young daughter.

As we talked, the subject turned to the fate of young girls and traffickers. This triggered my attention toward the human trafficking I had been hearing about. This was where Tanya became my teacher.

Tanya told me there were many other working girls like her there that night. I kind of thought so. She turned to wave at others who waved back from their dimly lit tables.

"All girls here same like me. We come to make friend and to make money, no just for fun. It is work," she explained. "But sometimes is fun, too."

As we talked, I asked graphic questions. Her answers were even more graphic.

Tanya was a *working girl* with an actual day job. She came to places like this to earn extra money, albeit part-time. She explained that men gave her money to be their girlfriend. She admitted they sometimes had sex. Other times, the man just wanted companionship. He might take her to dinner or buy her some nice things, maybe even some groceries. She came to Tanamur occasionally and when she did, it was only on Saturdays after she finished her tailoring work. Even though there was an exchange of money, she did not consider herself a prostitute.

"*Prostitute sama Ayam-Gila,* (prostitute is like a crazy chicken)."

I asked, "You mean like *Kupu-Kupu Malam* (night butterfly, a more respectable term for lady of the night)."

She quickly corrected me, "*N'gak, Tanya sama burung manis,*" (No, Tanya is like a sweet bird).

I could see that.

Tanya pointed out which girls were the house dancers. They were easy to distinguish by their halter tops and tight skirts or their one-piece, super-short dresses that offered a teasing flash of bare derriere. These sexy house dancers were paid by the management to keep the place rocking, reminiscent of America's Go-Go dancers from decades before. At least eight were there early. Another eight arrived before 11:00 p.m. If they worked the whole night, they could hustle tips and also receive around four dollars from the house. That was quite a lot compared to what Tanya made in 10 hours as a seamstress. The girls could also hustle men on the side but if they left before closing time at 3:00 a.m., they wouldn't get their four-dollar house wages. Those tips and those four dollars were significant. As such, house dancer hookups usually had to wait until after closing.

Tanya seemed to know many of the arriving patrons. Many seemed to know her. As the night progressed, more and more arrived. She waved at the new arrivals, saying hello with handshakes and air kisses. She pointed out who were guys dressed as girls, and vise-versa.

Tanya whispered and alerted me when *'Ayam-Gilas'* (prostitutes) came in.

She told me who to be careful of, including "Girls from Sulawesi who carry knives in their waistbands," she warned.

I asked if she knew about the labor worker girls, the tenaga kerja wanitas (or TKWs) and if they were treated badly?

"Oh ya, TKW," she said with confidence. "Yah, not good for them."

Tanya told me in detail how young girls, especially pretty girls are lured from their small, rural towns and remote villages. There are various layers of traffickers who place ads in newspapers and publications around the country. Recruiters promise domestic and foreign work, making it sound more like a career than a job. From first contact, recruiters begin applying heavy debt to their victims; debt that will later be used against them. The girls are *charged* the equivalent of thousands of U.S. dollars for communication, transportation, food and housing as they are taken to various locations. Most girls don't even realize they are accumulating debt until they are shown the overwhelming charges.

Across the country, unsuspecting families often pooled their meager resources to send their daughters away to work, hoping someday for a return on their investment. Traffickers especially preyed on girls who were trusting of authority, honestly innocent and naïve. Listening to her stories, assessing her knowledge, I wondered if this had happened to Tanya in her earlier years. Had she been caught in these traps and managed to survive?

It's important to understand that throughout rural Indonesia, a young girl is raised to prize and hold onto her virginity at all cost. She is religiously taught that losing one's virginity out of wedlock immediately disqualified her from meaningful marriage and happiness with a nice man. Right or wrong, this is a strong lesson, deeply ingrained in the girl's mind throughout her rural childhood. At some point, a trafficker may use this against a girl.

Tanya continued her story. Sadly, many girls were instead, sold directly into prostitution. The recruiters brought attractive girls into large *prostitute villages* found throughout the country. In the beginning, the new recruits were treated nicely. Girls were provided with a tiny but nice private room and free food. They were encouraged to socialize with the other girls. The 'Bapak' (*in this case, referring to the village "father figure"*) wanted the new girls to feel comfortable and become part of the community.

All the while, the other girls were forbidden to warn a new arrival. Over a couple of weeks or so, the Bapak gradually tried to convince the girl to voluntarily submit. He knew a virgin was worth more. He coaxed his other girls to keep up the pressure. He might even offer her a portion of the maybe $50 *bonus* he received for providing an agreeable virgin to one of his visiting, foreign customers. These numbers sounded huge to a young village girl who had nothing. Many agreed and were tricked into the business this way.

If the girl continued to resist and hadn't *joined* within a month or so of her recruitment, a stronger approach would follow. Girls were often raped to break them in. Traffickers would arrange to take their prized virginity in order to break their spirit and force them into submission.

Tanya explained in sickening detail how one of these methods worked. The girl's close neighbors in her building would be subtly invited to go somewhere as a group so they could be removed from the immediate area. This was often on a Sunday afternoon when the village was officially closed. The place would be virtually empty and quiet. The lone girl would answer a knock at her door and encounter a group of a half dozen masked men who would quickly, violently pushed their way into her tiny, now isolated room.

These men were not there for sexual gratification. They were a rape squad. This was their purpose and they were paid to do it. They had one goal: to take away her virginity, her most prized possession. They would quickly restrain the girl. Each man had an assigned task. Most would restrain her limbs so she could not resist or injure herself. She was no match for one of these men, much less the whole squad. Another man would subdue her head, cover her face and muffle her screams and cries. They were skilled at preventing injury. Once subdued, the girl's lower clothing would be quickly removed; her legs would be spread and held back. She would be penetrated by one of the men who wore a condom. The perpetrator would ensure he had sufficiently penetrated her enough that she knew she was no longer a virgin. They would taunt her, telling her just that. That was their only goal.

The rape would be complete within a couple of minutes. Then quickly, the men would systematically release her and leave, disappearing into the surrounding, outlying communities. She would be left there with no serious physical injuries but completely terrified and distraught over the attack and at losing her virginity.

As if on cue, the neighbors and the Bapak would return and pretend to be horrified at what they found. The girl would be quickly comforted by the community of other girls. She would be hugged, bathed and lavished with lots of healing attention. Ironically, some of the other girls caring for her would have endured the same thing. They knew it was going to happen. But talking about it, warning someone would have severe consequences.

The victim would not be left alone, having other girls who had been assigned to take her under their wing while providing security and comfort. The police or other authorities would never be called. They would never take the side of a girl living in that village.

The Bapak would continue with his fake, fatherly advice. Gradually, she would begin to feel safe again. Over time, the now hopeless girl would again be approached to join. The other girls would show her the money. They'd tell her "It's fun, it's easy." They'd teach her and help her get started. The Bapak would remind her she owes a whole lot of money. He would continually remind her that she no longer has anything to lose. After presenting her with all this over time, she'd most likely accept her fate and become a sex worker.

Tanya went on to tell me about other local, nighttime venues where girls worked as prostitutes. She mentioned small showrooms where men went to select from a waiting group of girls. Apparently, these showrooms existed throughout the city and at all levels of *quality*.

As long as these girls paid the showroom a hosting fee upfront, they were free to come and go as they wanted. If they didn't have the upfront money, the showroom had control over them, keeping them as virtual slaves. When there was no customer, the girls might hang out in the back, talking, laughing and helping one another with their hair and outfits.

When a customer arrived, the decorative lights went on and the girls entered into the showroom where they sat on velvet, display-style seating, did their best to look attractive and offered themselves for selection. The customer was under no obligation to follow through, the girl was. The negotiation was between the two. If a deal was reached, she either left with the customer or joined him somewhere later.

As bad as this was, Tanya told how other girls were sent overseas and suffered an even more dangerous fate. "Many girls buried in the desert.

Tanya have family member in Middle East, five year. She always work seven day. It was being a slave."

She told me that those who did come back were usually robbed of any money they had earned. More is written about these victims in the newspaper articles below.

Tanya spoke of the children left behind by young prostitutes who had no way to care for them. The children were not welcome in the prostitute villages and the mothers couldn't leave the villages. That created still another industry as well as an abundance of infants, and orphans, such as those I saw along the road to Merak.

Tanya's stories were shocking. That said, I had been in-country long enough to understand their validity. I had not expected the education I received that night. It wasn't what Tanya had in mind, either. Still, we both came away with something.

By this time, I had overstayed my plan and my evening at Tanamur was rapidly coming to a close. Perhaps to soften the awaiting crowd to the looming dragon, the DJs closed out their singles with Gloria Estefan's, *Tradicion*. The place was nearly full. Powerful house music had taken over and I could no longer hear Tanya.

I managed to thank her for the stories. She bowed, hands together, humbly accepting the folded money discreetly slipped into her hand. It was more than a tailor earns in a month. I waved goodbye and started for the exit. At the top of the rickety stairs, I turned and looked back long enough to see Tanya fade into the insatiable dance floor, absorbed by the draconic beast that was the Tanamur.

Outside in the warm night air, I grabbed the first taxi I saw and told the driver, "Kebayoran Baru, 'Pak."

As we were pulling away, he asked, "*Showroom, Meester?*"

"No, 'Pak. *Bawa pulang.*" (No Sir, take me home).

It was well after midnight when I got home. I spent the next hour making detailed notes of what Tanya had told me. Below are unedited, published case studies that support what she said.

～ ～ ～

Case Study, *The Jakarta Post* **1994** – Indonesian authorities are battling a growing trade in child trafficking, including a recent case where hundreds of babies were sold overseas, a report says. The report, by the Indonesian Ministry of Women Empowerment, found that efforts to retrieve the children in baby trafficking cases were flawed. The report said one woman was caught in South Jakarta last year after having sold 880 babies abroad. A further 25 babies were saved. The babies, she explained, were re-sold when they arrived in Singapore. If the traffickers were caught in action at sea, the babies were often thrown out of board so as to wipe the evidence. Other victims might be promised jobs in Jakarta as domestic workers, but then flown to West Kalimantan province on the Indonesian side of Borneo and taken across the border into Malaysia, often using false travel documents.

Article, *The Strait Times* **1994** – "Debt bondage." Some labor recruitment companies, known as <u>PJTKIs</u>, [agencies specializing in overseas contract workers] operated similarly to trafficking rings, luring both male and female workers into debt bondage, involuntary servitude and other trafficking situations. Some workers, often women intending to migrate, entered trafficking and trafficking-like situations during their attempt to find work abroad through licensed and unlicensed PJTKIs. These labor recruiters charged workers high commission fees—up to $3,000—which are not regulated under Indonesian law and often require workers to incur debt to pay, leaving them vulnerable in some instances to situations of debt bondage. PJTKIs also reportedly withheld the documents of some workers, and confined them in holding centers, sometimes for periods of many months. Some PJTKIs also used threats of violence to maintain control over prospective migrant workers. Recruitment agencies routinely falsified birth dates, including for children, in order to apply for passports and migrant worker documents. Internal trafficking is a significant problem in Indonesia with women and children exploited in domestic servitude, commercial sexual exploitation, rural agriculture, mining, fishing and cottage industries. Women and girls are trafficked into commercial sexual exploitation in Malaysia, Singapore and throughout Indonesia. Indonesians are recruited with offers of jobs in restaurants, factories, or as domestics then forced into the sex trade. Young women and girls are trafficked throughout Indonesia, via the Riau Islands, Kalimantan, and Sulawesi, to Malaysia and Singapore. Malaysians and Singaporeans constitute the largest number of sex tourists, and the Riau Islands and surrounding areas operate a "prostitution economy," according to local officials. Sex tourism is rampant in most urban areas and tourist destinations. The employer or agency "holding" the worker's passport, to prevent them from leaving is common.

Article, *The Jakarta Times* 1995 – The Indonesian NGO, KKSP Foundation and Anti-Slavery International have long been concerned about the use of children on hundreds of rickety fishing platforms, known locally as "jermals," in the seas off the northeast coast of Sumatra. Apart from a supply boat that comes every two weeks, there is no contact with the shore. Each jermal is likely to have three or four children on it who haul in and mend the nets as well as boil, dry and sort the fish. The children stay for a minimum of three months and are not free to leave. In this time the children obviously cannot see their families or go to school.

Children can fall or be carried off by large waves during storms and there are no life jackets on the platforms. The children suffer from fatigue because of the very long hours they work and interrupted sleep patterns.

Article, *The Strait Times* 1996 – A 25-year-old Indonesian guest worker will have several of her fingers, toes and part of her right foot amputated because of gangrene after being tied up for a month in a bathroom by her Saudi sponsor. The Indonesian Embassy noted that 2,000 housemaids have been repatriated to Indonesia so far this year, with many alleging maltreatment, nonpayment of wages or physical abuse. Girls from the villages are lured into cities or neighboring countries with promises of lucrative jobs as waitresses and domestic helpers, only to end up in massage parlors and karaoke bars. Others are flown as far as Australia, Japan, South Africa and the United States to be kept as slaves in brothels—beaten, drugged, starved or raped in the first days of their reclusion to intimidate and prepare them for customers, the experts say.

Case Study, *The Jakarta Post* **1996**

The agent came to my house and promised me a job in a house in Malaysia… He promised to send me to Malaysia in one month, but [kept me locked in] the labor recruiter's camp for six months…. I think one or two hundred people were there. The gate was locked. I wanted to go back home. There were two or four guards, they carried big sticks. They would just yell. They sexually harassed the women. Interview with Fatma Haryono, age thirty, returned domestic worker, Lombok, Indonesia, January 24, 1995.

Case Study, *The Jakarta Post* **1996** – I worked for five people, the children were grown up. I cleaned the house, the kitchen, washed the floor, ironed, vacuumed and cleaned the car. I worked from 5 a.m. to 2 a.m. every day. I never had a break; I was just stealing time to get a break. I was paid just one time, 200 ringgit [U.S. $52.63]. I just ate bread; there was no rice [for me]. I was hungry. I slept in the kitchen on a mat. I was not allowed outside of the house. — Interview with Nyatun Wulandari, age twenty-three, returned domestic worker, Lombok, Indonesia, January 25, 1995.

Headline: *The Jakarta Post,* **25 November 1997** – In 1996, 17 young Indonesian women working as housemaids abroad were killed or died under mysterious circumstances and 46 others were tortured or sexually abused. The women were possibly sold or traded to buyers in several Middle Eastern countries before their deaths. (Women's Solidarity report, "Seventeen maids have died abroad.")

Headline: *Kompas,* **7 February 1997**- In mid-1997 hundreds of Indonesian women, most under 20 years of age, were in prostitution in Saudi Arabia. (Mien Sugandhi, Minister for Women's Affairs in Indonesia reports, "Hundreds of RI's women believed to work as prostitutes in Saudi Arabia")

Additional information regarding human trafficking can be found at the following link:

The United Nations Office On Drugs And Crime: https://www.unodc.org/documents/human-trafficking/2015/Recruitment_Fees_Report-Final-22_June_2015_AG_Final.pdf

13

CROCODILES AND TOMATOES

AND NEVER THE `TWAIN SHALL MEET

January of 1994 had been a busy month. The project was in full swing and we were intensely focused on getting all the supply contracts issued in time to prevent delays to the overall schedule. As always, our partners were not making it easy.

I was venturing into the nightlife even more, finding a few late-night restaurants, bars and music venues near Blok M. I knew when they were having a good DJ or an occasional band. I wouldn't say I was reckless but at times, I put myself in risky places and circumstances. There were times during a weekend when I left a bar at 1:00 a.m., taking a shortcut walking through the seedy dark alleys on the back side of Blok M. There were always shady characters lurking there. I walked fast and straight, purposely keeping in the shadows. That didn't give a bad guy time to plot or get a fix on me. I was careful not to set patterns or take the same route along that 20-minute walk home.

Sometimes walking home at night, I'd stop by a popup roadside *blue tent*. These makeshift, open-air restaurants were usually in the vicinity of the lone operational streetlight in a community. They got the nickname because they were nothing more than a blue plastic canvas propped up and tied to some rickety poles. A blue tent might show up one day, operate for a month or two and be gone as quickly as it arrived. Local food was cooked on the spot, often employing a propane canister attached to a burner under a large wok.

Most times they served only one item. If I wanted something different, I'd go find a different blue tent. They were plentiful. If the food was good, the locals gathered for late night meals and omong-omong (*talking-talking*). If the locals didn't eat there, neither would I. I sat with them on old milk crates or wooden slats between concrete blocks. We shared food, told tall stories and sometimes passed around a rusty-stringed guitar, singing until the wee hours of the night. Some of the Jakarta boys had some really good licks. They liked my southern blues.

I continued to graciously accept those name cards from girls in the retail and business stores. I followed up on some. It was nice to go with the flow for a change. Seemed everywhere I turned, there were nice girls available for activities. I usually didn't have to ask and if I did, my invitation was usually accepted. With all the social engagements, scheduling became essential. Dating also required respect, consideration and paying close attention to what I was doing.

Getting to know someone, hanging out at home or around town was as simple as taking advantage of the puzzling Equatorial Effect, and I wasn't about to complain. Meeting a new girl could happen quickly and often. For example, one Saturday morning I climbed the stairs up a foot bridge, crossing the busy roadway below. Even before reaching the other side of the bridge, a girl approached me and introduced herself. Then and there, she invited me to her home for dinner with her family that evening. I had other plans that evening, but that's just how fast a meeting could happen.

During this time of exploration, Arlita and I gradually saw a bit more of one another. We weren't what I'd call close but we were getting along well. We were not intimate or exclusive. She was smart but still a rather innocent young girl.

She was busy with friends and family and understood that I saw other girls. Although cool with it, she never missed an opportunity to tease me about it.

Many of the ever-curious office staff lived on the premises. Late at night, they'd sit outside around small fires and gossip with the jagas and security satpams from my apartment building across the street. Consequently, Arlita heard about my every move, including any guest I might have had over. And yep, the whole office heard about it the next morning.

Referring to my social activities with Indonesian girls, Arlita and our staff affectionately nick-named me, '*Buaya Gila*,' (Crazy Crocodile). I came in one morning to find a two-foot long, stuffed-toy crocodile on my desk. It was all in fun.

One Sunday morning, a small group of us planned to go to Ancol, a large park and amusement area north of the city. We were just going to hang out and paddle around in the small skiffs at the park. Turns out, Arlita and I were the only two that showed up. We spent a little time on the water then walked around, talking and making jokes. We were sitting on a park bench swatting mosquitos, when I slowly leaned in for a really light, first kiss. She responded sweetly and for the moment, we left it at that. I enjoyed her company, but that was no time to abandon consideration or caution with a girl and her family who trusted me.

Another week, another afternoon, I asked Arlita if she'd like to see a movie with me the following weekend.

"Sure, why not?"

The crocodile in me wondered, "Hmm, does this young lady really want an answer?"

But again, she knew she was safe with me. Her parents knew it, too. I may have been a little less sure.

The one and only time I ever picked up a girl at a bar was in Jakarta. I didn't set out to do this but knew it was common for expats and other consenting adults. So late one evening when the flirting and conversation turned into an opportunity, I gave into my dark side and went with it. I didn't have to, I wanted to.

I got this, I thought. *It's Saturday night and I'm gonna' have some fun.*

As the evening advanced toward midnight, I flagged a taxi and took her to my apartment. We sat on the edge of my bed for a few nervous moments before I excused myself to the bathroom.

"*Kembali moment* (return in a moment)," I assured her.

While in the bathroom, I could hear the unmistakable sound of my dresser drawer squeaking as it closed. I finished quickly and went back into the room as the girl abruptly sat back down on the bed, playing with her hair and pretending to have been there all along.

Hoping to be mistaken, I sheepishly walked over to the dresser and opened the squeaky drawer. My dozen or so CDs were gone!

The girl looked at me like, *I don't have a clue what you're thinking.*

I had no experience with this. I promptly grabbed her large purse and emptied it onto the bed. There were my CDs, along with other small things she'd lifted in just the minute or so I'd been in the bathroom. I gathered my things and separated them from hers. I put her stuff back into the bag and asked her to leave as I handed the bag to her.

But no, this wasn't gonna be that easy. Like crazy, she made a big scene, insisting that my stuff was hers and she wanted it back. She was yelling at me in one of the Indonesian languages I could not understand. She pushed at me, grabbing at the things I had separated away. She was breaking glass, wood carvings and trashing the apartment. She hit and scratched anywhere she could find bare skin, biting hard into my arms. I could have hit back but didn't.

I struggled to restrain her wrists as she yelled, fought, kicked and bit, still trying to get at my belongings. To stop her from biting, I got her into an arm lock and practically dragged her to the door. She was tough as nails. I felt like I was trapped in a pick-up truck with a porcupine! I managed to get the door open, pushing her and her bag out of my room.

She instantly turned and swung at my face with something in her hand. She missed. I recoiled at the sound of metal scraping against the door just as I got it closed. With my shoulder against it, I opened the door just enough to toss her a generous amount of money for a taxi. Then I locked and secured both bolts. She didn't stop yelling, banging and kicking the door. My head was spinning as I leaned against the wall, wondering, *what should I do next?*

If they hadn't already, in just a couple of moments all my neighbors and coworkers living in the building would peek out to see what was going on. This was terribly embarrassing. The satpams would have already heard the commotion and be on their way. There was also a possibility that the police might be in the area. Who knows how they might react, but it wouldn't be good for an American expat.

Then I remembered the narrow servant's entrance on the front side of my apartment. I quickly turned off all the lights and sneaked out that small door, quietly locking it behind me. In the darkness, I crouched over, moving along the front of the building to the metal fire escape on the side. I took off my shoes and quietly tip-toed four stories to the rooftop. I could hear the noise for a couple of more minutes, then silence. Perhaps the satpam had gotten to her and sent her on her way.

I hid out for an hour or so, trying to slow my breathing and nurse my wounded pride until I was reasonably sure she was gone. Back inside, I saw that the apartment was a mess but I wasn't turning on any lights. Even in the dark, there wouldn't be much sleep.

As dawn approached, I slowly crept back out that small door in front. One step at a time, I checked around each corner, calculating how quickly I could get back inside if it became necessary.

One of the satpams saw me and came over, grinning like a hound dog eating a pickle.

He shook his finger left to right. *"Sulawesi, 'Pak?"* he asked, teasing and inquiring if I had just encountered one of the fiery girls from the island of Sulawesi.

"Yah, 'Pak. Maybe so," I sheepishly admitted.

He walked me around to my main door and pointed. There was a 12-inch-long knife gash, scraped across the exterior of the door, parallel to where my face would have been the night before. Message received!

Of course, this didn't end there. The office staff couldn't wait for Monday morning.

"Heard you got laid...out," Wilder teased.

Someone left a pencil sketch on my desk; a crocodile being swung around by an Indonesian girl holding onto its tail. This friendly badgering went on for more than a week. Grin, bear it and acknowledge the humor. What else could I do? After the hoopla settled, I found it funny too, but privately. The incident did not deter me from dating Indonesian girls. But I'd never, ever bring home another total stranger. A less-than-total stranger perhaps, but not total. I could be taught!

As it turned out, this fiasco was a catalyst to search for another place to live. My initial lease was nearly up and I had begun to experience bouts of cabin fever in that tiny studio that had served me well.

The owners had restored and updated the remaining apartments. The building now housed a lot of other expats. I knew the guys from our team. But others, I didn't know. They were from other companies working in the region. With expats come expat attitudes. The once euphoric, fragrant lobby now smelled of cigarettes and beer. Just two doors away from mine, loud, intoxicated people hung out until after midnight, turning the lobby into their own noisy pub. Whenever I went to the pool, it was the same thing, fat guys skinny dipping, beer bottles floating. The solitude was gone.

I had lived in Indonesia for a year. With a little more than six months left on this now-extended assignment, the once comforting amenities and environment of my first apartment had gradually lost their charm. The biggest downside to moving was that I'd have to forfeit those lunchtime naps. But as convenient as the apartment, lobby and pool had been, the whole place just wasn't the same.

I started my house search by asking my Indonesian co-workers. Not surprisingly, there were a lot of houses suitable for Western expats. The houses were not big, modern or fancy. But they were certainly livable.

These landlords were not part of the organized clique that had pushed me toward the expensive places when I first arrived. They were independent and willing to negotiate. In mid-February, I looked at a house about five blocks from Blok M. The walk to the office was only 12 minutes. The mostly-furnished house rented for just over half the price of my apartment. That included water, electricity, refrigerator, telephone and a two-burner cook stove.

The house had a small front yard and an eight-foot, concrete and rock wall. Like so many houses in Indonesia, the top of the wall was lined with dangerous glass shards embedded in the concrete. The solid steel gate was secured by a large keyed lock. That was the only way in or out of the property. Built into the concrete wall was a small fireplace of sorts. It had a removable grill and its chimney extended to the top of the wall. It looked more like a place to burn trash than to grill food but it had potential.

Modifying my environment was a good opportunity to change my routine. This cozy, older home and the neighborhood seemed secure enough. Because of that, I saw no need to hire household help or a jaga for security. I'd carry my laundry back to the apartment and pay the ladies there to take care of it. I'd clean up after myself and tidy the house as needed. I'd carefully lock everything when I left so there should be no problems with intruders. With the financial savings, it easily seemed like a win-win.

I agreed to a six-month lease and arranged for complete payment in advance. The gracious owner was so happy to rent to an American that he provided new bedroom furniture and had his family move all my belongings for me. Within a couple of days, I was completely moved in, organized and operational. I was finally able to set up my Bose 201s, amplifier and CD player.

The neighborhood was all Asian and very welcoming. Most residents were older Indonesian families. There were grandparents in the community who took care of their grandchildren while their adult children were at work. Next door, a younger Korean expat family lived with their two middle-school-age children. Over the coming days, I learned that the husband was the director for all Nike operations throughout Indonesia.

~ ~ ~

In early March 1994, a message reached me that my father was not doing well. I quickly arranged for my work to be covered so I could fly to South Carolina. Years before, Dad had suffered a stroke and had achieved only a partial recovery. He was unable to take complete care of himself. He had been living on and off with my oldest brother Garland and his family. That seemed to create tension and had not been going so well.

When I arrived in South Carolina, I saw that Garland had pulled his small camper trailer about 10 miles to Dad's place so Dad could live in it. Another brother, Johnny, and my sister, Charlene had been sharing responsibilities for his care. Seeing him alone in that cramped, dirty little trailer was a heartbreaking realization.

Dad was in and out of cognition, but we shared some meaningful communication. He had kept up on where I was working and was happy that I had gone out on my own a long time ago. He told me that he was proud and saw me as a success. For a while, he played a few tunes on his old ukulele. Johnny and I sang along. I felt especially guilty, not being there to help take care of him. Johnny, Charlene and I hatched a plan to improve part of his old house; to at least get him back into a more comfortable shelter.

In better days, Dad had been locally famous for growing tomatoes. Get him going on tomatoes and he'd talk all day.

"You hafta' take you some of them Big-Boy tomato seeds and show them folks over there in Jakarta how to grow 'em."

Before leaving South Carolina, I stopped into a feed and seed store and bought two packets of Big-Boy seeds, along with a small box of powdered Miracle Grow fertilizer.

When I got home to Jakarta, I dug some good soil from the edges of the rock wall. Working on my kitchen counter, I filtered out the small rocks and mixed in just a touch of Miracle Grow to make a nice bed for the seedlings. The container for the bed was a cardboard lid from a spare Xerox paper box. I placed three seeds into each hole, setting the holes two inches apart and one-half inch deep in the soil.

Using a spray bottle, I lightly watered the surface with bottled water infused with a wee bit of dissolved Miracle Grow. The mini-garden remained on my warm, tiled counter in the kitchen. Twenty-four hours later, I was astonished to see rows of young plants already one-and-a-quarter inches tall. Within a week, there were 30 plants, six inches tall and healthy. I chose 10 plants and gave the rest away to neighbors, who seemed a little unsure what I was up to.

Before long, the plants were nearly ready to transplant outside. To protect them from 12 hours of vicious Jakarta sun, I bought some green, flexible, screen door material and built a shaded lean-to for cover. That reduced the direct sunlight while still allowing plenty to filter through. I connected a garden hose for drip irrigation and prepared some large bedding pots to receive this foreign vegetation. The plants loved it! Within the next three weeks, they rapidly grew into tall, bushy sentinels with stalks the size of my thumb. The irrigation, shade and Miracle Grow were doing their thing. In another few days, beautiful, healthy, yellow blooms sprouted throughout this thick, front yard jungle. This is where the tomato story took a sad turn.

I didn't know, therefore did not consider that Indonesian pollinators—bees and other essential insects would stay away from these succulent yellow blossoms. Apparently, the local pollinators did not recognize or make any attempt to get acquainted with these plants from the other side of the planet.

I watched day after day as the oldest blossoms withered and died. I had one more idea—a crazy something my dad might pull out of his hat.

What if I took a blossom from a plant at one end of the row and touched it gently with a blossom at the other end?

I doubted this would make any difference but repeated that process a dozen or so times before accepting defeat. Guess what, it sort of worked. While hundreds of blossoms did not survive, a dozen or so morphed into little green tomatoes.

As the weeks marched on, I harvested an entire *five* of the best-tasting tomatoes ever grown in my own front yard! My dad saw the photos I sent of those beautiful plants—the yellow blossoms and the few tomatoes they produced. I skipped the details of how they came to be, Dad was proud.

14

EASTER ON CHRISTMAS ISLAND

Red Crabs, Robber Crabs and Spiritual Moments of Solitude

As March 1994 came to a close, a couple of our expats heard about a local charter flight that had space for 10 or so additional passengers. It was a promotional trip designed to increase public tourism at a new resort on Christmas Island in the Australian Territories. Luckily, our office had a three-day weekend and for only $240 each, we could get three days basic accommodations and a round-trip ride on a large, private jet.

Christmas Island? Yikes! I had always thought Christmas Island was a nuclear test site. Turns out, that was a different island with the same name somewhere in the Pacific. This tiny, remote island was in the Indian Ocean and luckily, not radioactive.

It is in fact, the actual tip of an ancient volcano rising more than 500 meters (1640 ft.) from the ocean floor. Unlike the many small islands I had visited north of the Indonesian mainland, this one was far south, just over 300 miles southeast of Jakarta and 960 miles west of Perth, Australia. It is exceptionally isolated.

Observed and named by the British on Christmas Day 1643, humans were first known to have actually set foot on this unique island in 1688. While some exploration took place here and there, it remained uninhabited for another 200 years. The island is heavily forested. More than 250 endemic species can be found there. These fragile plants, insects and animals exist nowhere else on the planet. They depend on the delicate balance they have mastered over hundreds of thousands of years. But then came man.

By the early 1900s, British ships had contaminated the island with a voracious, uncontrollable species called the *yellow crazy ant*. While these now-established foreign ants attack many of the island's defenseless species, their primary target is the red crab. Since the 1990s they have been known to kill tens of millions of red crabs during a single migratory season. There appears to be no way to stop them. And if nothing succeeds, eventually, the entire ecosystem will collapse and one by one, many of the island's important creatures will vanish forever.

In a relatively short historical period, the results of man's presence and actions will impact this fragile island and its irreplaceable habitat more than all the waves absorbed since its earliest creation, millions of years ago.

~ ~ ~

Christmas Island's main attraction was its one unique luxury resort and casino. Clearing for the resort had begun in the late 1980s, but it had not been completed until December of 1993. We were arriving barely four months after it opened.

Including the resort staff, the island had less than 1,400 residents. Most worked in some association with an old, barely-operating phosphate mine. The resort included two pools, two restaurants, two nightclubs and its ultra-high-limit casino. Not only was the Christmas Island Casino the island's main source of income, it was also immensely important to Australia's overall economy. Far outside most territorial waters, this discreet little casino generated more money than all other casinos on the Australian continent combined.

Just over an hour after departing Jakarta, our plane banked hard for the final approach into Christmas Island. I was surprised to look down on the huge runway ahead of us. Curiously, this little island had a long, wide runway fully capable of landing anything from a single-engine plane to a fully-loaded 747.

That exceptional runway had two primary purposes. The first had to do with strategic military purposes. The second was to accommodate the larger, unregistered jets bringing in anonymous, high-rolling gamblers and partiers along with wives, partners, mistresses and girlfriends from all over Southeast Asia. I'm talking about serious, ultra-wealthy gamblers including presidents, government ministers, politicians, super-rich playboys, business leaders and oligarchs—the kind of folks who arrive for a discreet evening via a private aircraft, drop $500K, then jet-set off to another discreet party in another secure casino hours away.

This casino had three gambling salons: one 'secret,' one 'private' and one 'public.' A secret patron and his entourage could arrive and depart unseen, with no record of them ever being on the island.

Although the resort was built on Australian territory, it was owned by an Indonesian business tycoon. This gentleman was famous throughout Southeast Asia and eminently close to Indonesia's President Suharto. During this time, Suharto and his extended family along with most of the Indonesian hierarchy were among the casino's patrons. Gambling had been outlawed throughout Indonesia but for the wealthy or well-connected, flying to Christmas Island was one way the affluent bypassed that law.

There were private, fortified meeting and conference rooms throughout the complex. So if big dogs from any country wanted to get together to sell, buy, party, plan or plot without anyone knowing about their meeting, this was the place. It offered isolation, confidential transportation, secure accommodations and discreet, well-armed security.

These people were uncommonly serious about anonymity. Being recognized or photographed here would not play well back in their home countries. They certainly didn't want anyone anywhere knowing about their money, choice of travel companions or vulnerabilities. It was that kind of casino.

There were around 60 people on our charter flight. Most had come here for scuba diving. The frighteningly deep, turquoise waters were beautifully clear and filled with towering coral reefs along the island's steep, subsurface cliffs. My fellow travelers were not high-rollers, but some came to gamble at the *public room*. Other travelers were here just to get away from the busy, dirty city in Jakarta.

Most of my visit to Christmas Island was spent in near solitude. That was fine with me. I came to walk, explore this remote island and take nature photographs. I wanted to take in everything I could, knowing I'd likely never pass this way again.

Before my time on this island was done, I spent late nights chatting with the young, Australian staff, tipping well and asking enough questions to understand a lot about this mysterious resort, literally in the middle of nowhere. I learned that Australian Immigrations did not scrutinize the diplomats, anonymous guests or the ultra-high rollers. Their arrivals and departures were always pre-arranged.

Economy flights like ours were not as privileged. Upon our arrival, Australian Immigrations greeted the passengers at a series of newly built, tightly controlled open-air shelters not far from the runway. The shelters offered shade from the intense, direct sunshine. They had us queue up into four narrow chutes, each wide enough for a single person.

The authorities were notably stringent and precise with their deeply probing questions. They took time to carefully examine baggage and gear, including things in our pockets. This exceptional level of scrutiny for such a small, isolated island did not seem to be for the protection of the people on this flight or the residents. The agents looked in detail at every stamp in my passport, commenting that I would need to get more pages added when returning to Jakarta. They made notes and counted my rolls of film, video tapes and batteries. They made sure I understood that no cameras were allowed in restaurants or casino. They cautioned that while on the island, "You are subject to observation and questioning at any time!" This vetting was unusual, but I had no problem with it. Their motives seemed focused toward identifying and monitoring any elusive journalists, professional photographers, international authorities or others who might identify, expose or harm their primary clientele.

Quickly enough, we understood we were secondary. It took well over an hour to clear passengers from our flight.

We were shuttled about two miles from the Immigration Arrival complex to the resort by four small, air-conditioned buses. Along the edges of the well-compacted gravel road, I saw hundreds of live red crabs doing whatever they do in the vegetation and debris. There were also hundreds of unlucky crabs smashed along the roadway. In another six months, 40 to 50 million of these red crabs would begin their annual, three-week migration to the sea. Christmas Island is the only place in the world where this phenomenon takes place.

Photo courtesy of Gary Tindale

~ ~ ~

Above a tall cliff, the resort sat on a well-manicured 160-acre clearing along the southeast face of the island. It was at least 40 feet above the ocean which roared and constantly hammered the jagged, volcanic formations below. There were no fences to keep anyone from falling. I suppose they relied on people being smart enough to respect the cliff's edge, dangerous shorelines and razor-sharp rock.

After check-in, I followed the winding, concrete path to my assigned room. It was early-dorm style: beyond basic and bordering on spartan. There was a small bathroom, one twin bed, a little wooden table and a straight chair. Should I even mention the small bar of soap and single roll of toilet paper left for me on the bathroom floor? The one window was covered by a thin, pink curtain hung with push-pins above the ground-level air conditioner. There was no TV or telephone.

It wasn't the kind of place that would impress a date. That would take one of the $1,000-a-night villas, off limits to us on the other side of the resort. Coming to such a lonely, faraway place was for me, a once-in-a lifetime opportunity. Economy room or not, I was seriously happy with this deal.

It took all of five minutes for me to settle in. Then everyone went their separate ways. I walked the shoreline wherever I could. Incoming waves created awesome blowholes in the rocky formations, but getting close required too many risks. A couple of minor cuts were entirely convincing. Later, some of the folks from our group met at the shaded, open-air restaurant near the pools. The staff serving us was mostly young, clean-cut, college-age Australian men and women. It seemed like a great place for a summer job, even if these kids were nearly 1,000 miles from home.

The Australian beef burgers and draft beer hit the spot. We looked out beyond the pools, over the cliff to the beautiful, blue ocean that went on forever. No planes, trains or automobiles, no dirty buses, no horns blowing, no blaring house music. There was only the sound of the wind, the ocean and the big, brown birds diving for a cool drink from the pools.

~ ~ ~

On day two, I planned more exploring. After a quick brunch, I grabbed my cameras and walked north, following the paved shoreline road toward Flying Fish Cove. A dozen or so nice, old rock homes sat high on the hillside on the inward side of the road. They were not the norm and were likely built for the early executives of the mining operation. They were on larger, manicured lots with old-growth trees and decorative shrubbery. The 19th-century, covered concrete porches had long stair-steps leading down to the dusty roadway.

I stopped at both of the little T-shirt and trinket shops along the way but saw nothing that piqued any interest. I supposed they operated on an honor system since there were no shopkeepers around.

Flying Fish Cove, also known as *The Settlement,* appeared to have some small businesses and a port that seemed to be hardly used. Aside from the trinket shops, the other businesses in the area showed no signs of activity. But it was after all, late on a Saturday afternoon.

Christmas Island had not (yet) been developed for general tourism. The resort grounds were really the only thing this sleepy little mining island had going for it. The vehicle license plates as well as the landline telephones used only four digits. The island's phosphate mine had, for the most part, closed years before; it was still barely operating. Most of its dusty old rail tracks, processing and administration buildings around The Settlement were unused and overgrown by an ever-encroaching jungle. This whole area became quiet and ghostly as evening approached.

Walking into the thickets, I wasn't sure where The Settlement ended and the jungle began. I picked a spot to enter the undergrowth then broke a dead branch from a tree, using it to rattle the bushes ahead. Nothing resembling a trail was obvious. Crooked, narrow little pathways edged with spiky foliage and decades of plant litter lured me further into the quiet forest. Forward progress was deliberately slow.

The little island was home to 30 different species of spiders. At each turn, I saw the island's unique variety of spiders had staked out their territory, weaving strong webs between most available spaces. Older webs responded, giving way to my trusty dead branch, but the more recent webs often brought the brisk attention of the critter that designed and built them. The larger Orb-Weaver spiders were all around. With their centered bodies, their leg span could reach more than 6 inches. I knew they were there. They knew I was there. I fastened the top button of my shirt and continued.

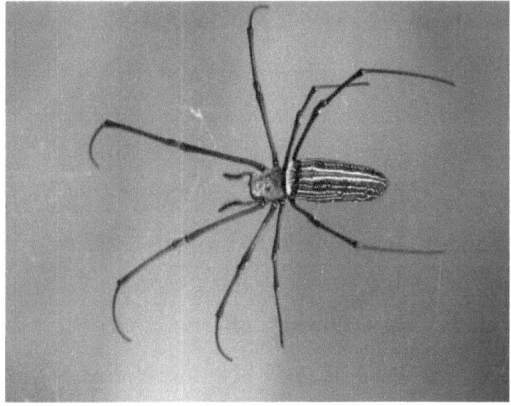

Photo courtesy of Gary Tindale

With each step, I ran the risk of stepping on a small crab or other critter just under the surface of the debris. *This isn't the right thing to do and this isn't the smartest way to continue.*

Just then, another good reason to question this little excursion unexpectedly developed. About three yards ahead, two enormous crabs-- nearly three-feet across with two long vice-like pinchers and 18-inch, spidery legs, two on either side and another back-up pair behind—blocked my path. Their eyeball stalks were trained on me. Their pinchers went up and so did my heart rate. At that time, I had never heard of these monster-looking giants—Coconut (Robber) Crabs. I had no idea what I was facing. They weren't moving. For me, that was the end of this path. I captured a couple of photos and slowly backed away. I backed up until I could turn-around. Catching quick looks back, I wasted no time exiting that thicket.

Back at the resort, I found out that coconut crabs are non-aggressive, slow movers. They are plentiful on the island and encounters are common. *That's alright; I'm still not going to pet one.*

Photo courtesy of Gary Tindale

According to a map at the resort lobby, there were a handful of beaches around the island. At that time, most were undeveloped and not accessible. Trails were few and not improved, so getting to these places seemed unlikely. South of the resort grounds, there were a couple of small but alluring beaches along the eastern shore. These beaches were not safe for swimming. The volcanic rock and attractive flora were dangerously deceptive. Inches below the beautiful sand were thousands of sharp, jagged fragments and razor rock requiring high-top water shoes to protect your feet. Even then, swimming out 100 feet or so from shore placed you in water that was nearly 1,700 feet deep.

There had been enough foot traffic to create vague, narrow pathways leading from the high cliff, through the lava rock formations, down to the water's edge. Ethel Beach was the closest to the resort, less than a quarter-mile. The setting was nice but the beach itself, including far out into the water, was paved with sharp, broken coral fossils and shards of the ever-present, black razor rock. Through the tall, prickly brush and briars further south, the more intimate Lily Beach was carved into the shore like a keyhole between two tall cliffs. Moving carefully to avoid the tall, spiny grass, I lingered there in solitude, taking in the blue sky, listening to the waves break over the reefs. So far, this was my favorite place.

As Saturday evening approached, the blue sky had gradually grown dark as a thick, heavy cloud bank engulfed the entire region. The grayness appeared to absorb the fleeting light and continued in either direction, as far as the eye could see. After dinner, the lobby and restaurant began to close and most visitors settled in for the evening. I went into the public casino for about 20 minutes but found nothing interesting. Tomorrow morning, the resort was hosting Easter events for the children. Our flight would depart in the afternoon. But this was my last night on this entrancing, far away island and I wasn't the least bit sleepy.

The lights of the resort faded into the distance as I walked south, back toward Lily Beach. I moved slowly through the tall brush, making use of what little light my camera offered. I already knew what the island's scariest creatures looked like and didn't want to say 'hello' again.

Arriving at the secluded little beach, the darkness was so complete I could barely see the ocean or the sky. But somewhere out there in the night, ocean and sky melted into an eerie horizon and although I couldn't see it, I accepted it was there.

The tide was in and the waves pushed much further into the keyhole, finding their way over all but a few feet of the still-warm sand. A couple of hours and a couple of beers went by. I enjoyed the tranquil aloneness, the vast Indian Ocean, the reliable rhythm of its large waves pushing steadily against this solitary island. There was plenty of time to ponder its future and perhaps my own.

Using the light from my camera, I left the beach and walked back through the brush, avoiding the sharp rock formations and briars on the crooked little pathway up the hill. On the manicured grass at the top of the cliff, I paused to look back, unable to see the little beach hidden in the night far below.

Over the ocean to the east, slight traces of light appeared as a break in the clouds unfolded. On the distant horizon, the break was narrow. And directly above me, it was especially wide, fanning out in the shape of a V. The clouds within the V thinned and there was the moon: full, bright and beautiful. I stood in awe at the clarity of that moon, framed precisely between its grey curtains on either side, casting its soft, soothing reflection across the miles to where I stood.

I'm not a particularly spiritual man, but that moment felt as though I was closer to the depth of our universe, a depth within myself. I felt as one with the Cosmos.

15

FALL INTO ROUTINE

COMPLETING THE INITIAL ASSIGNMENT

By the time I returned from Christmas Island, I had travelled so much that my passport needed more pages. This required an in-person appointment with the U.S. Embassy in downtown Jakarta. When I arrived that afternoon, the embassy was still buzzing with news, planning and ceremonies regarding Richard Nixon's death on Friday, April 22, 1994.

While I was waiting there, one of the American ladies on staff asked, "Would you consider serving as a warden to the embassy? Since you're here longer than a lot of expats, you'd be a good resource for us."

"Sounds interesting, what's involved?"

"Don't let the title scare you," she said. "It's a volunteer role, mostly a back-up for us to have a few responsible Americans around the region in case of emergencies. Our wardens have rarely been called on, so it doesn't require much time. Basically, you'd assist with communication, disseminating embassy information and if needed, help assimilate reliable contact information for Americans visiting, working or living in the region. In an emergency, you might be asked to visit an American citizen in a hospital, a jail or perhaps assist in finding someone who is missing. Once again, let me assure you that under normal circumstances it takes very little time, and wardens are seldom activated."

It seemed like a good idea, so I agreed and signed their Letter of Assignment. Consequently, emails with more direct information on activities and news of interest to Americans showed up. I was cool with that.

This new connection was how I first heard the news about the French "Chunnel" opening on May 6. This important, international project had been underway for years and was finally complete. It connected the U.K. and France via rail, in a tunnel under the English Channel. Someday I would take that ride.

~　~　~

Our work felt as though it had become routine. By now, I understood what it took to *encourage* these partners and their associates to follow through with sign-offs and approvals. I dropped by their offices, spent time and asked about things going on in their lives. It wasn't always timely or simple. But having a closer relationship with these folks allowed the work to move forward even if the pace remained frustrating.

As Eid Al Adah, The Feast of Sacrifice, approached, Arlita invited me to come to Muara Karang and witness preparation for this particularly important part of the Islamic faith. It's one of the major holidays celebrated by Muslims and commemorates Abraham's willingness to follow God's command to sacrifice his son, Isacc. The event also included the *humane sacrificing* of farm-raised animals. The meat is shared with the hungry as well as with anyone else in need. Similar events were taking place on May 20, 1994, all across the Muslim world.

People who had the means raised and donated animals for the cause. Others donated money or their time and energy to transport the animals from outlying areas. Often that meant walking for miles with a tethered goat or lamb. No matter the task, all work involved in making it possible was equally respected.

That day's event was held under a series of shaded tents in the community near Arlita's home. It had begun pre-dawn and was well underway when I arrived. The Indonesians were happy to have an American in attendance. The leaders were welcoming and talked me through the process. Veterinarians were on hand, checking the health and well-being of the animals. They were sincere in this work and in caring for the animals as they were led to their demise. During my childhood, I had watched my parents kill chickens, wild squirrels and rabbits. I understood it. The taking of an animal's life wasn't pleasant back then and it certainly wasn't now as I stood far too close, witnessing this bloody ritual. I stayed for an hour or so before making a donation, excusing myself and heading home to clean my cameras and take a shower.

In the dusty, dry heat outside our office that night, some of our drivers, office workers and satpams had gathered fallen limbs and built two fires in the ditch next to the street. In one fire was a large pot of boiling water. In the other, a long broomstick held a goat's head from one of the day's offerings. Jamitri was burning all the hair off in preparation for the head, along with a selection of vegetables, to go into the boiling water.

Jam told me, "*Sup Kepala Kambing*, 'Pak." (Goat's head soup). "You want eyeball?"

He was offering me one of the *cherished* eyeballs when it was ready. This level of authentic, Indonesian food was a bit much for me. I wasted no time assuring Jam, "No 'Pak, you have earned it with all your hard work. It must go to you."

Jam humbly shuffled and accepted. I had lucked out, no eyeballs, no goat's head soup for me. I'm not sure what I would have done if he had insisted.

~ ~ ~

By now, some of our expatriates were getting close to completing their initial assignments and rotating back to the Missouri office. Indonesia was not hard on single expats, but as more and more families returned to the States, they carried with them stories and experiences, including difficulties they had encountered. Add to that, the world was starting to hear more news about Indonesia's war in East Timor (*currently Timor-Leste*) and stirrings of periodic, government and civil unrest. That news tended to dampen the enthusiasm for recruiting replacements, especially those with families. As new replacements arrived in-country, I often helped them get settled in and showed them around.

Many things American expatriates needed/wanted, such as specialty foods or personal care items, were not available in Jakarta. But if someone was looking for something and Jakarta had it, I could most often find it. I had a good network and knew my way around. Moving through the neighborhoods, shopping, dining, walking and using cheap, local transportation was pretty easy for me. The more useful I was, the happier I felt.

~ ~ ~

Notable events at work and in my personal life seemed to be occurring more and more rapidly. And as my time in Indonesia grew shorter, each day felt as though I should be writing more. At the end of most days, I opened my Lotus spreadsheet and made brief *tickler* notes of significant occurrences. There were at least a hundred lines by now: short reminders of things I might one day use in chronicles or short stories.

There were less than three months remaining on this extended work assignment. I was leaning toward remaining in Indonesia, but with Dad's living conditions, a tenant who was talking about moving, and a slew of other little things needing my attention in the States, the internal pressure was growing by the week.

Beyond that, I was comfortable with my routines in and around Jakarta. Too comfortable. One Saturday afternoon, I flagged a bajaj and headed to Pasaraya to get a haircut. Nearing the massive, always overcrowded department store, my driver found an unusual opening in the normally congested drop-off point outside the main entrance. He drove us right into the center of that circular opening where no one was standing. Most times I'd have to walk about a block, so this was rare to get this close to this particular drop-off area. *Lucky day*, I thought.

I paid the driver and was halfway out of the bajaj when something came into my left view and hit me hard on the side of my face, glancing to my shoulder. Rolling with the impact, I realized what the locals called an '*Orang Gila*' (crazy person) had taken a swing at me. I had seen this character, one of Jakarta's mentally challenged people in the community before but never close and certainly not with his fist in my face.

The image flashed quickly as this growling, filthy being with cave-man hair and no clothes was lifting his greasy hand to make a second strike. Instinctively, I ducked his next incoming swing. Instead of hitting me, his second strike went hard into the metal frame of the bajaj. I could hear bones and metal colliding as I rolled further to escape the situation. I stumbled to my feet and saw that my driver had bailed out the other side of his little vehicle. The attacker was hopping up and down, snarling, screaming and shaking what had to be a badly injured right hand. His presence explained why there was so much space for the bajaj to get that close to the building. The crowd knew he was there. My driver did not.

I was shaken, dirty from the greasy hit and not sure about injuries—his or mine. But I knew there was nothing I could do to help him. I moved away from the scene as quickly as I could, heading to the first floor at Pasaraya and on to the salon on the second. I told the ladies what had happened. They locked the door and promptly went to work cleaning me up, using antiseptic on the scratches. They continued doting over me throughout the haircut, offering further assistance if needed. I even received another name card and an invitation to call from a new stylist working there, so all was not lost.

As with many developing countries, Indonesia did not incarcerate their mentally challenged or seriously deranged people. Given the vast population, the number of mentally challenged people was relatively small, yet the country could offer them no help. These unfortunate folks existed as best they could on their own. As far as I knew, they received no care and little assistance from any organizations. They roamed Jakarta's streets while the general population simply tried to keep their distance.

After getting some dinner, I walked home that evening a bit more apprehensive than usual. I was acutely aware and cautious of anyone nearby. I would make mistakes again but not this one. A sore jaw was a great reminder to stay alert, look over my shoulder and never get too comfortable.

Arlita and I continued to go to restaurants, movies and other events in and around the city, most often with other friends. She sometimes invited me to her family's home for a meal or just for *omong-omong* (casual talk). I entrusted her with a key to my house, inviting her to come and go as she pleased. At times, she and some of her friends dropped in. We had a slowly growing, casual friendship that was important to me. We were buddies who enjoyed hanging out, uncomplicated and meaningful.

Since I no longer lived across the street from the office, Arlita no longer got the daily crocodile reports from the satpams, jagas and office workers. She understood I was still seeing other girls and not exclusive to anyone.

Although she was free to date others, I started to sense she was not happy about me doing so.

Around mid-day of June 13, our office received sketchy news reports that apparently, O.J. Simpson had murdered his estranged wife and her boyfriend. At night, people flocked to the big hotels where they watched the live TV feeds coming from the U.S. and other countries. This story dominated the news there for weeks. People with good television reception could monitor every detail. On my little TV at home, I could see fragments of the story late at night on CNN-Philippines. I guess if I had been back in the States during this time, the news would have seemed more significant, but I wasn't and it didn't.

Around this same time, my Indonesian friends were becoming increasingly concerned about growing tensions and public protests against the government. We expats were also watching these obvious developments, but silently.

Seemingly out of nowhere, Indonesia's President Suharto issued a decree banning three of the nation's most popular, influential newspapers. He warned others they may face a similar fate. Long established publications *Tempo*, *Editor* and *DeTik* were shut down for exposing broad corruption and veiled criticism of Suharto, his family and close associates.

The U.S. Government expressed serious disappointment in Suharto's actions but as expats, we were advised to keep our heads down and mouths shut. Word of these tensions quickly reached our offices back in the States and further affected the ability to recruit replacement employees.

I could tell Wilder was getting concerned. He was trying to keep an experienced team together in Jakarta but was watching that experience evaporate as political tensions increased.

"We've got a lot of people leaving here and there are not as many employees interested in coming to Indonesia as before," he said.

Apparently, Wilder had already had conversations with our Missouri office management regarding staffing. It wasn't long before he approached me about accepting still another extension and continuing to work in Jakarta.

"Missouri is good with you staying here as long as our partners are happy and right now, they're happy. But if you repatriate to the States, they're going to expect you to remain there."

I felt like I was wedged between two worlds. On one hand, I was selfishly enjoying my work and having the time of my life in Indonesia. On the other, the realities and responsibilities called me to do the right thing; to take care of family back in the States.

I told Wilder, "It's not that I don't want to stay in Indonesia, because I do. But life is starting to crumble back home. I've got some personal matters in the States that will take quite a while to resolve. My dad's health is declining. I need to meet with my siblings in South Carolina and evaluate how to best meet his needs. Also, my tenant in Missouri has given notice. There's a lot of work to do to prepare for a new one."

"Yeah, and I know you've already been in Jakarta beyond your original agreement and I understand what you're up against, needing to take care of things back in the States," Wilder said, doing his best to be understanding.

"I see it too, Rick. I get it. You're already short-staffed here and it's not getting any better. I know it bugs you because you mention it a lot."

Wilder brainstormed, "What if we devise a *loose plan* that gets you to the States long enough to get your stuff done then brings you back to Indonesia if you're not happy being back in the States?" he asked.

At this point, I couldn't make any promises, nor could he. So we agreed to talk later.

By July 1, 1994, my departure date was only two months away. It was a hot Friday afternoon. The air was stagnant. The scorching, equatorial sun was still peaking in the blue, cloudless sky. I finished work early and headed out, walking home.

As I approached my metal gate, something was obviously wrong. The gate was opened just a little bit. The padlock was cut and lying on the ground. I walked onto the porch and saw broken glass and wooden debris scattered around the open front door. There was a flash of utter defeat. For the first time in my life, I felt helpless and violated. I was hesitant to step inside but the stillness and quiet that hovered above the mess assured me whoever had broken in was gone.

Due to my own carelessness and economizing, I had chosen to not hire household help. With no housekeeper or jaga to guard the place, my house was an easy target, even in broad daylight. My heart was sinking because aside from my other valuables, I knew what else was in there. In preparation for leaving Indonesia, I had been drawing down on my local bank accounts. Among the papers in my nightstand was a plain, white envelope with $4,000 cash. Even before going any further, I knew it was likely gone. *My bad for being sloppy.*

I quickly surveyed the visible results of the human storm, then carefully eased back out the gate to where the neighbors, frightened and upset, had gathered to tell me what they had seen. According to neighboring housekeepers, a group of 10 or so young men on six motorcycles arrived right at the *Call to Mosque*. This special weekly religious call occurred every Friday at noon. Because most of the population was deeply focused on the extended noontime prayers, Friday's Call to Mosque provided a weekly opportunity for robbers to hit homes and businesses anywhere across the country.

Around half of these bandits had stayed outside while the other half broke in. No doubt, they had already cased the neighborhood, discreetly learning from other housekeepers and jagas that I had locks, but no security. They were in and gone within about two minutes. The neighbors offered to call the police for me. I agreed and thanked them.

Knowing the crooks were gone, I eased back in the house to more carefully assess the damage and loss. The first things I noticed missing were the electronics. They had taken a Canon AE-1 camera system including undeveloped film, a rare, Realistic gold-faced amplifier and that stack of a dozen or more CDs I had wrestled away from that girl six months back. I guess those CDs just weren't meant to be mine. They took items that were relatively small and easy to sell. Most shoes and clothing were gone. But some of what they left behind was surprising: my 1971 Yamaha acoustic guitar, a pair of Bose 201 speakers and a Sony Hi-8 video camera that was charging in the kitchen.

I swallowed hard and slowly made my way into the bedroom. The thieves had taken the four pillowcases from the pillows, apparently sharing them among themselves in order to carry away their stash.

Smart move, I thought. *They've done this before.*

The mattress and bedding had been overturned and tossed, covering the nightstand that had been completely dumped onto the floor: its contents pilfered. I dragged the mattress back onto its bedframe. My papers were scattered all over the place: torn, wet and marked by grungy shoe prints. Broken water pitchers, cups, mirrors, wet loose socks, underwear and shaving gear were scrambled among shattered glass all over the ceramic tile.

But there among the trash, overlooked by thieves preoccupied with gadgetry and escape was the plain, white envelope partially sticking out from under the debris. "It can't be," I said aloud.

I inched down onto my knees to pull it from under the rubble. When I felt its weight, I knew. I opened it to find all forty of the one-hundred-dollar bills nestled securely inside. None of it was missing. These guys had completely missed what would likely have been the biggest haul of their criminal career. And at that moment, with my house turned upside down and inside out; my possessions in the hands of nefarious thugs, I was the luckiest guy in the world.

The police arrived about an hour later. The stinky, sweaty officers smelled like they hadn't bathed in a month. Their uniforms were filthy. They walked through the house making an even bigger mess—smoking, mashing cigarette butts onto the white tiled floor. The black powder they recklessly used for finger printing was everywhere. I gave the lead officer a list of what was missing.

"All is common thing, Bapak. I think we will not find any of this."

"You want to pay for investigation and we will catch the robbers for sure?"

I flashed back to articles I had read every week in the Jakarta Post about thieves being "shot while trying to escape the police." These shootings were far too common to be coincidental. As pissed off as I was, this had been partly my fault. None of that stuff was worth someone's life.

"No, Bapak," I said. "I do not want to investigate."

That was the end of it. I had a lot of cleaning to do.

A couple of days later, my Korean neighbors invited me next door for dinner. They were sorry about what had happened. Their children and housekeepers had hidden inside and watched as the house was being robbed but fearing for their own safety, they didn't know what to do.

After dinner and a gentleman's toast with soju, they presented me with a pair of brand-new Nike Air Alarm sports shoes. These were not scheduled to be released until 1995, months from then. Once again, lucky me!

As July came to an end, still more of our solo expats and expat families were completing their assignments and making plans to return to the States. Add to that, two other families had recently encountered some scary issues. One involved an overdose, which required the parents to take their child out of Indonesia for treatment. The other required the family to immediately and permanently return to the States because of a house fire. Wilder was involved with coordinating support for both of these families. This added even more to his already short-staffed load.

"I'm not sure how much longer I'll remain in Jakarta, myself," Wilder said. "I expected to be here another year, but my wife is having health problems." He was concerned about wrapping things up so that he'd be in a better position to respond to her needs. I understood that at any time, her health might become his most important priority.

Wilder and I worked well together and had one another's back as best we could. My extended completion was just around the corner and if I went back to the States, he'd be left in Jakarta without adequate support. We reopened our discussion about the possibility of me extending a second time.

"Let's talk about that *loose plan* you mentioned before. Do you think there's a chance I can go back to the States long enough to get my stuff sorted out, then return to Indonesia if I change my mind?"

I waited but Wilder didn't respond. I continued. "I know this puts you in a bind here in Jakarta, because you're going to be short-staffed for three months or so. But I need this option," I explained. I paused again. I knew he was struggling so I gave him time. Then quietly but firmly I repeated, "I need this option."

He thought for a minute then said, "Well, our partners will have to approve anything you and I propose. Let me see what I can get wired up, but you'll owe me one."

"Copy that!"

Right away, Wilder met with our Indonesian partner and discussed his Jakarta staffing issues with them. In turn, our Indonesian partner discussed the matter with everyone my work had been supporting at the primary level. It was my understanding they had reached out to eight or more of the partner's key personnel. This included Ibu Niniek, Arlita's mother. The partners told Wilder that they would rather hold the position open for me, even at the risk that I didn't return. They cited my good relationship and value to the project. Together with our Indonesian partner, the primary partners agreed that if I needed to go to the States, then it was OK with them. Then, if I wanted to return to Indonesia within three months, they would approach our Missouri team directly and request my return to Jakarta. This was the welcome option I needed. I was honored by their confidence. To have so many key people agree to this unusual opportunity was simply unheard of. Their belief and trust in me was touching. It made me proud.

Wilder said, "When our partner gave me the go-ahead, he also told me I owed him one. You know what that means, right?"

"It means I owe you one, as well," I said.

"Sure does. Don't forget it. You're clear to go back to the States with the possibility of returning to Jakarta. I'll make do here."

Wilder liked to say about me, "At least he won't get you into trouble." It was true; I had gotten lots of our folks out of trouble, including him. He depended on me a bit more than he wanted to. I was good at bringing people together, having been there longer than most of the staff, especially the short-term engineers. I knew my way around the partner's staff and could drop in uninvited just to chat. As a trusted liaison, they relied on me to diplomatically get word to our team regarding sensitive matters. And that was a two-way street. If our team wanted to convey information privately to one of the partner's people, I could do it discreetly. That trust turned into good visits and fostered long-term business and personal friendships.

I went into my last month with the *loose plan* I wanted. Wilder and I both knew it was risky. Anything could happen in three months. Any little variation or glitch in the work or the relationship between Wilder and our partner could derail this plan.

"It's wired as best as I can get it. Anything changes; I'll let you know immediately. If you want to come back, send me a message that just says *push the button*, then hold on to your hat," Wilder said.

After 18 months, I was on the path to departure.

~ ~ ~

Over the next few weeks, I didn't see any girls other than Arlita. We spent more time together, just the two of us. Because my leaving was making us both a bit sad, we felt an urgent sense to make the most of every minute together. In her short life, Arlita had witnessed many expats leaving their friends, loved ones, even families behind in Indonesia, never to be heard from again. Far too often, that was the norm. She didn't say it, but I expect she felt this was her turn to watch a close friend fly away into Jakarta's blue horizon. I promised her that I'd write and call frequently. I'd also keep her posted on my possible return status. I meant it. She let me know she'd miss me, but cautiously made no promises.

~　～　～

There was a long list of things I needed to complete before leaving, and they needed to be done in a manner that assumed I would not be back. I created a list and began checking off the items. Most personal tasks were simple. Work items were more complex. I contacted the embassy and resigned my role as warden, providing them with the departure date and stateside contact information.

In Jakarta, I gave away a lot of items. My larger personal effects were packed into one cardboard container and commercially shipped. Essentials were packed into an oversized suitcase and a backpack that would travel with me on the flight. Back in Missouri, the relocation department arranged one of their temporary apartments for my return.

The now-70 or so letters and photos I received from girls across the country, along with a cigar-box of name cards had to be dealt with in a secure way. This was sensitive, trusted information that could not be thrown into any trash bin where Jakarta's scavengers would dig it out and somehow exploit or embarrass the senders. Nor was it right to take the letters to America. I was closing the book on that chapter and knew I'd never follow up on any of them. That's where that little fireplace in front of the house became useful. I thought it best to simply, privately burn them myself. Best and simple, yes, but not so easy.

The paper burned quickly. But the photographs would not ignite unless there was oxygen and fire on both sides, simultaneously. Holding and looking at the individual photos while they burned seemed weird. I couldn't put my finger on why, but destroying them didn't feel right. Regardless, reluctantly, it had to be done.

I set aside three of the photographs, at least for a moment. Two of the three, I had no communication with at all. I just liked the images. I suppose it was a guy thing, since they were both attractive young ladies. The third photo was of Susan, my pen pal standing at the Borobudur Temple in Central Java. She and I had written back and forth several times, but had never met. We weren't close so there was no need to let her know I was leaving. I casually thought I might someday write her from the States. Of the three remaining photographs before me, hers was the only one I kept. I didn't know then that this was a key decision. The melancholy process of disposing of the rest of the images took more than an hour. I stoked the fire, trying to push away the tinge of guilt that kept surfacing, unable to thank so many deserving girls who had reached out to me. I watched the fire until there was nothing left but ash.

I'll never know whose idea this was, but it was fun for the expats and Indonesians. With my departure just over a week away, the gang got together to arrange a *Surprise Progressive Bajaj Party*. As work came to a close, I heard what sounded like a whole lot of bajajs revving their engines in the street out front of our office. That's exactly what it was. Apparently, Wilder and some other folks had pitched in to hire these guys for a couple of hours. They led me outside to a dozen or so wildly decorated bajajs. They were decked out with flags and natural vegetation such as tree branches, palms and banana leaves. Our entire expat staff and many of our Indonesian friends loaded up and drove off toward the first of three stops.

Our noisy little orange motorcade paraded its way through Kebayoran Baru's usually quiet streets, drawing residents from their homes to see what all the commotion was about.

Three expat families had opened their homes for drinks and hors d'oeuvres. At the first stop, they presented me with a large, hardback photo/story book entitled, *Indonesia, Paradise on The Equator*. The book was filled with beautiful photographs and exquisite narrative from the writer and the photographer who had spent years trekking throughout the country's most remote areas. That would have been the epitome of an adventure. Inside its cover, the Indonesian and expat staff had written cherished farewell notes of appreciation. This was an exceptional gift I'd treasure from that moment on.

At another stop along this little adventure, they gave me a handmade, authentic scaled replica of a bajaj. I think that was to tease me for using the bajaj taxis more than any expat they had ever known. Whatever the reason, that too would be forever appreciated.

The final stop was drinks, jokes and tall tales. The party ended just after 9:00 p.m.

This farewell party was a wonderful, unexpected treat. The future was uncertain, but the rare opportunity to live and work in Indonesia had been exceptional and fulfilling. I lay in bed that night, looking through the book they had given me, appreciating the beautiful, exotic photos that captured the cultures of dozens of tribes across the 3,000-mile Indonesian archipelago. But more than the book, the photos or the narrative, I was touched by the writings—ink stains dried upon the pages of time, affectionately penned by my dear friends and associates

On Thursday morning, September 1, 1994, Arlita and I loaded my belongings into a taxi and headed for Sukarno-Hatta Airport. She accompanied me on the solemn, one-hour ride. Avoiding sentiment, we made small talk and traded lame jokes. Those last moments together went by in the blink of an eye. Perhaps that was for the best.

The taxi stopped curbside; we got out with my belongings, exchanged a quick kiss for luck and went our separate ways.

In a little over an hour, I was out of Indonesian airspace heading back to the States.

16

CHOICES, CHALLENGES AND DECISIONS

THE IMPORTANCE OF HAVING OPTIONS

Descending into Los Angeles, there was an actuality, a significance that could not be ignored. In one way, I could see myself getting back to life in the States. But I wasn't elated. It felt more like regret. I had left a foreign country where I had been accepted, embraced and made to feel special. Some of that was earned. Most was simply given by warm and gracious people. Reflecting on the innocence and kindness of Indonesia, I felt that something important was being left behind.

If I remained in the States, everything on my road ahead needed to be earned. Life would again become competitive. Most of me was up for the task. Clearly, some of me wasn't.

The flight continuing to Kansas City landed late afternoon on Thursday, September 3, 1994. The weather was still hot and the leaves had not yet begun to turn. I planned to take a couple of vacation days to get myself organized, then report to the office on September 8.

Leigh picked me up in my Nissan she had been keeping for me. She had it cleaned and fueled, having driven it only enough to keep it maintained. For all practical purposes, it was still new. Heading south back into the city, we decided to have dinner and catch up.

After a pleasant visit, I dropped Leigh off at her home, again thanking her for all she had done. After a long hug, she handed me the keys to the car, storage unit and the house at Pleasant Valley. The documents she had taken care of on my behalf were on the back seat.

"You know, you don't have to be a stranger," she said. Whether she actually meant that or was simply making polite conversation was no longer important to either of us. In a round-about way, we were telling one another goodbye. I would never hear from Leigh again.

~ ~ ~

It was dark as I drove over to the duplex where I would stay for a while. It was one of a dozen duplexes just east of Mission Road, on the Kansas side of the border. In the headlights, it looked as though it had been built in the late 1960s. The driveway was broken and patched, some asphalt, some concrete. I left the engine and lights on as I walked to the front. A rusted, wrought iron handrail swayed when touched, its anchors long ago worked loose. I fiddled with the lockbox and was soon inside.

Indoors, the place was clean and furnished. The land-line telephone was operational as was the clunky, old television. The accommodation was not a five-star joint but that's not what I needed. It was a much-appreciated perk and would do just fine until I could get myself re-established.

Before crashing for the night, I organized my belongings and walked across the street to stock up on some basic groceries. I was wowed by the cleanliness, volume and variety of the huge Dillon's Grocery store.

The next morning, I went out to look at basic cell phones, which were becoming more available in the States. I had gotten used to pocket communications, but my Indonesian pager would not work in the States. I settled for a flip-phone that cost a little over $100. It had no call back, voice mail or text capabilities. Additional costs included $30 per month for the network connection and 75 cents per minute for each call. And if I went into *roaming* outside my network range, calls increased to $1 per minute. I now had a portable phone, but casually using it could quickly become expensive. Some calls were worth it. For most calls I'd find a landline.

Later in the day, I drove north to Pleasant Valley, Missouri to check on my rental property. The tenants were not home, but I was able to see the yard and exterior were OK. They would be moving out soon.

~ ~ ~

Heading back to my temporary duplex, the Nissan wanted to take a different route that took us way out east on Highway 210 which paralleled the Missouri River.

This long, straight stretch of two-lane road was rural with very little traffic. I'm pretty sure that's why the Nissan chose it. I deny any responsibility for this decision. For the first time in a year and a half, it was me, my car and some steam to blow off. The Nissan came alive, all five gears powering us to well over 100 mph before re-entering the safe zone. That couple of minutes was enough recklessness for me. But the car had been itching to do it, just this once. So had I.

I'm sure most of it was me, but everything felt different. Each day reminded me that indeed, it was. Compared to the Indonesian food I had grown to enjoy, American food was initially boring.

Some friends had moved away to other towns, other states. Some were still local, but the closeness had waned. When I lived here before, I was in a significantly active relationship with Leigh. That too, was gone. Rebuilding something from scratch was going to take time. I wasn't particularly lonely but I definitely felt alone.

The next Wednesday morning, I was ready to go to work, sort of. Dragging a mixed sense of excitement and anticipation, I walked halfheartedly across the parking lot and through the main entrance into the division headquarters.

The office was unfamiliar. The elevator delivered its cargo of silent strangers along the way to my floor. I knew no one. I spent my first day back, debriefing with a friendly project team who seemed to get along well, with or without me.

New engineering and construction business was exploding and domestic energy projects were plentiful. The overall staff had grown substantially. In fact, the business was leasing buildings in downtown Kansas City to make space for all the new projects and staff. I used to know one out of every five people in the building. Now, I was lucky to recognize one out of 20, and maybe one out of 20 had a clue who I was: some new guy coming in here with all these stories, ideas and lame jokes.

The computers, networks and servers were all fully operational and my coworkers seemed to be old pros at using them. We had worked with older computers in Jakarta but these new machines seemed loaded with opportunities to expand. I was looking forward to this.

Desktop telephones were gone. Banks of operators no longer transferred in calls. Everyone had these flimsy little headsets with wrap-around microphones that plugged into USB ports on their computers. They built digital contact lists instead of business card files. The Rolodex was a thing of the past. They made, received and sent calls to voicemail with the click of a mouse. *What planet have I landed on?* I comically thought. Day one at the Missouri office was now history.

Getting ready for bed that night, the TV was still on, the laundry was spinning and I was wondering if I should adopt a dog. I understood that I had to keep moving forward and carve out my new existence here in the States. It deserved a fair shot. I knew how, but there was a tinge of dread at all the tasks lying ahead. At that moment, I wasn't excited or thankful. Then the TV flashed with breaking news. U.S. Air Flight 427 had just crashed on approach to Pittsburgh. There were no survivors. I promptly adjusted my perspective. The next morning, so would a stunned nation.

I entered day two running head-on into re-acclimation. Overseas, locals and expats were accustomed to crude talk. Jokes and raunchy language were rampant and seemed to be widely accepted behavior. Recklessly, we paid little attention to their impact and didn't notice anyone being hurt or offended. I didn't notice because I wasn't paying attention. *My bad.*

Here in Missouri, I noticed coworkers turning and rapidly walking away whenever I started to crack a joke; even before they had a clue of the theme, even if it was a clean joke. Expats returning from overseas ahead of me told of being called to HR and reprimanded for their language and attitudes. *Was I missing something?*

Turns out that while I was away, employees and management had gone through *sensitivity training.* With their new awareness, it became evident that I had returned with some habits and behaviors that no longer fit in. I hadn't changed, they had.

I had always tried to maintain my vocal respectability and was certainly far from the worst. I didn't mind cleaning up my act. That was good for me. *A little maintenance will fix this before it breaks,* I reasoned. What I did mind was this odd feeling, like walking through a mine field blindfolded. *People turning and walking away?* It made me feel like an outsider. There I was, a grown man tripping over glitches that didn't exist in the workplace just a couple of years before.

For the next couple of weeks, I continued assisting the Missouri engineering team that supported Jakarta. I appreciated the opportunity to interface with the folks in Indonesia nearly every day, but the project did not have enough work to keep me busy and billable full time. Staying billable was vital. Each week, my new digital timesheet needed to reflect what I was working on and to which projects I was charging time. The timesheet had a line for *Unassigned Time.* No one wanted to be on that line. It was closely monitored and too much time charged to that line would adversely affect my overall performance rating. I certainly didn't want that to happen.

At the time, there was no centralized department to manage work assignments. It was more or less left to the employee to *knock on doors* and find their own gigs. Crude, but it worked.

I was a new cog in a large, unfamiliar wheel that was revolving every week. At least for the time being, I needed to visit with other project managers and offer my services. If a project was fully staffed, rejection was common. No one took it personally. I picked up an hour's work here, a half day there, but so far it was all bits and pieces. It was not unusual for my timesheet to reflect hours worked on up to 10 projects during the week. Thankfully, I didn't need to report any unassigned time. Eventually, I worked on a larger project where my contributions provided something closer to full-time billing.

There were other disturbing issues I encountered while being in the Missouri office. I expected some readjustment and felt no need to rebel. But compared to working overseas, the regimen here seemed at times petty and oversensitive; again, *mine field, watch your step*, I thought. Uncomfortable stuff.

Overseas, I was accustomed to having trust among my coworkers. We worked as a team. But when it came to getting our core work done, each of us was capable of functioning independently, effectively and accurately. That was different here in Missouri.

Here, processes and procedures were in many ways stringent down to the smallest detail. Even if an employee like me knew how to quickly achieve a goal, he or she couldn't just reach out and solve most challenges on their own. Too often, a committee was required. The committee would evaluate, agree on a solution, prepare a written report, obtain approval then execute the solution. Our processes were in place for good reasons. We were serious about it—well, they were. And although I had a bit of a maverick streak, I harnessed it and fit in well as long as everyone was following the same playbook.

In addition to our often-mundane work back in Jakarta, there were times when each of us expats took on unusually high-level tasks. We coordinated activities and solved problems that at times involved direct meetings with government ministers, global financiers and foreign manufacturers. We didn't have to be told. If we needed to go across Jakarta or out to the site to accomplish something, we just did it. We communicated as necessary. We always got the job done and no one consistently questioned where, what or how we met our responsibilities. We were trusted representatives of one of the world's largest and most renowned engineering construction companies. We lived that trust. We felt it and it felt great. To borrow a military recruitment phrase, each of us was "An Army of One."

One afternoon, I was chewed out, up one side and down the other by a main floor receptionist. She was irate that I didn't tell her I was going to the dentist. I suppose there in the office her complaint had a degree of validity, but her delivery was loud, condescending and purposely humiliating. That was uncalled for and had no place in a professional work environment. Clearly, trust held a different meaning in this sensitive office. I had stepped on a mine. More awaited.

~ ~ ~

As I was re-acclimating at work and re-entering life in the States, I continued to follow news of Indonesia and other Southeast Asian countries. The British held a long-term lease on Hong Kong and after 156 years, were returning the incredible city to China. Reports of wealthy and connected citizens leaving Hong Kong ahead of the coming turnover to China were becoming more frequent. The Chinese government had installed a large countdown clock on the mainland. That clock was ticking more loudly every month.

I stayed in touch with some of the Indonesians and expats still there. As promised, I used the DHL pouch and wrote to Arlita every week. I didn't hear back from her. I reckoned that to be natural, as she had witnessed plenty of expats come and go throughout her young life.

I spent additional time cleaning my rental home and readying it for a new tenant. That went well and several people were interested.

Some weekends found me going to nice restaurants on the Kansas and Missouri sides, then on to a movie by myself. The film, *Forrest Gump* was still headlining in most theaters. A new television series, *Friends* was making its debut on NBC. Another sexy but looney film I enjoyed was entitled, *Pulp Fiction*.

On October 19, the evening TV news had a 20-second clip about the opening of the latest Planet Hollywood in Jakarta, Indonesia, of all places. *Small world*, I thought.

In one of my weekend drive-arounds, I wandered needlessly into a jewelry store at Rosana Square in Overland Park, Kansas. The gentleman behind the counter was viewing cut diamonds from a velvet tray. Because I showed an interest, he took me through a tutorial of sorts, showing the different grades, weights, styles and inclusions.

I was in there well over an hour. To make a long story shorter, I dropped more than four grand on an elegant three-quarter karat stone that had a natural, microscopic inclusion, just because it somehow spoke to me. This was a classic case of money burning a hole in my pocket. So was the custom, 14-karat gold ring I sketched for them to forge as a setting. I did not need or have plans for the gender-neutral ring, but this acquisition, along with authenticity documents would be ready in about 10 days. After picking it up from the jeweler, I stuffed it in a locked bag and never gave it another thought.

Bored and a bit lonesome, I flew to South Carolina in October for a three-day visit with my family. Most of the old family home was not livable but my siblings had fixed Dad's bedroom and moved him out of the little trailer back into his house. Charlene, Johnny and Bobby had installed a vented propane heater system that would safely keep the room warm during the coming winter. I hadn't been there for the actual work, but Charlene and I had financed it.

I brought in some food, and we all talked and ate as Dad lay in his bed. A hard life, compounded by the effects of his earlier stroke and the relentless cruelty of age had never given him a plateau on which to rest, even for a moment. Dad was frail. Behind the occasional smile, he was so tired. I saw it in his eyes. He saw the reflection in mine. He was not long for this earth and there was nothing anyone could do to change that course. It was as though he was just waiting. As we held hands, I wondered if this would be the last time we'd see one another.

It was tough being in the States when my mind was somewhere else. That was nobody's fault but mine. It wasn't true, but in regard to both my professional and personal life, I felt as though I had experienced more during my time in Indonesia than in all the years before. I thrived in that environment. I felt more alive and wanted it back. I was conscious of the three-month deadline I had promised Wilder. There was one month left to decide.

Allowing for bias, I still felt as though I had done my best to equally weigh my opportunities in the States. I understood clearly, I could fight myself and fight to comply with these valid routines. I could buckle down and make the adjustment. Or, I could possibly return to a life that had proven much more interesting—a life where I could be happier. As before, my only responsibilities were to myself. I had been back a little over two months when I decided to try to return to Indonesia.

"I'm pushing the button," I messaged Wilder.

"Hang tight and I'll see if everything is still in place," Wilder responded the next morning.

We both knew this would have to be a win-win for our partner's and for our company. The company couldn't just send someone over without the partner's specifically requesting that position. While picking up various billable tasks, I waited patiently for any news.

On November 17, I received an email from Wilder saying only, "Wheels in motion."

The next morning, I was called to the offices of the Jakarta project team and heard, "The partner's want to know if you'd consider coming back to help them with their invoicing."

"Yes," I answered without hesitation.

This was that win-win for everyone. This was another key decision that would have incredible consequences for my future, even if I didn't know what they were at the time.

I began wrapping up my Missouri project work. There were plenty of other qualified professionals happy to earn those fragmented hours.

I found a new tenant for my house at Pleasant Valley and got them settled in. I made another quick trip to South Carolina to visit Dad. Again, we held hands, talked about wintertime and shared memories.

On November 22, Mount Merapi in Indonesia erupted for the second time in as many years. I received a message from Ibu Niniek that her parents (*Arlita's grandparents*) had to quickly evacuate their rural home. Merapi was remarkably active. This was a particularly dangerous eruption that went on for days. Massive rivers of boiling water and pyrotechnic flows cut through the valleys leaving deep, wide gashes in the hillsides, destroying roads, bridges and killing 64 people. The tragedy served to remind me of my ties to the country. Those ties were hard to ignore. I was concerned because there was still no word from Arlita, but Ibu Niniek assured me she was fine.

In the final days before departing for Indonesia, I sold my Nissan, my new cell phone and renewed my contract with the long-term storage facility. I still had my pager from Indonesia, which would come in handy. Some of the boxes I had brought to the States had never been unpacked. I simply changed the labels and routed my personal shipment back to Jakarta.

On December 6, 1994, I again left the U.S., heading back to Indonesia. It felt more like going home than when I had come to the States three months before.

17

HOME TO INDONESIA

FOLLOW YOUR HEART

I arrived back in Indonesia on December 7. My semi-permanent resident's visa still had a couple of months left on it so getting through immigration and customs this time was a breeze. It also helped that I knew the ropes. My $20 bills were discreetly concealed in two plain, white envelopes. They did their job. Even with the luggage, this arrival was far less intimidating than when I'd first landed in Jakarta 22 months ago.

The taxi ride to the hotel had not changed. Once we entered the city, it was congested and chaotic. But this time I barely paid it any attention. Once I was checked in and had secured my luggage, I flagged a bajaj and headed to Block M to get something familiar to eat.

By early the next morning, I was back in the office, on the phone with our partners, processing through a stack of invoices and enjoying my warm tea. Coming back was the right thing to do.

Once more, the hotel would be my home for the next couple of weeks. Through an arrangement with our company, our partners covered the cost of accommodations along with a temporary car and driver. This was much appreciated. Aside from the work, my immediate goal was to find a more permanent place to live. I put out some feelers among the expat and

Indonesian communities and looked for a house right away. Knowing the area made this much easier than last time.

After looking at four or five houses, I settled on one at Jalan Cililin II (*Cililin Street 2*), not far from the house where I had lived before. It was basically the same distance to and from my office, but a much nicer property. The house needed some serious cleaning and would be available toward the end of December. There were two bedrooms, bath, kitchen and living room on the ground floor. The rooms were not large, but the layout was good. The outside walls surrounding the house were lined with beautiful plants and fragrant flowers. The servants' quarters (*their term, not mine*) were unusually large and well-appointed. But an exceptional feature of this place was its two rooms with baths on the upper floor of the house. Access to these rooms was through the kitchen, making them ideal for rent-sharing with other expats. I would eventually explore that possibility.

~ ~ ~

From last July, I learned the hard way that trustworthy, domestic housekeepers are the only thing keeping marauders from robbing me blind. So this time around, I hired housekeepers. An expat family from another company was returning to the U.K. and wanted to find an employer for their two housekeepers. I was happy to oblige.

Somewhere in their past, one of the expat families had named them Minarti and Winarto. I asked if they would like to use their real names. Both liked their new names so Minarti and Winarto it was. They were a young, highly-recommended husband and wife team. The pair spoke little English but I could help fill any gaps in communication. As soon as I hired them, they moved into their quarters and went to work, cleaning the newly rented house while I stayed at the hotel for another week.

~ ~ ~

Around the office, my friendship with Arlita was stable. Turns out, she had started dating a British guy while I was gone. I understood that for all she knew, I was never coming back. Most expats didn't. I now understood why she didn't write or respond to my letters. We didn't talk much about it; both just readjusted to one another's presence.

Many of our expat families were preparing to go away for the Christmas and New Year's. Those of us staying started picking up their critical work so progress could continue. As we got closer to Christmas, the contractors and suppliers brought in special holiday gifts for key partner personnel and at times, for us expats.

I was at my desk one afternoon when the American representative for Mitsubishi Construction came around the partition to my area. He was acting sneaky—totally out of character.

"Steele, I've got something for you waiting out in the car," he whispered.

"What you got, man?" I asked.

"Shhh, I got you two 16-year-old redheads."

My antennae immediately went up. Red flags were flying all around in my brain. I instantly recalled the time a lady had actually brought two Indonesian girls to my door. I also remembered what I had learned about human trafficking.

"What have you done, Tony?" I asked.

"Shhh." He looked around to see if anyone could hear us. "You want me to take them to your house? C'mon, I'll show you what I've got."

I didn't want to walk out to his car, just the two of us. I honestly didn't know what he had done, or what he was capable of so on the way out, I asked Jamitri to walk with us for a moment. Tony was parked on the street and as we approached his car, I didn't immediately see anyone inside. My warning flags were still up.

"They're in the trunk."

"Jesus, Tony," I said, thinking the worst.

Jamitri picked up on my apprehension and moved a little closer to me as we followed.

Tony popped the trunk and moved off to one side as if to say, "Voila!"

Jam and I carefully inched closer to the open trunk, neither paying attention to the shit-eating grin Tony was struggling to conceal.

Lying on a towel inside the trunk were the two, 16-year-old redheads, i.e. two 750ml bottles of Kentucky Maker's Mark bourbon. Tony was rolling, totally pleased that this naive American idiot, who wasn't the least bit familiar with this good whiskey, had fallen for his shenanigans. Indeed, I had.

"They're yours for the taking," he giggled.

I didn't drink distilled spirits at that point in my life, but other expats in the office quickly recognized the distinctive red wax tops of the 16-year-aged Maker's Mark bourbon. When evening came, we'd all partake in a smidgen before taking the whiskey to my home.

Over the next couple of days, I returned from meetings with our partners to find additional bottles of fine spirits had been delivered by various, generous contractor reps. The holiday gifts included single malts, blended whiskeys, more bourbons, brandy, cognac, saki and soju. Like other expats in our office, I had been gifted a dozen bottles of some of the finest spirits from around the globe. In addition, someone had stuffed a large, heavy-duty cardboard box under my desk. It was secured with metal straps, marked *Fragile* and labeled, *Hankook*. Jamitri told me it was delivered to me by Samsung Construction, the Korean contractor on the project.

It was a couple of days before I had time to cut the straps and peer into the cardboard box. Inside was a complete, six-serving set of formal, Hankook china from Korea. The imported spirits were expensive enough, but this beautiful china was over the top. Some quick research told me the set of dishes was in the range of $150 per setting. This offering was way beyond what our company considered appropriate.

My first call was to the representative, my contact with Samsung Construction. "Mister Dal, this gift is very much appreciated, but we're not allowed to accept such exceptional presents," I respectfully explained.

"Oh, but you must, Mister Steele," he insisted. "Our leader here would be insulted if a gift is not accepted. It is our culture."

I thanked him and told him to please thank his leader for the wonderful favor. I didn't want to make a mistake so I checked with my company, explaining to them what had happened. I was not at all sure what to do in this situation.

The message that came back from the Missouri office was, "We don't ever want to insult our associates out there, so it looks like you have some china."

I repackaged the china, then carefully boxed the bottles of spirits. I wasn't sure what I would ever do with any of this bounty, but I took it to my house, placed it in a closet and pretended I didn't know it was there.

~ ~ ~

After the dust settled on Christmas, I offered to take some of the office staff to Ancol for Jakarta's tremendous New Year's fireworks display. I planned to explore the food booths and other activities ahead of the display. Arlita was the only one to accept my offer. I picked her up the following Saturday evening; we took my temporary driver and left in plenty of time, I thought. We were still four miles from Ancol when the traffic began to back up. Painfully, we realized we weren't the only ones with this idea.

The traffic was going nowhere, slowly. Making use of the time, we caught up on my three months back in the States and she told me about things that had gone on locally.

She apologized when I asked why she didn't answer my letters and she didn't want to talk much about the British guy either; only to say that he drank a lot. She implied there was a chance she would stop seeing him but she hadn't yet decided.

We switched subjects and talked about—of all things—cars. Why were the prices so high in Indonesia? According to the locals, the government placed exceptional tariffs on all imported, high-quality vehicles and other essential manufactured goods. The majority of those tariffs went straight to the first family. Japanese automobiles were the most sought after and they held their value. The basic, used Toyota Corolla we were riding in was considered high quality. It was six years old. The same used car in the States sold for around $4,000. Used in Jakarta, it sold for $20,000.

Arlita told me that while I was gone, someone approached her offering to buy her a new car if she would steal them an advanced copy of a competitor's bid package. She had turned them down and reported the matter, but nothing more ever came of it.

After more than an hour stuck in traffic, we agreed to call off our little field trip. I asked the driver to watch for any opportunity to turn around. This was perhaps the only time this driver ever shined. He didn't wait for an opportunity. He created one, inching the Corolla back and forth, left and right a dozen times before finally squeezing out of the lane, bullying his way across the lines and into the empty, opposing lane.

Arlita and I had dinner, then I dropped her at her home around 10:00 p.m., much earlier than expected. We were both OK with that. If we had actually made it to Ancol, it would have been at least 2:00 a.m. before I got her home.

A week into the New Year my household shipment arrived from the States and was delivered to the house. That afternoon, Winarto came to my office to tell me that my temporary driver was at the house, opening the boxes and going through everything in my entire shipment from home. The driver had hooked up my VCR and TV and was sitting on the floor, drinking Bintang beer, going through my things while watching videos. I went home to find him still at it. I politely terminated him on the spot, a week before my allowed time was up.

Most of my nights were spent setting up the house. The bathroom mirror was attached to the mortar wall by two L brackets at the top and two at the bottom. With a little pressure, I discovered the mirror would slide a foot to the left or right. I slid it as far as it would go to the left, then used a small hammer drill to carve out a deep, six by six-inch hole in the mortar wall behind the mirror. This created a hidden niche to store smaller valuables and documents.

I continued shopping for essentials that made the place more comfortable. This meant repurchasing some of the items I had given away just three months before.

I worked out a plan for Winarto and Minarti to keep the two small upper rooms clean and ready for guests, should we have any. If I leased them out, the rooms would be offered at an exceptionally low price so that any expat tenant could keep most of their allowance. There would be no minimum stay, no curfews and the room would include breakfast. I would supply coffee, tea and groceries. Winarto and Minarti would prepare breakfast, take care of laundry and keep any tips the guests would leave. They'd also receive 25 percent of any proceeds. They were thrilled with this arrangement and eager to get started.

~ ~ ~

On Tuesday morning, January 17, 1995, our office received sketchy reports of a horrendous earthquake in Japan. Our Japanese associates in Jakarta were having a hard time getting information themselves. The communication lines were down. By mid-morning, we were being told to expect delays on Japanese electrical and steel products bound for Western Java. Throughout the coming days, we learned that this 7.3 quake had struck the area around Kobe and was believed to be the largest to strike Japan in more than 70 years. By the time the areas were cleared and searched, more than 6,000 souls were lost.

About this time, Arlita moved out of her family home in Muara Karang to a boarding house two miles south of Kebayoran Baru. This reduced her daily transit time by more than half. She had reached a point where she wanted to live on her own as well as study at Universitas Nasional (UNAS), the oldest private university in Jakarta.

Before long, she let me know that she was considering breaking it off with her British friend. We remained on happy, friendly terms, occasionally grabbing a meal or seeing a movie; sometimes with the group, other times just the two of us. Neither of us were anxious to start a formal relationship. My return to Indonesia along with our friendship was right where I wanted it to be.

18

LOSSES, GAINS, CARS AND PLANES

MILESTONES WE'D RATHER NOT MEET

O ver the last couple of years, I had made several trips back to the States and had taken the opportunity to visit other countries whenever concurrent vacation days allowed. I was now convinced I never wanted to live or work in the U.S. again.

Between my network of expatriates and global employment publications, the foreign employment outlook was bright. Offers kept coming without my needing to inquire. I could easily see Southeast Asian opportunities had the potential to keep me employed another 10 years. Knowing I would likely be in the region long term, I decided to invest in a few more household goods to make my world a little more comfortable and efficient: a new television and some better kitchen appliances to begin with. The biggest purchase was a new Suzuki Katana. The Katana was a basic, two-door, jeep-style vehicle that was cheaply made, but considered reliable. Unlike the expensive Japanese cars, Katanas were far more affordable.

The auto dealership arranged for the registration, license plate and a year's maintenance for the car. All I had to do was hand over two straps of new $100 bills. *It's only money, right?*

I also bought a battery-powered wireless doorbell. I planned to put the bell in the housekeeper's quarters and keep the pushbutton in the Katana. Whenever I was getting close to home, I'd push the button and Winarto would come out to open gates and the garage. In essence, he'd be the motor for my *Indonesian garage door opener*.

With my own vehicle, I'd need an Indonesian driver's license. That could be accomplished in one day, as long as I was being *referred* by a business. I arranged for our local administrative manager to accompany me to the downtown license office. She'd take care of the *official gratuities* and make sure I was properly referred.

The parking area was really congested with lots of new drivers who had taken numbers and were waiting in their cars to be called for processing. Many of the drivers were as young as 17. They sat in their vehicles with radios blaring and engines running. Since our administrative manager had arranged a referral expedite fee, I didn't have to wait.

I followed her around the edge of the parking area and toward the first tier of concrete steps leading into the offices. Just as my foot landed on the first step, I heard an engine rev somewhere behind me. I rapidly looked left just enough to recognize a car had jumped the step and was already upon me. I twisted myself enough to land my hands onto the hood of the car, pushing down in order to lift my feet off the concrete. In less than a second, my torso folded forward onto the car's hood with a bang. But my legs had made it off the steps, high enough to keep them from buckling under the car.

The young man waiting in the sedan had succumbed to inexperience and accidently hit his accelerator while his vehicle was in gear. A group of men gathered around him, helping get the car safely down off the steps. He was concerned that I was OK. I assured him I was, although it occurred to me, *he might need a bit more coaching before becoming a licensed driver.*

Most times in Jakarta, I'd been lucky enough to dodge moving objects. This time, I was not. I was not outwardly injured and after settling down, continued inside to get my driver's license. The next morning was a different story. My arms ached and my ribs were so sore that it hurt to breathe. My chin and upper legs were purple. Walking was painful.

Great way to start off with a new car. Hope this isn't an omen.

I was better in a few days.

Arlita was especially happy about the Katana. Turned out, she already knew how to drive a stick and was anxious to borrow it. Her driver's license experience went a lot smoother than mine.

As the first month of 1995 was coming to a close, the country was again preparing for Ramadan. Once this important event got underway, most official agencies naturally slowed down. Since it was nearly time to renew my semi-permanent resident's visa, I thought it wise to do that before Ramadan. We had another rare lull in our workload so I made plans to fly to Singapore on Thursday, January 26. I'd renew the visa on Friday and be back before work began the following Monday.

Arlita surprised me when she asked, "Is it OK if I go with you? I would like to visit Singapore."

She had a travel document that allowed Indonesians to visit Singapore for short stays, but it was customary for young women to consult their parents, especially if leaving town with a man. If I agreed, she would approach her parents for permission. I agreed. Her mom was all for it but her dad was a bit more hesitant. I gave them my word that I would take care of her; that she'd be safe. With my assurance, they both agreed. They trusted me more than I trusted myself.

Arlita and I left Jakarta that afternoon, arriving in Singapore in just under two hours. We got some street food, shopped some of the many stores including Tangs, and walked around the pristine city until well after dark. We were really enjoying ourselves. Showing her around, seeing her take in the sights and sounds on her first trip away from her homeland was especially fun for me.

In our room at the Hilton, we snuggled under separate blankets and talked until way after midnight. Sometime just after 2:00 a.m., I was jarred awake by the persistent ring of the house phone. I stumbled around to find and answer it. Our office manager in Missouri had used their resources to locate me and with sincere condolences tell me that my father had passed away on January 26, just hours before.

Family is a priority; my visa renewal would have to wait. Before dawn, Arlita and I headed back to the Singapore airport and caught the first flight back to Jakarta. We were both disappointed about missing our time in Singapore but she was very understanding. I needed to see her back home, then ready my travel bag for a quick turnaround.

Arrangements went in my favor. By 3:00 p.m., I was back at Jakarta's airport, boarding still another Singapore Airlines flight. With layovers, it was a five-leg, 44-hour journey that would take me from Jakarta to Hong Kong and Los Angeles then onward to Kansas City, Charlotte and Greenville, South Carolina. Somewhere among this chaotic aeronautical scheduling, somewhere along the way, there would be time for mourning. Hopefully time for some sleep, too.

My longest layover was in Hong Kong. I checked my one small piece of luggage as far as L.A., then wandered aimlessly around the crowded concrete city, taking in the heavy night air, the noise and the endless colored lights. A sidewalk kiosk made noodles with chicken for me while I pondered the future of this unique place. *What would it become under China's authoritarian rule?*

That night, I was a proverbial grain of sand, alone in a sea of millions of people, 8,400 miles from family. My heart was heavy yet strangely at peace; my spirit very much in sync with my father. Between us, nothing had been left unsaid; our memories, our understanding of life, our responsibilities and the love we often, openly expressed. I managed to snag four hours of half-sleep in a tiny Hong Kong hotel room with barely enough room to squeeze through the door. The next leg across the Pacific would begin boarding at 8:30 in the morning.

19

RECOLLECTIONS AND LITTLE PRAYERS

BYGONES AND LUCKY BREAKS

Saturday, January 28: When boarding completed the next morning, the heavy 747 moved to its place in line for takeoff. I settled in and prepared to attempt sleep. As we waited, a flight attendant came to my business-class seat and introduced herself.

"Mr. Tollison, my name is Kiera. Are you interested in moving to the first-class cabin?"

Did I hear that right?

Kiera continued, "You have been identified as an SAL preferred customer. There is space available and the chef is requesting additional passengers in order for him to prepare proper portions."

I wasn't so tired that I couldn't recognize this once-in-a-lifetime gift.

"Yes, thank you," I politely answered. "That would be wonderful."

I retrieved my carry-on from under the seat and was immediately escorted to first-class.

The first-class cabin on a Sing-Air trans-Pacific flight was reminiscent of the bridge on the Starship Enterprise—elegant, beautifully appointed, low ceiling and all too alluring. Although they had brought two of us forward from the back, the majority of the 12 seats remained empty. These were not ordinary seats. They were more like *areas,* or personal cubicles. Mine was along the starboard wall of the cabin. Spacious was an understatement.

My area had two windows, a lighted teakwood rail table with slots and cubbies for drinks, writing essentials and small personal possessions. The TV/monitor and magazine rack were built into a beautiful, teakwood panel more than two arm-lengths ahead. I could follow the aircraft's progress or watch any of the dozen films. There were soft blue, private lights that dimmed to my preference. The wide, tanned leather seats allowed for curling up into any position. With the touch of a button, the seat automatically transformed into a surprisingly comfortable bed with pillows and blankets provided. The touch of another button raised a teakwood/upholstered panel on the left side of my area to provide nearly complete privacy, retract for full openness, or anything in between.

The first-class cabin was attended by a maître d' and four flight attendants. After I was seated, Kiera offered a brief tutorial, ensuring I knew how everything worked. Over the next few minutes, she brought warm, moist white cotton hand towels, a zippered case with toiletries, a sleep set consisting of soft, blue sweat-style pajamas along with a pair of slippers. She offered French wines, Champagne, Scottish spirits and international beers including American and Irish. The chef could even prepare custom cocktails.

Beverages were served in formal glass stemware appropriate for the drink. During the 13-hour flight, the chef would prepare a light lunch, a more formal dinner and a light breakfast just before the flight reached Los Angeles. Between meals, orange, mango, papaya and tomato were among the many juices and beverages available on request. In first class, I didn't have to wait for the next round of service; custom-made sandwiches, any beverage and any snack I wanted were quickly available just by asking. Clearly, this airline's goal was to care for, pamper and impress their first-class customers. From where I sat, they were right on target.

Across the wide aisle to my left, a Chinese family of four was already settled in. These folks were dressed to a T. Even the two children were impeccably dressed. They reminded me of bygone days when Americans dressed in their best for a flight, but that era had ended by the late 1960s. Style obviously still meant something to my first-class neighbors.

They had been settled for a while before I arrived, so I assumed the family must have paid the $4,500 per person this privilege cost. I couldn't help but do the math. Their area was more like a suite, contoured to accommodate the two adults and both children. The section was modifiable and had perhaps been specifically arranged for them prior to boarding.

At 9:30 a.m., the big engines roared to life and within moments, the massive aircraft lifted from the runway. It made a lumbering, sweeping turn; gaining speed and altitude as it headed northeast out over the South China Sea.

Upon reaching altitude, Kiera came by and asked, "May I bring anything for you, Mr. Tollison?"

"Sure, some water, orange juice, champagne and a freshly-made BLT sounds really good."

Within 10 minutes, all were delivered with a sincere smile by this warm, friendly flight attendant who had only one passenger to take care of. I wished I could tell Dad about this.

Did he set this up?

A little later, I noticed the Chinese family taking their PJs and heading back to the restrooms to change, leaving a bunch of their personal belongings spread out all over their seats. Without leaving my seat, I could see four brand new American passports, onward tickets to Vancouver and a bunch of other loose paperwork along with an open gym bag. While visiting Indonesian banks, I had seen large blocks of paper money from around the world being handled and from where I was sitting, this bag appeared to contain at least eight *bricks* of new, $100 U.S. dollar bills. Once again, I did the math. A brick contains 1,000 bills. So that meant I was looking at a minimum of eight bricks of $100,000 each.

I never considered touching it or even looking closer, nor did I dwell on it. I figured these were diplomats or perhaps some wealthy Hong Kong residents re-establishing themselves elsewhere before the Chinese government took over in a couple of years. I silently wished them luck. They were going to need it, especially being as trusting and careless as they appeared.

After the activities and events over the last three days, I needed some serious rest. More than two days had passed since having anything other than a fragment of sleep here and there. Closing the window blinds, extending that comfy bed and closing my privacy panel was easy and comforting. I took off my shoes and shirt, put on a sleep mask and pulled that blanket over me. Sleep came quickly.

~ ~ ~

I awoke mid-afternoon, having slept nearly five hours. Opening the blinds revealed beautiful white cloud banks in the distance and the blue Northern Pacific Ocean seven miles below. Before long, we would fly into the darkness, searching for tomorrow's sunrise.

I made myself presentable then walked back to the private restroom. Even the restrooms were spacious. To stretch a bit more, I went through the curtains, walking further back into the business-class section. Just inside those curtains, I noticed two clean-cut Chinese men sitting with their backs to the bulkhead at the front of the business-class section. With buzzed haircuts, both were in their mid-30s, give or take. Oddly, they were wearing the exact same, non-descript street clothes and jackets. They seemed to follow my every move. Shortly after I returned to my seat, one of the two guys came into first-class. Unchallenged, he slowly walked past me to the front of the cabin, across to the left, then back out the other aisle. I'll never know for sure, but this suggested that these two guys were likely escorting the Chinese family. With personal bodyguards watching over them, these folks didn't need me wishing them luck.

As dinnertime approached, I could choose from a variety of meals and combinations that were prepared fresh. I chose grilled steak with roasted vegetables. The meals were timed so that no one waited for service. My private table was adorned with a white cotton tablecloth, stainless steel flatware, spice shakers and a petite, wide-based vase with fresh, live flowers. The chef came by to make an appearance and say hello. *Nice touch.* After dinner came desserts. My first was crème brulee with burnt sugar topping. Kiera made sure my first dessert wasn't my last. Ask me about Singapore Airline's apple pie with vanilla bean ice cream!

The cabin quieted and in the darkness over the Pacific, I finally allowed myself to think about Dad; time to remember, reflect and shed a tear.

Mom and Dad had flown only once in their lives, accepting my offer to fly them from Greenville to a small puddle-jumping airport in North Platte, Nebraska where I was working. Back then, I worked as an electrician, moving state to state, building new power generation plants. Sitting on this plane, I recognized that I had flown more times and to more places than I could count. Knowing how I had grown through my travels, I wished my parents had seen more of the world.

My mother's last years were broken and sorrowful as she faced terrible health issues. She passed 10 years before Dad who at that time, was not in the best of health himself. After her passing, he went further downhill.

I often wondered if my parents even realized that they had life choices. Many of their decisions seemed not well thought out; each more like a reaction than a conscious choice, each leading them deeper into hardship. Mom was the eternal romantic. Dad was the perpetual dreamer. Year after year, Mom supported Dad's dreams as best she could. In their early years together, his biggest dreams were songwriting, musical success, building a home and working their way out of poverty.

Mom was always there, supporting his dreams and setting his songs to music. But too often she was in the shadows. She wrote short stories and occasional columns for *The Greenville News*. One of her long-term goals was to write a book. Before she passed, she managed to pen a short novel entitled, *Song of the Angel Oak*. Her novel didn't win any awards but completing it meant a lot to her. I later discovered her novel was listed in the Library of Congress.

During my early childhood, Dad taught me to sing and play instruments: ukulele, guitar, mandolin and harmonica. It was all by ear, only Mom could actually read music. From the time I was four until around 10, he and I performed around the region. In some performances I was solo. Most times, Dad accompanied me on guitar while I sang.

We played business openings, assemblies, Saturday morning TV and radio programs. In my short life, we had been on stage a lot: an audition here, a performance there and more small-town talent shows than I could remember. Sometimes, brothers Bobby and Johnny joined us for performances put on by the PTA.

Dad sent original sheet music, songs and demos to the major music companies of the time, dreaming of the day when his efforts might land something big. But none of his undertakings ever came to fruition. Dreams were always calling Dad, but just beyond his reach.

At some point when the 1950s were making way for the `60s, a regional entertainment promoter contacted Dad about an opportunity. In the past, Clint Griffith had booked some minor talent gigs for Dad and me in and around Greenville and Spartanburg. This time he was rounding up young, musically talented boys to audition for some kind of television show. I was around eight, maybe nine. Mom washed, ironed and dressed me in the nicest clothes she could find.

Clint picked Dad and me up in his big, black '58 Cadillac and we headed northwest on Highway 25 over the mountains toward Ashville. I barely knew what was going on but to Dad and Clint, it seemed important.

Along the way, Clint laid that Caddy into those sharp, mountainous curves while Dad, I and Uncle Willmon's Gibson guitar slid from side to side across that enormous back seat.

In Ashville, I barely remembered the bright studio lights; friendly but serious strangers with clipboards asking me to, "Read, talk, laugh, be happy, be sad and sing a half-dozen songs," while Dad played guitar. We must have been there a couple of hours and that was the end of it.

Night had fallen when we left the studio and I was hungry. Clint stopped at a rundown, roadside store with one Esso gas pump out front. He filled the Caddy while Dad took me around back of the store so we could both pee. Dad got us a little snack cake to eat along with a five-cent Dr. Pepper. We stood outside that store quickly finishing our substitute supper before getting back into the car. I don't remember the ride home that night. I barely remember Dad carrying me from the car into the house and putting me to bed. We never heard anything more about that audition. At least I didn't and it didn't matter to me.

Another year or more went by before Dad brought home a well-used, stand-up black and white television that Aunt Hazel had given him. She had just gotten her first color TV, passing the old B&W on to Dad. I remembered sitting on Aunt Hazel's floor watching Elvis's first TV appearance on that old TV.

That winter, some of us were sitting around that scratchy old TV, trying to adjust the screen from rolling while we watched a show Mom and Dad had come to enjoy. I guess Dad had found out by talking to someone that this was the show I had auditioned for in Ashville a couple of years back—*The Andy Griffith Show*. A kid named Ronnie Howard had been selected for the part and he was really good in it. But another one of Dad's dreams had gone by the wayside. By this time, even I could sense the toll these losses were taking on him and Mom.

In the late 1950s and early '60s, my oldest sister Mattiphene lived with our grandparents across the broom straw field from our house. Mom, Dad and the other five of us six kids lived in a four-room house between two sets of railroad tracks. Years earlier, Mom, Dad, his brothers along with some distant neighbors had used reclaimed lumber to build the house from scratch. The Northern Pacific Railroad was 300 feet behind us and the

Southern Railroad was about 500 feet in front. We somehow made peace with the deafening whistles, bells and constant shaking. Mom named the place, *Echo Ridge*.

We got by on hand-me-down clothes from our cousins, drew water from a well outside and made use of a rickety old outhouse shared with field mice, wasps and the occasional snake which you never seemed to spot until you had your britches down.

In the later part of 1960, Mom and Dad sold Echo Ridge and borrowed some money from Aunt Hazel to buy another piece of remote, heavily-wooded property a couple of miles away. It was a quarter mile off the nearest paved road. There was enough money to have a small 'kit house' built on it. The materials for the house were delivered to the site and the builder finished the exterior, leaving the rest of the material stacked outside. Mom and Dad could not afford to have the interior finished by the builder, so they took the option to finish it themselves. The interior work began after we all moved in. The subflooring was in place, but we could see the ground below through the cracks. The two-by-four studs and part of the drywall were up, but there were no doors or plumbing. There was no insulation in the walls or ceiling and there never would be. Mom named this place, *Timberest*.

Shortly after we moved in, Mom and Dad added a fireplace in the main room. The guy building it didn't seal the flue joints and one night while we were all asleep, the house caught on fire. We were lucky no one was hurt. The fire was relatively minor but because of the necessary repairs, the other work was set back months. In addition, the chimney had not been built high enough, causing even the slightest wind to push smoke back through the fireplace, into the house. Dad always said he was going to make it higher, but he never got around to it.

So, there we were again, seven of us living in a small unfinished house, this time deep in the woods. Progress was slow—I'm talking years. There was no refrigeration or running water. We carried drinking water from a natural spring an eighth of a mile away. We cut wood to heat water and keep warm. We used kerosene lamps for light. We cooked over the fireplace. Winters were brutal.

Once again, the toilet was an outhouse or more often, just some isolated spot deeper in the woods. We trapped rabbits and squirrels until there were none. We kids walked the highways looking for pop bottles to sell. There was limited electricity with only two outlets and three incandescent lamps on wires hanging from rafters above. But even that didn't last long if we couldn't pay the electric bill. By the time I was 11, our electricity had been completely cut off. It was months before we could pay the $45 bill and reconnect.

On weekends for a couple of years, Dad tried to flip old worn-out cars he'd buy cheap at local auctions. He had little success. Most of the cars had been patched just enough to get them through the auction before breaking down shortly after he paid for them. More than a dozen of these old cars sat rusting among the many trees around our property. Us boys piddled with them, trying to keep them running. In the process, we learned a lot about working on vehicles.

The following year, we lost electricity again, this time living without power for the next four long years. Isolated deep in the woods, there were a couple of summers where we didn't even see other people until school started again. During those hot summer nights, Johnny, Charlene and I took a 12-volt battery from one of the old cars that didn't have a working radio and put it into another car that didn't run but its radio worked. This way, we could sit outside at night, swat mosquitos and listen to music over the local stations. When that battery ran down, we'd put it back into the car that ran so it could recharge.

In 1964, the Beatles dominated America's airways. FM radio was making its debut and if we tied a long wire to the car's antenna, we could listen to the Grand Ole Opry on WSM way out in Nashville.

NASA was working on plans to send men to the moon yet we still lived in an unfinished house—that never would be finished. Our family had a clunky, 1948 four-door Chevrolet with mismatched wheels and black paint peeling off. It seemed to burn oil at the same rate it burned gas. In a cloud of blue smoke, we looked like the Beverly Hillbillies coming down the road.

Beyond Timberest, other families seemed to be doing well, but we weren't. Dad earned $1.85 per hour at the Piedmont Shirt Company in Greenville. For a while, Mom worked 12-hour days as a housekeeper making $25 for a six-day workweek. Whenever she brought home leftovers from her housekeeping job, we'd share them with the dogs. Mom was sick a lot, required surgery, and was in and out of the hospital.

Without question, our parents bore the weight of six children. They were two bright, compassionate people but they couldn't even take good care of themselves. They lacked parenting skills and resources. Both wanted better for our family, they just couldn't make it happen. They didn't know how to plan for the future until it was upon them. We kids were not a lot of help. We didn't know how to step up and do things that would make the family's lives better. We didn't know it then, but our family was coming apart. On some level, every one of us was suffering.

Mattiphene was the oldest. After high school she attended night classes at Furman University before joining the U.S. Air Force. Shortly thereafter, she went to nursing school and became an LPN. Garland and Bobby were beginning to venture, perhaps to stumble into their own individual destinies. Johnny, Charlene and I were still at home full time. It was tough enough on us boys, but even harder for Charlene, a very young girl robbed of a normal, happy childhood. We were hungry, dirty and always smelled like smoke. We had no dental care, no decent shoes or clothes. The three of us looked and felt the part, especially at school. It was painfully embarrassing.

Our county didn't have middle schools so at 14, I was in high school. Like other kids in the area, I was driving illegally and lying about my age so

I could work nights in the local manufacturing plants. The plant managers knew we were underage and let it slide. I didn't have much of a plan but I sensed opportunities for those who were hard-working, open-minded and willing to learn new skills. By the age of 16, that had unintentionally become my M.O.; listen, watch and learn.

Despite the hardships, our life at Timberest still held sweetness, a romance of sorts. It was the only home we really knew and there was always love. We'd seine the creek for small fish, wade and swim during the summer. We built forts in the high broom straw and rode our rickety bicycles to distant communities. At night we'd sit around that fireplace with the dogs, ducking the smoke, singing and playing our worn-out instruments until something broke. With three of the guitar strings missing, I learned to make pretty good music with those that remained. On occasion, Johnny and I were asked to perform on a couple of local television programs. Dad made sure we had all the strings for those events.

Later in her life, Mom went to nursing school and like our oldest sister Mattiphene, became an LPN. Mom told me once that being a nurse, her writing and her children were her greatest sources of happiness. She didn't mention their marriage. We children knew that because of the hardships, real happiness had always eluded her.

Dad loved Mom and all his children. He seemed especially close to his first-born, Mattiphene. After the birth of her first child, Adrian in the mid-1960s, Mattiphene became ill. After the birth of her second son Vincent, this mystery illness immobilized her. Her husband was overwhelmed by the responsibility and abandoned the family, never to be seen again. Years went by before she was finally diagnosed with myasthenia gravis. During those long years, Dad drove himself to work, then stopped off to sit with her in the hospital until late in the evenings. Mom worked at the same hospital and spent her break time and time off there with them. It seemed that the rest of us kids could only look on, unable to help our parents as their hearts broke; unable to help our sister as the disease slowly stole her life.

Our parents were broken and there was nothing we kids could do to fix it. Too quickly, each of us found our own pathway forward. We had no choice. Some of us fared better than others. Whenever the siblings got together we'd remind ourselves, "Hey, at least nobody's in prison."

Then came Vietnam amidst a divided Nation. Garland was the first to be drafted. A few months later, it was Bobby. After a serious bout with asthma, Garland received an early discharge. Bobby was sent on to Vietnam. Thirteen months later, he came home a changed man with a broken spirit that never healed.

My turn came in April, 1970. Fortunately, I served stateside and was sent directly from basic training to work on vehicles at Fort Carson, Colorado. By working on old junk cars, I had inadvertently prepared for this role throughout my childhood.

By day at Ft. Carson, I plied my mechanical and electrical skills repairing and maintaining tanks, armored personnel carriers and an array of other infantry vehicles. By night, I sat with emotionally troubled soldiers who had returned from Vietnam with several months to go before being discharged. My role was whatever it took to keep them from hurting themselves during their long, frightening nights. Aside from six weeks of basic training, I had no formal instruction for the roles I covered. But during that war, the Army offered very little in the way of advanced training. If a draftee was identified as having even a hint of aptitude, the job was his.

When I was discharged in 1971, America had become even more divided. Returning veterans were too often a target of ridicule, employment discrimination and even violence.

I quickly hid my military affiliation and grew out my hair. Like many fellow veterans, I was careful never to reveal my service. It made non-veterans uncomfortable. I didn't acknowledge it on any applications, forms, or other documents; as though it never happened.

For the better part of the next four decades, only a select few knew of my service—a silent echo in a time when that was safer to remain hidden. It wasn't until some 40 years later when a doctor at the VA hospital in Kansas City uttered the simple but profound words, "Thank you for your service," that I began to acknowledge that part of my past. For the first time, I broke down hearing those words. It was as though his gratitude, offered so long after the fact had unlocked a door I had kept shut.

I went on to work full time during the days. At night, I attended college and trade school where I earned a Journeyman Electrician's license that would support me for more than a decade before finding my way into business and engineering.

For Mom and Dad, the decade between 1961 and 1971 left them with heavy hearts, heavy debt and emotional burdens from which they would never recover. They suffered far too many sleepless nights, worrying about each of their four military children serving during wartime and the younger two still at home. They were devastated by the long, gradual loss of Mattiphene and the struggle to take care of her two children. All the while, their hopes, dreams and moments of joy slipped away.

From my first-class seat in that nearly empty cabin, my sleepy thoughts circled back to Dad and the loss I was realizing. He had been a perpetual, unfulfilled dreamer. *What made him that way?* Only the angels knew. But it seemed his role in life was to dream; to create amazing, often hair-brained, sometimes annoying schemes from somewhere within. Now, someone else would have to take those dreams and try to make them into something meaningful. My father's life on earth, his role as a dreamer was over and no doubt, I had lost someone important.

As we flew into the darkness, I roused from my recollections feeling the plane tilt slightly as the pilots adjusted our bearings. A moment later, Kiera stopped by to see if I needed anything.

"A coffee and Baileys?" Of course! The rest of the cabin seemed to be sleeping as I sat and she stood, just talking. I felt taken care of, content in Kiera's company.

A couple more of the attendants stopped by and chatted with us. I asked about their exceptional mid-sleeved, full-length uniforms. "They resemble the Batik dresses in Indonesia."

"These are Sarong Kebaya," Kiera explained. "Yes, they are Batik."

The colors indicated the status of the attendant. Blue indicated the flight stewardess, green was the lead stewardess, red was the chief stewardess and burgundy was their supervisor. Kiera's uniform was a delicate shade of blue.

"They're really pretty. Are they comfortable?" I asked.

"Thank you, yes, and safe too."

In that moment, one of the other girls slowly undid a snap on her sarong, (lower skirt), the gesture both graceful and suggestive as she twirled, letting it slip away. Beneath it, she revealed a pair of form-fitting Batik spandex leggings that respectfully hugged her curves just above the knee.

"This is how we handle serious safety issues, allowing us to move more freely and respond effectively in an actual emergency."

Oh my, I thought. This gentleman kept his composure, but I was pretty sure I was having a *serious safety issue* right then and there. Kiera recognized my polite but pleasurable reaction, casting a blushing smile my way.

Throughout the night, Kiera drifted by to chat. We shared a lot about ourselves; learning and making small talk. She offered condolences on my father's passing, her soft words accompanied by a tender prayer, "May he be reborn into a world of happiness."

As dawn approached, we exchanged contact information, both encouraging the other to reach out sometime in the future. Neither of us ever did but during this time, it was comforting to know I could.

With regret and sincere appreciation, I said goodbye to Kiera and that luxurious, first-class experience. To Singapore Airlines I'd say, "Thanks, guys. What a ride!"

~ ~ ~

Back in daylight savings time, my flight arrived in L.A. around 9:30 a.m. With unfavorable layovers and connections, South Carolina was another 15 hours away.

Finally, after 44 hours of travel, I met up with family in time to attend the funeral and graveside services on Monday morning. The service was brief. The fiery Southern minister was determined to admonish the living of our sins. At first, it felt like he was singling me out until I realized he was pointing at everyone. Message received! Some ladies from the Welcome Baptists Church played and sang a couple of Dad's favorites, *Amazing Grace* and *I Saw the Light*.

Through my mental fog that morning, I saw my father forever laid to rest alongside my mother. I could only strive to live up to the gifts they had given me.

It happened that my brother Bobby and sister Charlene were with Dad when he took his final breath. He left this world cradled in the arms of his children, sunlight on his face through the window of the home he and Mom had built together. That tender image of his passing has always given me a degree of comfort, as has that little prayer offered by a young Buddhist flight attendant seven miles above a dark, Pacific Ocean.

During the next few days my brothers, sister and I got involved in clearing up final issues. There wasn't a lot I could do since I was returning to Indonesia in a couple of days. Charlene and I took care of the cost of the funeral, burial and gravestone plaque. Beyond that, someone else would have to divide any worthwhile items, clear out the closets, cupboards, and sweep the ashes from that notorious fireplace.

I hung out with family for a day or so, visiting their homes as well as Timberest, the old home place. We poked around the musty wooden out-buildings Dad had built by hand. As we walked through the woods around the area, I felt as though the spirit of my parents still lingered there. Whenever I visited in the decades to come, it always felt the same—a hallowed place.

Before leaving, Johnny helped me record a bootleg copy of Mel Gibson's film, *The Year of Living Dangerously* into the center of a two-hour, High-8 video tape. It was a highly controversial film so I recorded some nonsense stuff in front and behind it in case Asian customs got nosey. When the time came, I left South Carolina, made my way back to Los Angeles and onward home to Jakarta. I knew the way.

20

AN ACCIDENTAL TRIP TO ALASKA

GOING OUT OF ONE'S WAY

O n my journey back to Jakarta, I had an early afternoon flight out of L.A. on Singapore Airlines. The Los Angeles International Terminal was separate from the domestic terminals and it was larger than most airports by themselves. It was highly congested, chaotic with people from all over the world dragging mountains of luggage, lined up at perhaps 100 check-in points. Many people coming through here did not speak English, requiring assistance and extra time navigating the processes. For them, it was especially confusing.

Luckily, Sing Air was notoriously efficient. I completed the check-in and made my way to the gate area like I'd done many times before. It was Saturday, February 4, 1995. In less than two hours, I'd be airborne for the expected 14-hour flight to Hong Kong. My itinerary called for a plane change in Hong Kong before continuing south to Jakarta.

About 20 minutes into the flight, the staff called over the PA, "Any doctors or medical professionals please identify yourselves."

It was a while before we learned that someone on the plane was having a cardiac issue. Medical people had responded and the patient was quickly stabilized. This was where it got weird. I'll never understand why this flight didn't simply return to L.A., less than an hour away. Instead, the plane continued on its flight path.

The monitors showed we were heading northwest, which was right on course. However, in another hour or so, the captain announced we were diverting to Anchorage, Alaska. I scratched my head, so to speak: a guy with a heart problem, two hours back to L.A. or four-plus hours to Anchorage? To me, it seemed illogical and risky, but guess who wasn't flying the plane? Anchorage, here we come!

With a Sony Walkman, three CDs and some decent headphones, I did my best to occupy myself during the hours it took to get there. There were fantastic afternoon views of the snow-covered terrain as our 747 gradually descended. During the final approach, I could see hundreds of single-engine float planes frozen in the harbor ice like neat little rows of boats at a marina. They wouldn't fly again until the spring thaw, months later.

During the landing, I could see dozens of unusually large aircraft at different places around a maze of oversized runways. Most planes were 747s, including some that appeared to be highly modified. There were also four huge, Russian Antonov-style cargo planes. By asking around, I learned that

Anchorage was a global cargo hub. Instead of flying east or west, these large aircraft from around the world saved time and fuel by navigating over the North Pole, refueling, trans-loading cargo and continuing to other more southerly destinations.

Finally, our plane stopped in a holding area where an ambulance with paramedics took the cardiac patient away. The pilot announced we would refuel then continue onward to our destination. But it didn't happen that way. We sat there, waiting. Two hours later, we were still waiting. The pilots repeatedly thanked the passengers for their patience.

Then came the announcement no one wanted to make or hear. This incident had consumed nearly six hours from the original schedule. In compliance with FAA and international regulations, the Sing Air crew was required to stand down and rest. The passengers let out a uniformed moan. So did the crew, but this was a strict regulation. Everyone understood it was the right thing to do.

A short while later, an announcement came over the PA: "All passengers and crew will be taken into Anchorage, provided with evening and morning meals, any medical considerations and warm, safe accommodations. You will receive instructions for re-boarding during tomorrow's breakfast."

An hour or so later, a caravan of yellow school buses lined up in horseshoe formation outside the plane.

About this time, I realized another impending conundrum. I had been in South Carolina and L.A. and was heading back to the tropics. The last thing I expected to encounter was cold weather. It was 14 degrees out there. I was wearing a short-sleeve shirt, jeans and boat shoes with no socks. Other under-dressed passengers were starting to realize the same thing and started getting antsy. The crew came back on the PA, telling everyone to take the Sing Air wool blankets when exiting the plane.

Sing Air bussed the 400 passengers plus crew to several large hotels near downtown Anchorage. I went to the Regal Alaska Hotel (later known as the Lakefront Anchorage) where an ominous, stuffed grizzly bear stood guard over his domain in the lobby. I'm not sure how many passengers were there but it was more than I could count. Caterers were nearly finished setting up large buffets in an oversized conference room. It was obvious this kind of airline stand down situation had happened before. You don't just feed 400 hungry people on a moment's notice without having had the experience, resources and supplies quickly available.

The ground crew and hoteliers did an exceptional job. By the time everyone was fed and rooms were assigned, it was after 11:00 p.m. I had a good meal and a large room with a king bed, mini-bar and pay TV all to myself, courtesy of Singapore Airlines. I did not abuse this privilege, but I did partake.

Sing Air advised all passengers that because of the crew stand-downs and scheduling, we would be bussed back to the plane around 2:00 p.m. the next day, Sunday. Our expected takeoff was around 5:00 p.m. Passengers were instructed to meet back at the hotel no later than 2:00 p.m.

It turned out most businesses in the historic downtown corridor of Anchorage were normally closed on Sundays, especially in February. But when there was a planeload of 400 passengers with money and time on their hands, every store owner in the downtown area came in and opened their shops. Right after breakfast, the outside temperature was still hovering around 14 degrees. I threw my airline blanket over my shoulders and went shopping, taking advantage of the close proximity of the shops, ducking in and out to avoid the biting cold. What a strange, comical sight it must have been: 400 people walking around the frozen snow-packed city, all draped in the same blue wool blankets.

Our presence was a windfall for the shop owners; all these people wandering through their businesses, buying things they didn't need. I tried to buy items I could use. My first priority was a heavy cotton Alaskan hoodie and a pair of socks to supplement my warmth. Then, there were four cans of salmon packaged in flats. That salmon was edible for years to come. A couple of key chains, some chocolate, some hot chocolate; I continued through the shops just killing time before returning to the hotel. I kept that blanket with me everywhere I went.

At 2:00 p.m., there were those yellow school buses waiting to take everyone back to the plane. As usual, Sing Air was efficient and within 30 minutes, all the passengers were deposited at a convention-style gate area. The walls were glass and the views in three directions were exceptional. The Sing Air plane was sitting about 500 feet away. The building was warm and had basic facilities but there was no place to sit. I guess they didn't plan to keep us there for long. Bad guess.

The crew was kind enough to let us know they were working on some issues and hoped to board within the next hour. Everyone was tired, bored and ready to get underway. But here we were either standing, sitting on our bags or sitting on the floor while once again, we waited.

I moved over to sit on the floor and lean against the window. Others did the same. I struck up a conversation with a redheaded girl who was heading to Australia to study. Attie was maybe 25 and working on a master's degree in strategic communications.

"I'm quite Scottish," she said.

"I'd never have noticed," I playfully responded.

This was her first time living abroad and first time traveling this far. She had been visiting friends in the States and touring around for two weeks before moving on to Australia. We sat there as comfortable as anyone can be sitting on a hard floor. At times, we said nothing. Other times, we chatted aimlessly while swapping CDs.

We finally boarded and departed Anchorage around 5:45 p.m. Once we were well underway, an attendant announced that because of the flight's disruption, this bird would be making stops in Hong Kong, Singapore and Jakarta. That meant no further plane changes for me. But it was going to be a long night for all of us.

I was in business-class, which on Sing Air was nicer than first-class on most other airlines. The seats around me were empty so I asked the flight attendant if it was OK to bring Attie up from coach. She cheerfully agreed.

Attie was thrilled to get the nicer seat and the amenities that came with it. I wished her well when she deplaned in Singapore. She'd have a long layover before completing her flight to Sydney the next day. But if you had to layover in Southeast Asia, Singapore was the most comfortable place to do it.

I finally got back to Jakarta around mid-day on Monday, February 6. I had done enough flying, waiting and waiting some more to last me for quite a while. I'll never complain about that long trip to and from South Carolina, even the accidental trip to Alaska on the return. The good parts were amazing. The bad? Well, they were amazing, too.

The sadness of losing my remaining parent eventually found its place within me, resurfacing from time to time, as it should.

21

THROTTLE UP

THEN EASE BACK ON THE STICK

After returning home to Jakarta, I fell back into my routines. I ensured all invoicing business and bid packages were processed on schedule. Before month's end, I flew back to Singapore to renew my semi-permanent resident's visa. This time, traveling by myself, it was a quick turnaround.

One morning in mid-March 1995, I arrived at the office to find the local office staff huddled in sad disbelief.

"What's going on, guys?"

"It is Nike Ardilla, 'Pak Steele. She has died."

Nike Ardilla, an extraordinarily popular Indonesian pop star was killed in a car accident in Bandung. She was only 19 years old but over the last several years had won the hearts of Indonesians with her variety of heartfelt, romantic love songs and dance numbers. She was multitalented: a sincere philanthropist, actress, model and singer. At that moment I thought it strange that the local folks were so distraught until I realized it affected the whole country. I hadn't paid attention before but this young girl was a household name. All of Southeast Asia seemed to love her. Neighboring countries throughout the region held vigils in her remembrance. Indonesia honored her short life and mourned her passing for decades to come. With respect, I took time to learn more about this person who meant so much to my friends. That endeavor would expose me to other Indonesian musical talents I had been missing.

~ ~ ~

I continued dating, more broadly and more frequently. Through my business and embassy connections, I met a couple of American ladies I saw on occasion. One was stationed in Jakarta with the U.S. Department of Agriculture, the other, with USAID. There was a banking representative from Singapore and later, a doctor from Thailand. I also dated local girls. For several months, I had an exceptionally good time. None of the women I dated continued into a committed relationship and that was more than OK with me.

Occasionally, I traveled to other smaller islands to take photos and see the sights. Some of these places were remote, hardly developed and had no paved roads. Whenever I hiked the trails or walked through a remote village, I applied *Steele's Chicken Principle*. If there were plenty of chickens roaming around the village, it was usually a safe place to be. If I went into a village where there were no chickens and only a skinny old dog or two, I turned on my radar. Having *no chickens* was a red flag that the place was not prosperous and possibly desperate.

~ ~ ~

At my house, I rented the two upper rooms to a couple of young engineers who had come out for a three-month, short-term assignment. These guys received a generous daily per diem which covered their hotel but it wasn't enough to cover any entertainment, leisure or weekend travel they wanted to experience while in-country. I arranged for Winarto and Minarti to manage their access, make them a basic breakfast and tend to the rooms. Minarti also took care of their laundry on a tip basis. I covered all the supplies and breakfast food costs. The engineers saw more of the country while saving well over half of their per diem normally spent for a hotel. Winarto and Minarti added around 50 percent to their monthly salary during those three months. I made enough to pay my electricity.

The house turned out to be a win-win for Winarto and Minarti, for me and for the visiting engineers. But it required a lot of upkeep, security and critter patrol. Minarti was fearless when it came to Jakarta's critters: insects, lizards, snakes, bats and rats. Jakarta had really big rats. They were filthy, mangy, sometimes mauled, crippled and often diseased. Most times, they didn't pose an immediate threat unless they congregated in an area. Day or night, when it was quiet they'd get into your food stocks and sometimes trap themselves inside living areas. That could be thrilling. Housekeepers all across the country saw rat patrol as one of their responsibilities. Winarto and Minarti were both skilled at keeping the population minimized. They traded live-cage traps back and forth among other housekeepers. That way, no one had to invest in one.

I came out early one morning to go to work and noticed Minarti placing a cage by the drive out front.

Inside the cage were two of Jakarta's finest, hissing and looking at us like, "When we get outta' here, you guys have had it!"

"What will you do with them?" I asked.

Minarti pointed to the sun.

"Matahari akan membunuh dua puluh menit," (sun will kill in twenty minutes) she said.

She went on to tell me that they couldn't relocate the rats or do anything more humane. Some of the housekeepers poured boiling water over them. She preferred to let the sun take care of them.

Three miles south of our office, Kemchik's Grocery Market carried items of interest to the expat community. The Indo-Chinese owners were always helpful and friendly. They were also famous for placing new, stick-on labels over the original expiration dates. Most times, shoppers received a product that was still useable—most times.

Finding the thing I was actually going there for might not happen but I'd likely come away with something else that gave me a taste of the States, something different and not available in other Indonesian stores. Cereals, fresh veggies, canned veggies, soups, packaged meats, soft drinks, cookies and candies were some of the international items that appeared on the shelves from time to time.

I stopped by one evening to browse and thought I had hit the jackpot. There on a shelf with other oddball soft drinks was one remaining six-pack of Dr. Pepper. I was elated. I clutched it lustfully; leery of setting it down where some other opportunist might claim it for himself. I managed to get a couple of other items, including a box of Toblerone chocolates, before checking out and heading for the Katana.

When I got home, I grabbed a glass and the ice tray from the freezer, preparing to pour myself the first Dr. Pepper I'd had in ages. I put my finger in the loop, lifted and popped that top. There was no fizz or bubbly spray, nothing! It was totally flat. I checked another, then another. Same thing. I toyed with the idea of tasting it, but it didn't smell that great. I should have known better but I hadn't looked closely enough. I couldn't lay this crime on the shopkeepers because the information was right there on the can. I had been caught in my own emotional trap.

The printing and graphics on the Dr. Pepper cans were promoting a contest for a chance to win an array of prizes. It also told the buyer that the contest *Ends June 1991*. This was 1995.

It was a couple of days more before I got into the Toblerone chocolates. *Worms*! Lots of worms— discovered the hard way. There was no way to tell how old they were. It's not fair to the product, but I don't think I've had a Toblerone since. Kemchik's was indeed a risky market. Although most all the expats had similar stories, we still shopped there— just more carefully.

~ ~ ~

By now, I had been in the country long enough to justify buying a multi-system VHS tape deck. It allowed me to play and record PAL-system tapes from the region as well as NTSC-system tapes from the States. During my travels, I had returned with well over a dozen VHS movies. I and other expats often rented poor-quality, pirated videos from a local entrepreneur who had someone copying them from theaters around the country. The first clue was seeing the back of people's heads in the foreground.

I started a video library where expats and locals could check out and/or add their own VHS tapes of movies, documentaries and homemade films. This service turned out to be popular. I made sure Winarto and Minarti had a chance to see films before I returned them. I had to be careful about sharing controversial films like *The Year of Living Dangerously, Schindler's List* or anything considered too problematic for a sensitive government. I had those films but only shared them with people I knew well and could trust.

~ ~ ~

Arlita was still attending UNAS in the evenings. Sometimes I gave her a ride back to her place. Her boarding house closed its gates shortly after 9:00 p.m. so a couple of times I helped her climb over the fence. Other times, I jumped the fence just to visit. It wasn't a particularly secure place but she was happy to be independent and out on her own.

Within a couple of months, she moved out of there into a small apartment not far from the boarding house. There were no fences to jump.

~ ~ ~

Jakarta traffic cops standing around intersections were friendly but corrupt. I learned by watching the locals that when driving on multi-lane roads, it was wise to stay on the inside lanes away from the sides of the road where the police usually targeted vehicles. A couple of times, they walked in front of me during slow moments, directing me off onto the shoulder.

Then, they ticketed me for being on the shoulder where they had just directed me. The ritual was to roll down my window while the cop passed an aluminum binder through the open window to me. I would open the binder, insert Rp.20,000 (around $2.50 USD) then hand it back to him before he waved me onward. It was friendly and cheap enough. If you were local or expat, when the police stopped you, you paid. To challenge this daily micro-robbery would cost a person a full day at the police station where they'd charge you even more to process a claim.

One night in April, I received a pager message from the U.S. Embassy advising Americans to stay alert. A large federal building in Oklahoma City had been bombed and they were still gathering more detailed information. As the moments went on, we heard from folks back in the States. The tragedy had taken place at the Alfred P. Murrah Federal Building where 68 innocent people had died.

On a warm spring evening in May of '95, I surprised Arlita by taking her to an outdoor Bon Jovi concert at Ancol. I had bought the best tickets and we had arrived two hours before show time. But none of that mattered. It was money wasted. From the newspapers, we found out later that the promoters had oversold the concert by three times. This was standard fare for Indonesia. A Metallica concert a few years earlier ended in a deadly riot because of overselling. There was never any accountability.

When we first got to the Bon Jovi venue, we worked our way toward the front where our tickets placed us. People had overrun that entire area and were packed like sardines. I steered us toward other areas, searching for something with a view of the stage; not much luck. As the pre-announcements started, the crowds began compacting from all sides.

I sensed this was quickly getting out of control. So did Arlita. I pulled her along behind me, working our way from the front toward the back. Progress was extremely slow but there was no choice. We could feel the waves of people pressing and compressing. It was getting tighter and more dangerous by the second. I pushed, squeezed and angled my way inch by inch to escape the breathtaking crush. Arlita was tight against me, holding onto my belt as people were beginning to scream from fear and pain. We finally broke free of the mob, ending up toward the very back of the field, leaning against a crooked fence post.

Concertgoers passed the injured overhead, toward medical teams. As the concert continued, we could barely see or hear anything beyond the roar of the rabid crowd. But we were safe. The next day, we learned that dozens were injured including many smaller, young girls who had been trampled. I'll never understand how this show was allowed to go on.

~ ~ ~

In mid-May, I had some vacation time to spend. I decided it was a good idea to make a whirlwind trip to Europe, deliberately flying the other way around the globe. Instead of flying east, I'd go west. Somewhere early in the route, I picked up a food-borne stomach bug and had to see a doctor in Switzerland. I received two medications. One of them was charcoal. Of course it was! Aside from that setback, the next 10 days included visits to London, Zurich, Geneva, Munich, Austria, Paris and the tiny country of Liechtenstein. The Eurorail pass and rail systems were awesome, easy to use and consistently on time. This was the first time I had gone on vacation in other countries without even considering stopping off in the States. It felt liberating. Although I still had a few business and personal connections with the States, I never intended to live there again.

~ ~ ~

It would have been easy to continue with all the social fun I was enjoying. Considering my first 40 years of life, I had decades of catching up to do. But I was gradually being drawn toward something more meaningful. I wasn't cut out to be a playboy—that carefree *buaya gila*, as I had been nicknamed. I wasn't equipped to continue that astonishing single life that included the women and the pleasures we shared. I had seen what becomes of expats who succumbed to the omnipresent casual thrills, the commercial affection and lack of personal responsibility. I had ventured and respectfully partaken. Opportunities were still all around me but that wasn't who I wanted to be.

From somewhere within, a better part of me always wanted to be in a committed relationship, married or otherwise. I didn't yearn to be boring or mundane by any means, but a happy guy in love with the right, special partner. I longed to share life's adventures and its journey. It was this increasingly recurring thought, this inherent knowledge that eventually compelled me to throttle back on the amazing bachelor life and open myself to something more enduring.

Although we were not yet exclusive, I started spending more time with Arlita. We were enjoying ourselves. Her parents were both enthusiastic and pleased that she was spending time with me. She seemed every bit as happy.

In June, we took a speedboat out to Sepa Island north of Jakarta. The ride was especially choppy that day and I wondered for a bit if my equilibrium was going to hold out. Thankfully, it did. I had been to Sepa a couple of times, just for a day's getaway. It was always peaceful and quiet. At that time, Sepa was mostly uninhabited and undeveloped. Local folks arrived in the early mornings to sell food and beverages to others who visited throughout the day. But by day's end, most everyone left.

That day, Arlita was most attractive in her full-length, batik sarong and a buttoned blouse over her one-piece swimsuit. We walked, talked and played in the water. I was proud to be with her and couldn't have asked for a better day. Warm white sand extended far out into the sea. The clear blue water was perfect for swimming and snorkeling. Black sea urchins concentrated around coral or rock formations where currents were slight. These critters packed an unusually painful sting. Most times, they were visible along the white sandy bottom. We knew to stay out of their way, but water shoes were essential.

Sepa wasn't a big island. We strolled around the entire shoreline in an hour. As we walked around the back side, we saw a red-headed British guy who had ridden out with us that morning. He was sitting by himself, bottle in hand, totally naked in the sun. He was quite drunk. Later, we walked around again and he was lying half in, half out of the shade, passed out and sunburned, red as a lobster. I told the boat operators about him and before we headed back that afternoon, they had him up on his feet.

As the weeks went on, Arlita and I knew where our relationship was heading. We both did our part to steer it. There was no one pushing me. Her? I wasn't sure. It wasn't obvious to me at the time. There were often times when I made myself take a walk and honestly evaluate what I was doing—times when I searched my feelings, intentions and ability to make a relationship work. Overall, I felt mature and confident that I was ready to share a deeper relationship. Arlita and I talked for hours, for days. I knew she was evaluating as well. She trusted that I was intent on remaining in Indonesia; and in Indonesia, it didn't matter that I was 24 years older. It didn't matter to her, her parents, her friends, the community or me. As long as we lived in Indonesia, we'd always be just another common, Indo-expat couple. There were thousands just like us throughout the country.

Sure, I could have changed plans and gone back to the States to try to meet someone new. But I would be a 44-year-old man starting from scratch. Alternately, I could stay in Indonesia, become part of a family that believed in me and build a life with a bright, attractive younger woman who wanted to be with me. It was not a complicated decision.

The morning of July 29, Arlita and I took the Katana and drove to Ancol, where we'd first kissed while sitting on that bench more than a year ago. Again, we swatted persistent mosquitos and talked about the future. When I leaned in for a kiss, it was deeper, more deliberate and infused with the weight of all that had come before. Her response was tender and enduring, a silent testament to the journey we were pondering. For a long moment, nothing was spoken. Words were unnecessary. I reached into my pocket for the ring I had bought in the States the previous September. Back then, its significance had seemed distant, but now, it was laden with purpose. I placed the ring on her finger and asked her to join me in marriage. Happily, tearfully, she agreed.

Wilder's lease had less than a month left. His wife had already returned to the States the previous May and he needed a place to stay for three months. Repaying the *one* I owed him, I set him up in one of my spare rooms. Winarto and Minarti were happy with the same deal we had before, taking care of the room and breakfast while doing laundry for tips. Wilder stayed at my house as plans for a wedding took shape.

On September 2, Arlita's family arranged a large, formal announcement party at their small home in Maura Karang. To follow with Indonesian culture, the groom-to-be's parents usually accompanied him. Since I had no family there, Wilder stood in for me. He really enjoyed himself, hamming it up with the Indonesians. He wore a traditional Batik shirt, which was considered formal. I wore a dark suit and tie. Arlita wore a beautiful full-length, sleeveless red dress. Before the evening was over, more than 200 family, friends, neighbors and coworkers came by to visit, offer congratulations and share food.

The next few months would include a flurry of arrangements. Arlita set up a central location at my house where she, her family and friends could come and go, making wedding plans: preparing fabrics, invitations, gift trinkets and other ideas. My living room looked like a warehouse. I got the sense this was to be a big wedding. I didn't know then just how big! The ladies had control of the planning, letting me know when and what I needed to do. I was cool with that. We picked November 17 as the date, both thrilled at our decision to marry.

As I navigated the requirements for marrying in Indonesia, there were complications and surprises. I was asked to acknowledge Islam and have an

Islamic name. No one expected me to live the life, just give the family some clout and cover in a culture that was 90-percent Islamic. Arlita created an Islamic name for me. Somewhere there is a document under the name of *Wahu Sulaiman*, a spin-off of my initials, W.S.

I had to provide proof of my previous divorce, intent to marry and a slew of references from the embassy, the States and in-country. These documents were demanded by at least a dozen different entities from the local Roku Tetangga (*RT, who looks after the neighborhood*), to officials in the government and mosques.

Every entity, no matter their status, insisted on an *original* of my documents, including voluminous divorce papers as well as other pertinent documents. They would not accept anything stamped as *Certified Copy* it had to say *Original*. This obviously presented a problem. There were far more people asking for originals than I had original documents to give. I did not intend to deceive anyone, but the system was not practical or supportable.

Since I only had one original of everything, I simply went to Blok M and had a big rubber stamp made that said, "ORIGINAL." Going forward, anyone demanding an original of my documents received an honest, bona fide true copy, validated by a big red *ORIGINAL* stamp attesting its authenticity. That's all it took. It was never questioned again.

With two months until the wedding, the pace of activities accelerated.

22

CAUGHT IN A TRAP

STEP UP OR SHUT UP

Despite the excitement of planning our upcoming wedding, it was hard to ignore September's oppressive weather. For weeks, the approaching transition between Jakarta's dry and rainy seasons had once more wrapped the city in a heavy, filthy haze. The stagnant winds were powerless to carry away the smoke from burning garbage, particulates from rubber wheels and the endless emissions from low-grade petroleum fuels. This rapidly changed as the first rain clouds in months formed in the shrouded mountains to the southeast. With a crack of brilliant lightning, the season's first storm abruptly began. Every year the seasonal transitions happened just that quickly.

For hours, the torrential rain poured without mercy from opaque clouds so low to the ground they stole the last traces of sunlight from the menacing sky. On a dark afternoon, I was in my office not getting a lot done because as usual during storms, the electricity had gone out. The wall of leaky windows next to me allowed in what little light escaped the storm's wrath and with each clap of thunder, they rattled and let in more water.

Our local staff had completed all the work they could and were huddled in small groups, playing cards or chatting while secretly hoping the electricity didn't come back on this late in the day. I felt the same. From my window, I watched a man on a motorcycle arrive. Although he was wrapped in a poncho, he had no real defense against such a strong, blinding rain. I was surprised when a moment later our receptionist led the totally drenched man around to my office.

The soaked stranger bowed slightly, then opened his dripping leather satchel, handing me a badly wrinkled, previously used envelope. It was wet but intact. My name, our company's name and the city were written on it. On the outside of the envelope, it was written that I would pay whoever delivered the letter. The rider didn't or couldn't say anything, but our receptionist explained that he had ridden a long way and gone through considerable effort to find me. I thanked him and gave him a generous sum of rupiah equal to about two weeks' salary for a delivery person. He glowed ear-to-ear, then bowed out of my office and back into the rain.

The inquisitive staff stood around, anxious to help unravel this big mystery. Whatever it was, I didn't want to open the delivery in front of them. I put the soggy envelope in my pocket until I could regain my privacy. I pretended to go back to work, making notes, reading files and looking busy. They knew better, but they eventually drifted away.

When the perpetually curious staff finally gave me enough breathing room, I opened the envelope. It was a letter from Susan, my pen pal from a couple of years before. I read with surprise and disbelief as she wrote she was being held at a compound in some distant, mountain town and being processed to be sent overseas to work (not her exact words). She had sneaked the letter to a delivery worker who brought supplies to the compound, hoping it would find its way to me or anyone who could help. There was no optimism in this letter, no etchings or smiley faces drawn in the margins. The penciled scribbling was hurried and stark with fear and desperation.

To paraphrase her message, she didn't know exactly where she was but she remembered some of the agency's address from a newspaper ad she had answered. She had been there more than two weeks. She said they had lied to her and she was in big trouble. The people holding her would not let anybody leave. She conveyed her doubt that the letter would find me but she had run out of hope and was trying everything she could to regain some element of control. She pleaded with whoever found the letter to help her.

~ ~ ~

I slept a troubled sleep that night, realizing this was likely as real as it gets. I clearly remembered what Tanya at the Tanamur had told me about traffickers. I remembered what I had seen in the local newspapers; how young girls are tricked into servitude.

Yet, there I was trying to reason with myself, hoping that I'd find some solution that didn't include me getting directly involved. *These things happened to people all over the world*, I thought. *She'd probably be OK. And, even if there was anything I could do (which there wasn't), I couldn't go around saving every damsel in distress. I had never even met this girl. I was on a different, more focused course. I was supposed to get married in a couple of months and I was busy as a one-armed paper-hanger! She needed to fix this herself, right? After all, her letter had to have been at least a couple of weeks old and this whole thing had probably resolved itself, right?*

My reasoning made perfect sense—perfect sense for an average, well-adjusted person. But was that really me? I had always steered away from trouble and this situation was far beyond anything I knew how to fix. I definitely observed the world around me but had never needed to stand up to tyranny; to step up and make a difference or actually put myself in harm's way. This was eating at me. To do nothing went against my beliefs. *Could I ignore everything I had learned about this evil practice? If I walk away from Susan's distress call, this decision will haunt me the rest of my days!* I knew I had to help. But I had absolutely no idea what to do. I woke the next morning knowing that if I didn't at least try, I'd never forgive myself.

A wise man would have a plan. Wise or not, my plan would have to be developed as I went. There wasn't enough time or enough information to know what I was actually going to do.

First, I dug through my belongings to find that one photo of Susan I had decided not to burn with the others months earlier. *Found it!* Next, I went to my office and quietly asked our receptionist if she could help me track down the agency Susan had referenced, using the partial address provided in her letter. I didn't tell her why. She gave me the courtesy of not asking. I think that somehow, she recognized this was a serious, personal matter and should be kept private, away from the usual prying eyes.

Our receptionist found some addresses that looked similar. The names and a couple of the street digits were off, but there were many of these questionable employment agencies throughout the immense city.

I finished my pending work for the morning, cleared it with Wilder and left early. He didn't even look up from his desk when I told him I had some business to take care of. There was no need to tell anyone, even Arlita where I was going because I didn't know myself. I flagged down a taxi that looked to be in good condition and asked the driver if I could charter him for the rest of the day.

He grinned, "Yah, OK Meester."

I didn't know where we'd end up, but I got in and headed to the bank to get a bunch of cash. I remembered one of Dad's favorite sayings, *money talks.* I withdrew the rupiah equivalent of $4,000.

With cash onboard, I showed the driver the partial addresses we had uncovered. His identification card dangled from the rearview mirror as we headed off across Jakarta to see what we could find.

"Your name is Sukarno?" I asked the driver. "Like the former president?"

"No, 'Pak. I am Karni, because I do not like that president name." Given Sukarno's brutal history, I could understand why Karni didn't like him.

The remains of the day were spent in the northern part of the city, about 20 miles from my office. Karni stopped from time to time, braving the continuing rain while asking other drivers if they recognized any of the clues. By day's end, we were able to get a little bit of information on other agencies but nothing concrete. It was after 8:00 p.m. and dark when Karni dropped me off at home. He agreed to come back early the following morning.

~ ~ ~

It was still raining hard when I walked out of my house early the next morning. The air was still alive with thunder and lightning. Karni was there, sleeping in the taxi. In just seconds, my feet were wet from the flowing water inundating the streets. It was that way all over the city.

That day's search took us through the southern sections of the city. The first stop was golden. Two of the other drivers Karni asked recognized the vague information and gave me a correct name and address for the one agency we were looking for. After about 40 minutes of traffic, we arrived at a small, dingy office in a converted residence at Depok, a town on the southern outskirts of Jakarta about 15 miles from the office.

The small sign indicated it was an employment agency closely associated with the government. There were government-looking signs and placards on the gates and exterior of the building, but it was definitely not a government business. This agency was one of many private companies created by former immigration officials who knew all the tricks of the trade and had counterparts overseas, especially in the Middle East. These semi-official PJTKI labor employment agencies were all over the country, some licensed and legitimate, most not. I was confident this one was not.

Before getting out of the taxi, I folded two million rupiah and put the cash inside each of my shoes, re-lacing them tightly. This was insurance. I was relying on the fact that the locals believed one's feet were unholy. I kept the rest of the money in four envelopes inside different zippered pockets.

I was tense but focused and energized. The deeper I went into this endeavor, the more solitary and exposed I became. For a moment, I thought I should let someone know where I was, maybe even a little about what I was doing. But doing so would invite a lot of attention to an issue I wanted to keep private. I continued with my mission alone, hoping I wasn't making a serious mistake.

~ ~ ~

I entered the gloomy building and told the elderly receptionist why I was there. She asked me to wait. In about five minutes, an older man wearing a brown uniform of sorts came out and asked me into his office. The receptionist quietly closed the door behind us.

With his oversized eyeglasses hanging low on his face, Ardianto seemed to be in his late '50s. He was shorter than I was, balding and carrying too much weight around his middle. His nametag and uniform were quite similar to the immigration uniforms I'd seen at the airports. The insignia was slightly different. After some courtesies, I explained why I was there: I had come to find a girl named Susan. I showed him the crinkled photo she had sent years before. He studied the picture a moment then walked over to a window to hold it up to the light.

"No, nothing of this girl."

I sensed he might be positioning for compensation. Luckily, I was right. But this was not going to be an ordinary negotiation. I was dealing under the table. So was he. We were both taking risks. To show I was serious, I needed to start big.

"Bapak Ardianto," I said, looking him directly in the eye. "I would greatly appreciate if you would check with your associates." I placed a bulging envelope on his desk. "This should help cover the cost of your research." I pushed the envelope toward him then sat back, casually folding my arms, hoping they would hide the pounding anxiety in my chest.

Ardianto looked over the top of his glasses, keeping his eyes locked on mine as he reached for the cash. He looked into the envelope and saw Rp.500,000 (around $195). He slowly rose from his desk, cleared his throat and left the room.

Was it enough? I tapped my fingers on my knee and wondered how long he'd be gone. The ghostly receptionist brought me warm tea. While waiting, I noted several other men coming through the building—all dressed in similar brown uniforms with various insignia. After about 20 minutes, Ardianto returned to his office—without the envelope. He sat at his desk and leaned forward.

"Yes, we have found some information we did not recognize earlier." He handed me Susan's photo. "This girl has agreed to work for employers in Dubai and Saudi Arabia and is to be transferred there this week."

She's still here, I thought. *I've got a shot at getting her out of here.*

"She is with others being processed at a compound in another town," he said. "She will be gone tomorrow night."

"Her mother is very sick," I lied. "I am here to take her back to her village." I tried to remain firm and polite. "Can you release her to me, Bapak?"

"That is impossible. She is already committed to an employer."

We smiled at one another and politely argued over tea for a good 15 minutes more. During this time, Ardianto tried to justify holding Susan while outlining all the *costs* his agency had accrued in processing her to this point. Most of it was bullshit. This was a form of debt bondage, a common tactic for those trafficking in people. The agencies claimed she was indebted to them for room and board at astronomical rates, for the cost of bus transportation, which would have purchased a flight around the world, and for the cost of documentation that would have funded a small bill through Congress.

I was aware of the agency's process and what they were doing. Their scam on these unsuspecting girls was to indenture them, steal their first three years of salary and hold their immigration and travel documents as collateral. They would be offered as virtual slaves to wealthy, overseas bidders who would trade or imprison them as residential slave labor.

I pretended to make notes and look over the documents he laid out before me. Among them was an official *Special Worker's Passport* locking her into Dubai as a domestic servant. The passport photo was definitely Susan. In all, he claimed his agency had accrued thousands of dollars in fees.

I sat quietly with my arms folded, looking down at the documents, then back at Ardianto. "Bapak, I have one more envelope which is more than the first," I said. "I hope it will suffice so that I do not have to tell her family and all the other people looking for her that you are unable to release her." Ardianto examined the contents of the second envelope.

After some private promises and friendly dealing, I convinced Ardianto to sell me her paperwork, a release letter and directions to her location for the equivalent of around $400 on top of the $195 I had given him. Ardianto refused to sell me Susan's worker's passport, holding on to it tightly. Apparently, it was issued by the national government and had to be accounted for—likely turned back in to the real government agency that issued it.

This was a tremendous, personal windfall for Ardianto—a lot of untraceable cash in his own pocket. To me, it was peanuts. But to Ardianto, it was a whole lot more than he could personally gain from sending her on to the Middle East.

Another part of our deal was for me to give a ride to one of his officers who was transporting a new girl to the holding agency compound. Reluctantly I agreed.

Ardianto whispered—talking quietly to himself—I listened. He indicated that he needed to make up something to tell his associates at the agency. "They will be angry if they do not receive a share. Maybe she ran away, maybe she died," he said as he casually explored his options. I was stunned at how easily he mentioned dying. *Was death common among these captive young girls?*

Before long, Ardianto seemed to have his story assembled for the others in his agency. They wouldn't know the truth and he'd keep all the money. He fabricated a different story for the letter he was sending with me to the holding agency in the nearby town.

I understood Ardianto was ripping off his own crooked cohorts in Indonesia and the Middle East. I didn't care. Within the hour, I held the letter directing the holding agency to release Susan to me. I read over it as best I could, hoping that was actually what it said, but it was written in formal Indonesian so I wasn't absolutely sure. It looked favorable but for all I knew, I could've just been ripped off.

Within minutes, Ardianto brought the *officer* and the new girl into his office and nodded toward me, indicating our deal was done. The girl said nothing, keeping her head down.

Ardianto handed the officer a sealed manila envelope. "Take this man to the holding location, have them release the girl he wants to his custody and take this new girl to replace her," he instructed his officer.

A moment later, the officer, Susan's replacement and I joined Karni in the waiting taxi and headed into the mountains. It felt like I had just won the lottery, kind of.

23

EVEN MORE REAL

BECOMING SOMEONE ELSE

On the way out of Depok, we stopped for fuel, then continued southwest along a two-lane road into the distant hills. At first, the officer was quiet and expressionless. He kept the rear window cracked as he chained smoked, flicking the butts out the window without concern. I guessed him to be in his early 50s, his full head of black hair greasy and in need of a good washing. His demeanor lightened a bit as he and Karni communicated directions back and forth. He seemed a bit bored, but otherwise friendly. I sensed that his role involved getting new girls to various holding locations in the region; and that he had done this many times.

Our route intersected with a web of smaller roads, winding and sometimes unpaved. The journey took us through tiny villages, small townships and some high mountains on either side of the continually narrowing road. The last identifiable town I recall was Jasinga, with its buildings cuddled tightly against one another.

Along the way, Karni talked to the young girl. Rina was a slender girl although the long, white garment and jilbab covering her head concealed most of her features. My mind went back to 1993 and those young girls packed into that small van along the road to Merak. *Were those girls being taken to a place like this?* I tried to listen while Rina and Karni communicated in a mix of Indonesian and Javanese. I could sense her tension as she kept her head hung down, careful of whatever she was saying. She was from a small, rural village. Her family were poor farmers and needed her to work. She was a TKW (*worker girl*) and like Susan, she had answered an employment ad in the newspaper. This was the classic trap.

~ ~ ~

Maybe 20 miles beyond Jasinga, the officer directed Karni to turn left onto an unmarked, dirt road. This route took us higher and branched off onto more unmarked roads. Anyone would have to know where they were going to get into or out of this tangle of roads. There were no other vehicles in sight. In the last few kilometers, I counted three elevated checkpoints manned by guys wearing uniformed fatigues. There were likely others I didn't see.

The taxi strained to climb numerous steep grades and switchbacks. As the road turned back and forth, I got quick glimpses of grey, concrete structures on the ridges above us.

A few more switchbacks and we were staring at the front of an ominous, concrete fortress. The walls were around 12 feet high and the street-side facade was about 200 feet wide. Smaller buildings and watchful observation points punctuated the surrounding hillsides, casting long shadows over the landscape. At the front center of this foreboding edifice, three metal personnel doors and two heavy gates stood, their small barred windows giving away little of any secrets held within. It looked like a prison—ghostly and intimidating. But I reasoned it was likely an armory or a repurposed military compound of some sort, probably from the 1950s or `60s. There wasn't much distance between the front of the fortress, the road we were on and the dangerous cliff just beyond the narrow road.

As we arrived, the scene grew even more unsettling. Two austere figures in fitted black T-shirts and camouflage pants emerged from the compound, their movements precise and deliberate. They opened the rear door of the taxi and took Rina and her officer escort out of the vehicle and through one of the smaller metal doors in front. In a blink, they vanished into the compound.

Karni urged me, "Play tough and do not back down, regardless of how they come at you."

Play tough? Really?

Karni exclaimed, "I tell them I know nothing, because that is what I know!"

Again, I wondered, *what have I gotten myself into? Am I going to be able to get out of this?*

~ ~ ~

The guys in black were not the usual hired hands. They were clean, close-shaven, with buzzed haircuts. They looked like they ate well and worked out, muscular and in shape. They carried what appeared to be black, professional night-sticks. They resembled military or former military, although I saw no firearms.

They directed Karni to follow them as they walked ahead of the taxi into a long, narrow corridor with high, concrete walls on either side. The rusty hinges groaned as the colossal front gate slammed shut with a sinister clang, sealing us inside with an unsettling finality. Karni folded the mirrors back and the door handles nearly scraped the walls as we inched along behind the black shirts. We emerged into a courtyard surrounded by more buildings with high walls. I saw four doors but no windows. The ground was sandy with small gravel, like some kind of parade ground or arena. For the taxi, it was one way in, one way out.

Tension grew as more men approached from behind—my tension, anyway. At least six black shirts surrounded the car, directing us to get out of the taxi. After we were out, one of the black shirts went into the taxi and started nosing around. He opened the dash, looked over the visors and sort of strip-searched the interior. He came out with the microphone from the taxi's radio, in order to prevent any outgoing messages. He reentered the taxi and wrote the driver's name and license information on a notepad. Then he went to the trunk and searched there while another black shirt popped the hood and looked around. Then, they used a mirror to look under the car. Aside from the microphone, they took nothing else.

I assumed this was the enforcement branch of the trafficking operation. It was clear to me this wasn't going to be just a handful of trafficked people here and there. These were not small-time pimps and thugs running this fucking show. I had stuck my nose into an established, nationwide industry. This was more dangerous than I'd imagined.

The black-clad enforcers roughly frisked Karni and me before abruptly shoving us together with barbaric force. I staggered but managed to stay on my feet, while Karni crashed to the ground and lay there motionless. Before I could react, a sharp kick from behind sent my legs flying out from under me. I was hurled onto the gravel beside him.

The lead guy yelled in Indonesian, "What do you want? Who sent you?"

I stood to my feet, telling him in Indonesian, "Talk with the officer with us. He will vouch for me."

Out of nowhere, his slap was sudden and vicious, striking the left side of my head with an echoing crack. I heard my teeth slam together and the joints in my neck and shoulders crunch. My jolted vision gradually returned as I balanced on one knee, trying to keep calm.

"I talk to you, not to him," he yelled.

With my right arm held out to my side, my left hand slowly retrieved the letter from my shirt pocket. I transferred it to my right hand and gave a subtle bow, displaying submission. He snatched it, grunted unintelligibly, and moved away as he unfolded it. I stood, still reeling from the impact. Blood dripped from my nose. The more I tried to stop the bleeding, the worse it looked. I could see the fear in Karni's face as he stayed quietly on the ground.

Seconds seemed like minutes as the black shirt read, then re-read the letter. He refolded it then told Karni to get back into the taxi. As two black shirts led me through a door into one of the buildings, others directed Karni in turning the taxi around to return out the front gate. I didn't know what would come next.

They walked me through a narrow, tiled hallway, one black shirt leading and one behind. I tasted blood from the inside of my cheek, mouth and tongue. They led me to a rather spartan office with a battered, grey metal desk and a couple of wooden chairs, leaving me there to wait in solitude. The room looked like it might have once been some kind of operational office. Perhaps abandoned at one time, it was now repurposed. There were remnants of metal hooks and connectors still embedded in the unpainted, concrete walls: telltale of the military hardware that was once there.

Off to the side, a 35mm camera sat on a tripod facing a whiteboard screwed into the wall. I could see that there were two corridors leading out into the compound, one to the left and the other to the right of the hub where I waited. Each corridor had a heavy gray door opening into the office. The doors had peep-holes and being the curious type, I went and looked.

Each corridor, or wing, extended about 75 feet before opening into what looked like a circular pod with sleeping areas around the internal perimeter. The pods were arranged like a barracks. The sleeping areas were sheltered by a roof supported by wooden posts and an extended roofline protecting the interior. The front of the pod faced a circular dirt floor in the center that was open to the sky. That center area was perhaps 60 feet in diameter. Sunshine brightly lit the sandy courtyard, in contrast to the much darker room where I waited.

In the shade of the pod's interior, I could see bunks built into the concrete walls under the roofline. Some had thin, foam mats on them. Others only had rolled-out grass mats. My guess was that each wing could hold around 100 *guests*. The first wing I looked at was empty. The second was not. In its courtyard, I could easily see dozens of young girls milling about. It was clear to me that this particular operation focused on young girls.

In just a moment, footsteps on the tiled floor alerted me to someone approaching. I hurried to one of the chairs and sat down just in time to stand again, as the door opened.

"I am Marturak," he announced.

Marturak was dressed in a crisp, khaki uniform similar to Ardianto. He appeared stern, confident and business-like, resembling a military general with his garrison cap, insignia patches and sunglasses. He was taller than the average Indonesian and in good shape. His English was exceptional. Marturak motioned for me to take a seat while he kept standing. Reaching into the top drawer of the old desk, he pulled out a half-empty roll of toilet tissue and tossed it to me to tend my bloody face.

"So, you come here to repatriate this girl, Susan?" he asked.

"Yes, Bapak. You have seen the letter from 'Pak Ardianto?"

"I have seen," he said. "You have identification papers?"

I showed him my American ID, my Indonesian resident's card and my embassy contact card.

He had questions. "How do you know this Susan? What is your relationship with her?"

I told him we had never met but her family had asked me to help bring her home because her mother was sick.

"You do this for American Embassy?" he asked.

Without thinking, I quickly lied. "Sometimes."

"And you bring something for me?"

Here we go, I thought to myself. *Now, I'm getting my foot in the door.*

"Ma'af, (*sorry*) Bapak, I already gave this to Ardianto back in Depok," I said.

"I do not work for Ardianto," he countered sternly.

Marturak's interest in being compensated caused me to sense there might be an opportunity to get the new girl, Rina out as well as Susan. I would at least ask.

I humbly told him, "Ma'af, (*sorry*) I have three million rupiah left. I have to pay the taxi driver, but if you release Susan and give me the girl who rode here with us, you can have it all."

Marturak chuckled and balked, "There is no way I can do that."

Now I needed to give Marturak a way out. "Ah, but the new girl is not documented yet. She has no passport. She is not even in your system. I hoped what I said was true. "Here is an opportunity for you to have something for yourself and no one will ever know."

I had been lucky so far. That morning's negotiations with Ardianto had gone well. I would eventually recover from being smacked around. But would my luck hold? I was negotiating with a guy who could actually make me disappear if he wanted to. He held all the cards. I realized I was in a deeply precarious position. I was scared shitless, but I couldn't let it show. Inside, my heart raced. My head hurt. Adrenaline burned my bloody face. He knew I had three million rupiah on me. Why didn't he just rob me and take the money? Did he think I came there with backup? I had absolutely none. If I vanished, no one would ever know what happened.

Then I remembered my thoughtless, one-word lie, "Sometimes" -- to his earlier question about me working with the embassy. Was my meager connection to the embassy keeping him from whacking me? *Does he think the embassy knows I'm here?* Whatever it was, I felt as though I had become someone else off in the distance, watching this other *me* stay on point, moving forward.

I sensed light at the end of the tunnel when Marturak asked if I could pay him more.

"That is all I have, Bapak," I said, patting down my pockets to drive home the point. I still had other money in my shoes, but he didn't know that.

I continued, "Ma'af, 'Pak, but Ardianto has already released Susan and if I go back there without her, I must ask him for refund. Ardianto will not be happy about that if I tell him that you will not release her. The other girl is money in your pocket. I will say nothing to anyone about it. Three million rupiah, 'Pak. It is yours if the girls come with me."

Marturak thought for a moment as he paced around the room. "OK, OK Meester, but you must wait with taxi at the road and leave cepat-cepat (*quickly, quickly*) when I bring her."

I began to breathe a bit easier.

"What you want with other girl, Bapak?" he asked.

"That's my business," I said with a deliberately crooked smile. I was at a loss of what else to say.

He grinned back, nodding his head in approval.

Marturak fumbled through the desk then handed me a brown, manila folder for the money. Clearly, he didn't want his associates to see him taking cash, especially that much. That also worked in my favor.

"I will have the envelope ready when Susan and the other girl, Rina are in the taxi."

He didn't like that, preferring to have the money right then and there. But reluctantly he agreed. He still held all the cards. He and I both knew he had checkpoints in place along the only road out of there. I was certain that if he didn't want us to leave the mountain, we would not leave.

After our agreement, Marturak called on his radio and moments later, a black shirt brought Susan into the room, leading her by her arm as though she were a prisoner. She came in carrying a small cloth bag of her things, her head down, arms by her side, making short little steps. She looked clean but she was dressed in an oversized, long-sleeved shirt wearing loose pants that dragged on the dirty floor. Her black, shoulder-length hair was straight and unkempt. She was far too scared to look up or make eye contact.

It was clear she didn't know what was going on. For all she knew, I could have been someone buying her for any number of evil purposes. All she could do was go along with whatever was happening.

"OK Bapak, we go now." Marturak said.

I guided Susan by the arm and whispered in English, "You're going to be OK, It's me, Steele. Keep looking down and don't say anything." She remained silent as a black shirt led us out through the courtyard.

As we walked through the door to the outside, she looked up for the first time, still without expression. She had heard my name but when she saw my face, she still didn't realize who I was.

We walked onward to the taxi. Karni was nervously in place with the engine running. There were several black shirts standing guard, including in front of the car. Their faces stern, their eyes following Marturak, ready for any command he might make.

As we passed the menacing metal gates of the compound, other girls were reaching through the steel bars and begging, "Meester, tolong, Meester, tolong," (*Mister, please, please*).

One of the black shirts opened the back door for us. I guided Susan in and followed her immediately as he closed the door behind me. Near the same time, another black shirt brought Rina out and put her in the front seat with Karni. Marturak stood by my door as I rolled down the window and handed him the folder with three million rupiah. He opened the folder just enough to do a quick count of the money, then walked around to the other side of the vehicle.

Leaning in eye-to-eye with my driver, he spoke something in Javanese while Karni nodded, "Yes, yes!"

Marturak then waved for the black shirts to step away from the front of the taxi. Karni wasted no time pulling away.

The winding road out of the compound and down the mountain seemed much longer than it did going in. Each time we approached a checkpoint, I cringed, hoping some radio message to a sentinel wouldn't call the whole deal off.

When we cleared the area and accessed the main road, I breathed a sigh of relief. Susan still hadn't said a word. Both Karni and I kept looking behind us to see if we were being followed. We were not. I asked Karni what Marturak had told him as we left the compound.

"Forget you ever saw this place or your family will have no tomorrow," he said.

We were about 10 minutes into the long drive toward Depok when Susan began crying. I tried to comfort and assure her she was OK.

Through her sobs and tears she asked, "I am free?"

"Yes, you are free. I'm taking you home."

As we approached Depok, Karni found a large, open-air market and pulled over. There was a bus terminal nearby. I got some money from my shoe and wiped it with a tissue, simulating a feeble effort at cleaning it. I gave Rina some small money for food and transportation plus Rp. 200,000 for her and her family.

Speaking Indonesian, I told her, "Go home and never, ever sign up for any job like that again. And please warn your friends and family." With teary eyes, Rina nodded, thanked me and vanished into the crowded marketplace.

Susan took a moment to call her mother from a pay phone then the three of us continued toward Jakarta, where we eventually connected with her mother and her mother's boyfriend, Ronny. I provided them enough money for the night's hotel, some food and tomorrow's bus fare back to their village. I wrote my office address and phone number on a small piece of paper and gave it to her.

They were all sincerely grateful. It was the first and what I believed to be the last time I would ever see Susan. I was exhausted, dirty, sore and pretty sure I had at least one loose tooth. I didn't want to mess with it to find out. Karni left with a million rupiah. He earned every bit of it.

This whole rescue effort had been stupid, but successful. Susan was safe with her family and would never fall victim to that type of scam again. Still, I was deeply troubled by the desperation and the depths of human oppression. The last two days had shown me the monstrous face of human trafficking and taught me lessons I would never forget.

Reports of trafficking and human desperation are stories we see on television news. They're usually followed by risqué beer commercials, or polished new car ads that make us forget what we just saw on the screen. The idea of being entangled with traffickers, much less having someone's life hinge on my negotiation skills was something I could never have fathomed.

Despite putting myself in a place where the unthinkably worst could have happened, I somehow managed to change the lives of two girls, maybe even save those lives. Yet, in the coming months, I couldn't shake a powerful fear that they were still not safe; that the trafficking criminals might again turn their innocent lives upside down. Time would ease that fear.

But the vision of those girls desperately reaching through the bars at the compound would haunt me for years. Over time, I came to accept that there wasn't enough of me to help them, or to affect the kind of change that needed to happen. I will always wonder how many of them survived.

~ ~ ~

That night in the sanctuary of my room, I replayed the chain of improbable events that led to this moment—both trivial and monumental. *If I had known of the danger beforehand, would I have gone to find Susan? What if I had not returned to Indonesia after completing my first assignment? What if that soaked letter had not reached me? What if I had not kept that one photograph?*

If any one of these things had not happened, Susan would have never been delivered from those bastards. Within days, she would have been sent overseas, returning years later, abused and penniless. Or like some, she may have met an even worse fate—losing her life in a cruel distant country; swallowed into the darkness under the warm, desert sands, leaving her family with nothing but haunting memories and unanswered questions for eternity. Those were among the many assurances I sought that night. I was still scared; too scared and too pumped to sleep.

Part of me felt like a bumbling idiot who hadn't known what he was doing, faking it and talking out of my ass to the traffickers. Another part felt as though the right guy had been in the right place at the right time. And in spite of my bungling, I had somehow managed to pull this off and do the right things. In my life, that hadn't always been the case.

Over time, I would humbly accept that if nothing else, I had been made for that moment.

~ ~ ~

Over the next several days, I shopped around for a quality dentist who could repair my damaged tooth. The Indonesian lady I interviewed had been trained in Singapore before starting a modern practice in Jakarta. She did a great job on the repair but cautioned me it was temporary. We talked about this as well as some other important dental work she recommended. Over the coming months, I trusted her to help me.

24

THE DEPOSITION

Or Whatever That Was

As September 1995 ended, Rick Wilder completed his two-and-a-half-year assignment and returned to the States. Another project manager took the reins with the goal of completing the remaining contract award packages, while supporting start-up activities at the jobsite.

I was home one Friday night when I got an unusual, unexpected call from Stan Rothmeyer. Stan was a department head for a different construction-engineering firm back in the upper Midwest. I had worked with them for 10 years before joining my current company. Like many construction-engineering firms, an industry downturn adversely affected their business back in 1987 and '88.

As a result, they had to reduce their workforce from 2,200 to around 460 by the end of 1988. When I finished my work on the lineal power project in California, I was among the more than 1,700 who were gradually laid off. They covered my trip back to the Midwest, provided a couple of month's severance pay and that was the end of my decade with that firm. That was nearly seven years earlier.

Now, out of nowhere, Stan was calling to ask me for a favor. Sections of that gigantic Transmission line we built in the northern California desert had collapsed. The repairs had been completed and the issue had been turned over to a group of attorneys for further resolution and cost recovery. Stan and his management back in the Midwest were familiar with my legal support work over my 10 years with them. Whenever we had entered into or faced litigation, we prevailed.

"Steele, we don't need you to defend or support," Stan said. "We're asking you to honestly testify from your project knowledge on behalf of our firm. We're counting on you."

"Anybody else?" I asked.

"You are the only one in Indonesia they want to depose."

Just me? Wow, that's odd!

"They expect the deposition will take around a week. They're going to send a team over to depose you in Jakarta. We'll send one person to observe."

Jakarta? Really? "Wouldn't it be easier to bring one person back to the States than to fly an entourage of people halfway around the globe?" I asked.

"They want to see you in Indonesia," Stan reiterated. "The deposing attorneys are determined to come there," he said, unyielding. It was clear he didn't appreciate my skepticism.

"I'll discuss the matter with my people and evaluate your request," I said, trying not to sound defiant. "You'll have my response by the next Monday."

My team had only one issue with this plan. It was not fair for them to pay for a week of my time spent on another firm's deposition. If it were an hour or so, that would be one thing, but a week was asking too much. I agreed. My supervisors recommended that I charge unpaid vacation for all time spent on the deposition—time that I could not otherwise make up. I sent that message onward to Stan. I also told him that since I was not going to be paid by my employer, I required $130 per hour from their firm for my time. He understood.

Tuesday night, a call came in from a gruff-sounding attorney for the deposition. "Tollison," he growled. "Your requirements for compensation are outrageous if not illegal!"

From my exposure to legal matters years back, I remembered how much corporate attorneys charge. And most times, they earned it. My requirement was common and not out of line, but I was not surprised at his reaction.

"Respectfully sir, I have no interest in whatever goes on between legal entities in this matter," I held my ground and rather enjoyed my position. "Further, it is unfair to ask me to volunteer my time when all other entities are being well compensated for theirs."

The line was quiet. "Well, we don't agree, but I will look into it," he said abruptly.

"Please do, it is my requirement."

I further explained to the attorney, "Look, I can tell you everything I recall about that project over the phone from here. We can likely move through your questions quickly and minimize your costs," I said. "And if it turns out that a face-to-face is actually necessary, it's much, much cheaper to bring one person to the U.S. than to bring a team of people to Jakarta."

Again oddly, he wanted no part of my suggestion. It was a touchy subject for him. When this was all over, I'd understand why.

By week's end, Stan made one more pass at me, asking me to give this deposition as a favor.

"You mean my time given free to a wealthy firm and teams of well-paid attorneys that will no doubt make money from this litigation?" I snarked. "Respectfully, no thank you. You have my requirement."

Without being vindictive, I held firm. Back then, round-trip business class airfare to Jakarta was $2,958, first class was double that. These attorneys were about to drop at least $15,000 on airfare alone. This wasn't even considering the cost of ground transportation, business accommodations, personal accommodations, meals and peripherals. My requirement was peanuts in comparison. *Why were they even doing this, what was really going on?*

Without further discussion regarding my compensation, the deposition was set for October 3, 1995, in downtown Jakarta. The venue was a nice, rented ground-floor suite in a corporate business district. At 10:00 a.m., I was introduced to the deposition's team. It included two junior attorneys, a stenographer and one managing administrator who was also an attorney. He was the boss—the guy who had called me several nights before. These folks were dressed semi-formally. The last of the attorneys, Brady, was dressed in jeans and a long-sleeved shirt. He represented Stan's firm. Brady told me he was there to observe and help clarify any questions I may have. He was not there to direct or coach me in any way.

Right away, the deposition folks subtly let me know this was not a friendly get-together. Their group was comfortably seated in brown, leather-bound chairs, in a semi-circle. Their video camera, files, photos and computers were already on the tables in front of them. The stenographer was off to the side. I was seated in the center, opposite them at a small table with a straight wooden chair.

The boss told me to let them know if I needed a restroom break or to go out for some water. All the while, they were enjoying fresh coffee and the tables behind them were abundantly stocked with pastries, snacks, refreshments and plenty of bottled water. They made no offer to share.

This felt like it was going to be a low-energy grilling—more like a sleepy inquisition than a deposition.

That's all right, I'll take the high road.

No one made it clear who was suing who, or why. I didn't ask. But the environment they were creating was unnecessarily hostile.

Why? I wondered again. Seemed I was asking myself that question a lot.

The oddity continued to grow in my head. Why would five highly compensated professionals fly to the other side of the planet to depose one person who had a minor role on a project that went bad years ago? This whole thing smelled.

Before long, the boss called the group to order and asked me to confirm my ID information for the record. The stenographer was already typing and the others looked down, mindlessly flipping through papers on their table. I looked at the reminder note I'd scrawled to myself, then raised my hand.

"Gentlemen," I began, "I have not yet received a written acknowledgement regarding compensation for my presence here. I'm here in good faith to honestly answer all questions without prejudice. Other than that, I have no interest in the outcome of your issue."

Nobody nodded or looked away. It seems I had their full attention.

I continued, unyielding and beginning to take offense at their arrogance, "I am not being compensated for time away from my professional employment. Therefore, I require a valid, signed document confirming which firm, which person, and the contact information for the entity responsible for affecting and ensuring my compensation. In essence, I require a guaranteed, fully negotiable IOU. Neither handshakes nor word of mouth is sufficient.

Respectfully, you knew this before flying out here. You have my rate. We can begin when I have your written assurance."

The deposing group shuffled in their comfortable chairs, puzzled—looking back and forth at one another. Brady looked away and grinned. The boss acted as though he was about to blow a gasket when Brady halted him with a calming hand gesture.

I leaned forward, placed my forearms on the dinky little table, looked straight at the group and said nothing. After this deliberately disrespectful start to what should have been a simple, professional deposition, I was fully prepared, in fact *chomping at the bit* to walk out right then. I knew I had zero obligation, legal or otherwise, to any of these people or the clients they represented. They now understood that I knew it.

I waited outside the room for about 40 minutes. They asked me back in and presented a document for my review. It was as I had requested. The rate was correct. The firm's information, contact person and contact information were all there. They had added Stan's firm as an additional guarantor. The managing administrator and Brady signed it on behalf of Stan's firm.

"Gentlemen, thank you. I'm ready to proceed," I said, with a deliberate degree of insincerity. I offered my full name and contact information for the record.

~   ~   ~

The deposition went on for three days. We started at 10:00 a.m. each day, with them taking far more breaks than I did. Most times, it was just four of us in the room; one deposing attorney, the stenographer, Brady and me in a session. I never saw their boss again and didn't know where he went.

At times, 10 minutes would pass while one of the remaining deposing attorneys fiddled with his papers or his computer before asking me another question. Time dragged.

Regardless of which guy was asking questions, it was obvious he was bored out of his skull. Each day they took a two-hour lunch and we wrapped at 4:30 p.m. At least half of their questions related to things of which I honestly had no knowledge. They didn't seem to mind. They were already fully aware that I had not been involved in the project's design, planning, funding or construction at any stage. Before deciding to fly to Jakarta, they knew that my role had involved scheduling deliveries, unloading and assigning equipment to be hauled out to designated tower sites. It was no more complicated than that.

I was careful not to volunteer information that they hadn't asked about. There were plenty of opportunities for them to drill down, but they simply moved on to the next question.

At times, questions were real softballs like, "Where did you live while you were working in California? How often did you travel back to the Midwest?" and other meaningless questions. At times I wondered if they were going to ask me, "Do you like long walks on the beach."

I had been through many depositions during my career. Most drilled down to the heart of each important element. This one was casually galumphing along, going nowhere slowly. Perhaps they were serious, but they weren't asking serious questions. They were not prepared and fabricated questions, based on any clue that emerged from my responses.

On day three I was waiting in the room when the stenographer came back early from her long lunch break. The others were still gone. Separated from the group, she was polite and conversational.

"Are you ready to get back to the States?" I asked.

"Oh yes," she replied. "Four of us will leave tomorrow morning. The other is in Singapore meeting his wife and daughter. They'll come back the following week."

"I see. His wife lives in Singapore?" I inquired.

"No, she lives in the States, but she came with us on this trip. She has family in Singapore and Malaysia. This trip gives their family an opportunity to visit with one another," she said.

"Well, that's nice," I said, but I didn't mean it.

I excused myself and walked outside into the noisy city heat, processing the blockbusting information I had just been told. Now it made sense. *Indonesia doesn't hold a monopoly on corruption.*

This managing administrator was milking the system, perhaps even his own law firm, to cover up a personal trip for his wife, daughter and himself. He had dragged all these people halfway around the world for a senseless deposition. That's what this whole, lame three days of wasted time was about. He bundled this Jakarta sideshow with a real case in order to hide the expenses of a personal trip to Southeast Asia. If a crook had just half of an excuse, no one was going to investigate his actions over in Jakarta. This deposition and my participation was nothing more than his half of an excuse.

The afternoon session consisted of a half dozen more lame questions. The attorney took a phone call, then abruptly said, "We're done. You can go." There were no thank-yous or goodbyes.

That evening, I phoned Stan to let him know what had gone on and that the deposition was over. Turns out, Brady had been keeping him informed all along.

I offered details when Stan cut me off. "Look, I really do understand. I had my concerns. But it's best we not discuss this any further."

And so it was. I made notes and chalked it up to experience. If these people had been wronged by someone or some firm, it wasn't my business.

Stan thanked me for participating and asked me to send him my invoice. Within two weeks, I had a check. I never heard anything more about the lawsuit or the people who came to Jakarta for that deposition. But if the case ever made it to a formal decision, I'm betting Stan and his team prevailed.

On a side note, 30 years later I drove through that northern California desert and stood below one of the massive transmission towers we built out there. I remembered that deposition, or whatever that corrupt thing was, happy I insisted on being paid.

25

THE WEDDING

LONG ENOUGH TO LOOK BACK

The first week of November 1995 was upon us. Our wedding was just two weeks away. As time rapidly ticked away, it felt as though the days were barely more than hours.

I took a long, nostalgic moment to reflect back two years to late December, 1993. As I recalled, it was going on 7:00 p.m. and was exceptionally dark. Usual for Jakarta, a heavy storm had been going on for nearly an hour. Once again, it had knocked out electricity to many of the communities. Back then, Arlita and I had finished work and were heading to the Blok M area to meet other friends at a restaurant called Boncafe.

In the dim, amber light of the few streetlights that were still working that night, the road ahead looked like a swift, dirty river coming right at us. The little orange Bajaj strained to carry two passengers and our driver against the oncoming current. Its single, seven-inch wiper blade was no match for the torrential rain pounding against its scratchy, cracked windshield. Despite Jakarta being in the warm tropics, that night's relentless thunderstorm brought exceptional street flooding along with a chill that even a Westerner couldn't ignore. The driver guided the small vehicle upstream around debris while lightning exploded in the treetops all around us.

Arlita and I sat in the back of this little beast, holding the canvas side covers against the gusty wind, trying to shield ourselves from the direct sting of the heavy, blowing rain. Our clothes were getting wet. Our feet rested in water that had risen more than eight inches into the street and through the holes in the rusty floorboard. The lower part of the engine was submerged, and it coughed and sputtered whenever the flimsy little vehicle fell into the hidden potholes beneath the dirty water. If this had been a boat, it would have sunk.

Before that night, I had been living in Jakarta about 10 months and knew that the weather could change quickly. Just two nights before, I had been a warm, dry guest at the ambassador's home, helping his wife serve Christmas cookies to the 100 or so Americans who came for the tree lighting ceremony.

On other occasions, Arlita and I had gone with small groups from the office to the cinema or other restaurants without much trouble. But that night we were in the heart of the rainy season. Getting a taxi was nearly impossible. In fact, getting around town or planning anything that took us outside was risky. That night was a perfect example.

The Javanese are usually laid-back, patient people. Certainly, they experience a full array of emotions but centuries of cultural conditioning influenced how they display them. Their reactions often surprised even themselves.

On that dangerous night, Arlita's patience was keeping us afloat. She calmly offered instructions on better ways to hold the canvas or to position ourselves to stay dryer. If I had another idea, she politely let me learn the hard way. She kept her shoes over the biggest holes to minimize the water splashing from the road below. I took on the role of the panicked sailor, determined to keep us from being washed away by this turbulent stream. She had obviously done this many times.

Although quite wet, we made it safely to the restaurant that night and met with our other friends. That was 1993, two years ago and just one of many such experiences I recalled.

~ ~ ~

I had come to Indonesia with curiosity but quite reluctantly. I hadn't planned to drastically change my life's course. Had I not come, I might have filled these same paragraphs with stories of other occurrences from my home country, amazed by the things I discovered there.

I couldn't have known I would enjoy the challenges of daily life in Indonesia. I couldn't have felt what it's like to immerse oneself in another culture. I couldn't have predicted how the overall environment would invoke change and growth in ways I had yet to measure. Nor could I have known back then that two years into the future, the young woman beside me that night would become my wife.

~ ~ ~

Our exceptional, three-day wedding was now only a week away. It would take place at three large venues around the city. Most of the required processes and technicalities had been completed but there were still more rituals and rehearsals to endure.

Because Arlita's mother, Niniek, was an important, respected member of our partner's company and because her daughter was marrying a respected member of their long-time engineering firm, this wedding became a really important blend of cultures for our partners. Over two decades, many of their members had come up through the ranks with Niniek. She had dozens of friends and associates who were excited about this wedding of her youngest daughter, the first of three to marry. They stepped up to make this event exceptional and left no stone unturned.

Arlita and I spent days being fitted for elaborate, traditional costumes. There were different formal costumes for each of the three days. They were tight, heavy, hot and beautiful.

Each included head-gear; weighty ornate crowns and makeup specific to the day. Male and female costumes each included some form of traditional jacket and full-length batik sarongs.

There were a dozen groomsmen and bridesmaids, also adorned in gorgeous formal attire. Because my parents had passed and no one was coming from the States, an American couple, Pete and Lana Ashley, graciously agreed to stand in as my parental representatives. They were also fitted for the occasion.

A group of the men attached themselves to me. Each day, my happy entourage took me with them, checking venues, adjusting this, tweaking that. I went along with their good-natured teasing, giving it right back to them. Twice during the three-day wedding, they stayed with me overnight, following the custom of preparing the groom for marriage and of course, keeping him away from his bride. At times, I saw Arlita from a distance. She and I talked by phone, but we were not supposed to hang out with one another until the wedding was final. I was in no hurry. I just enjoyed all the attention and let myself get lost in the culture and traditions.

The partners provided the majority of the effort, logistics, arrangements, and finances. My financial contributions, although significant, were minuscule in comparison. They provided air-conditioned buses, sedans and trucks to shuttle family, technicians, support personnel, food and equipment to and from the different venues. They decorated the venues with elaborate traditional floral settings. Each of the settings was fully catered. They even brought in additional food to distribute to the surrounding communities, assigning a crew to ensure it reached the less fortunate. I was proud and thankful for their generous participation.

Aside from Arlita's family, there must have been 50 of the partner's people taking charge, working in parallel, directing the numerous activities. I knew many of these folks. Others, I had not seen before. They seemed to come out of nowhere, guiding the family, taking me under their wing, helping me with things I needed to do.

At each venue, they set up tables, hundreds of chairs, carpets, elaborate staging, lighting, audio systems and signage. Dozens of contractors dropped by with wedding gifts. Staff was assigned to secure the packages in a large, locked van. I was overwhelmed but grateful at the work others were putting into this production.

I would have been happy with a small gathering, but this was not about me. I wanted my bride to enjoy every moment of this once in a lifetime event. Arlita was the princess and this was akin to an Indonesian royal wedding.

The entire wedding party, including the family, consisted of 36 people all in formal costume upon a beautiful, burgundy and gold stage. In terms of weddings, this was one of Jakarta's larger ones. And as it got underway on November 14, 1995, all I could do was hang on. I certainly had no control.

Two smaller, all-day events were held—one outdoors at Arlita's parent's home, the other at a nearby facility. The main wedding was held throughout the third day and night of Friday, November 17.

Guests from surrounding provinces finished their workdays and traveled to the scenic wedding. The evening finale event was held in a 25,000 square-foot building closer to the city. There were speeches by the presiding MC, local politicians and dignitaries.

Inside the venue, decorators created an indoor garden, arranging vast swaths of modern and rustic greenery, large floral wreaths and beautiful botanicals unique to Indonesia. Many of the arrangements were coordinated with Arlita's costume, bouquets and the men's boutonnieres.

All eyes were on the beautiful bride, although I and all members of the wedding party were treated royally. Unlike many Western weddings, this one did not include dancing. From the large, elevated stage with its grandiose, traditional décor, we stood and received guests for more than two hours. We shook hands, received hugs and enough words of congratulations to last a lifetime.

~ ~ ~

After making it through the receiving lines, guests enjoyed a bounty of the best Indonesian foods in the extravagantly decorated arena. There were long, covered tables throughout the venue where guests could choose from many Indonesian beverages: coffees, teas, papaya, guava and mango juices. The tables were adorned with large, fragrant arrangements, banana trees and ice carvings. A full gamelan music ensemble played in the distance while guests enjoyed beef rendang, nasi goreng, bakso, gado-gado, chicken satay, ayam penyet and martabak. Well over 1,000 people attended.

When the wedding concluded, the family loaded into air-conditioned SUVs and were driven back to Arlita's parent's home where it was customary to spend the wedding night. And so we did, with nothing but a curtain separating us from other family members.

We were both exhausted from the three-day wedding, but elated.

~ ~ ~

The next morning, Arlita and I enjoyed a casual breakfast with her family. The next night was spent in a downtown Jakarta hotel before flying to Bali for our honeymoon.

"Now what?" we pondered.

26

THE TRIP TO AMERICA

Loading and Unloading Luggage

After our wedding, I wanted to take my new bride back to the States, introduce her to friends and family there and show her a little bit of the country. It was December 20, 1995. We had been married just over six weeks.

We awoke in Jakarta, beginning our day around 5:30 a.m. There were plenty of last-minute things to do. Arlita was tending to her parents, who had stayed overnight to see us to the airport. I busied myself heating leftover *nasi goreng* (fried rice) for our breakfast.

The flight was at 9:00 a.m. I estimated we should leave two hours ahead to account for likely delays in getting to the airport. After all, it was 25 miles and it was Jakarta. Our flight would stop over in Hong Kong in the late afternoon. We planned to hang out, shop into the night then take the 13-hour flight to Los Angeles the following afternoon.

Around 6:30 a.m., I felt the usual anxiety associated with taking such a long trip. But I was a confident, seasoned traveler and was on top of things, right? Still, that same question that haunts every traveler kept repeating itself, *I know I'm forgetting something, but what is it?*

On the kitchen table, my checklist of 20 or so items had been marked down to one or two remaining. We were packed. I had answered Arlita at least four times during the last two days, assuring her that I indeed had the tickets, passports and the money in my leather, continental wallet. Winarto had instructions and money to run the house for the next three weeks. The last item on my list was to call the taxi, which I planned to do right after we'd had a bite to eat. So, what was there to fret about?

The nasi goreng was especially tasty, except my portion contained a bit too much spicy sambal sauce. My mind was going over its own checklist while I ate. I talked to Arlita's folks and did my usual, last-minute mental organizing. I was chewing away and trying to adjust my mouth to deal with the hot sambal when damn! I bit right through the tip of my tongue. To say it hurt was an understatement. The searing pain of my skewered tongue made me forget my struggle with the spicy sambal. The next few minutes were focused on blood flow from this self-inflicted wound. My tongue continued to burn but after a couple of awkward moments and some ice, I was able to stop the bleeding.

Just in time! Five minutes later the taxi arrived, thus completing my checklist. The driver rearranged his trunk space and we loaded the luggage. Arlita and I rode in the back seat while her parents followed in our car. We emphasized to the driver that he needed take it slow so her parents could keep up. This turned out to be a constant battle as the grumpy driver had to be repeatedly called down from 85 mph.

It was on the last straight-away to our destination that Arlita turned to me and asked, "Did you get the money off of the bedroom cabinet?"

"Of course, I -----!"

That was the answer to the repetitive traveler's question! The money needed for our exit tax, Rp.500,000, (around $250) was still lying on the bedroom cabinet at home! This in itself was enough to disrupt the entire departure. With the chaos and pain from biting my tongue, I let my intentions take the place of action, forgetting an important, last-minute detail.

Things were tense in the back of that taxi. I was trying to restrain the speeding driver, reassure my new, usually calm bride and ponder the few possible schemes for getting my hands on Rp.500,000 when we reached the still-sleeping airport. We had U.S. dollars, but I knew the money changers weren't open yet. Arlita didn't have that much available on her bank card and trying to draw money from a credit card account was a waste of time. There wasn't enough time to go back for the cash. The solution would have to develop itself when we got to the airport. Meanwhile, we rode in silence. Seething, Arlita crossed her arms and looked out the opposite window. With a still-throbbing tongue, I looked straight ahead. Whenever she could bear it, she turned to glare at me.

All I could do was offer one of those, *I'm really embarrassed* smiles. "We'll work it out," I promised.

Entering the airport grounds, I saw the Jakarta Military Police setting up a roadside checkpoint for enforcement of the National Discipline Campaign. The police periodically hold these kinds of events to keep the population from breaking traffic rules. That was sure to make someone's day more pleasant.

The airport was designed for departing passengers to unload and check-in from the upper ramp approach. Arriving passengers exited the airport from the lower ramp. The speeding driver made a split-second decision before selecting the entrance for the upper ramp. Good move.

We unloaded the luggage and the driver, whom I'd nicknamed *Fireball,* seemed surprised when I gave him such a meager tip. His continuous speeding and ignoring my requests had frustrated me. Right then, I felt like the small tip was one of the few things over which I still had the slightest control.

Once inside the airport, I confirmed that the money changers were closed. I went back outside to search for Arlita's parents, who had gone to park the car. I searched the parking area but couldn't find them. I knew Arlita would be unhappy if I came back without her parents so I continued to look, acutely aware of every minute that passed. I had to finally admit defeat. Our departure was looking bleak.

I went back to tell Arlita and there they were, all together with the luggage and lots of smiles. Arlita's mom had recently received a year-end bonus and by sheer chance, had Rp.500,000 with her. We traded her for dollars and breathed a sigh of relief. Time to relax!

We said our goodbyes and proceeded through the security area. Arlita's parents saw us off and left the airport, heading back to their home. Thanks to Fireball, we were a little ahead of schedule so our check-in counter wasn't open yet. We sat on our luggage for a while, relaxing, two naive travelers unaware of the next disaster lurking just minutes away.

~ ~ ~

Before going to the counter, we needed to pay our exit tax at the immigration window. Thank goodness, we now had the rupiah to do it. I started assembling the documents to present at the window. *Let's see, we need the tickets, the money and the passports. Why weren't the passports in my leather wallet? I must have taken them out earlier and put them in my carry-on.* Arlita was giving me that look again. I felt the pulse in my neck start to race.

I can't explain how stupid I felt when seemingly all the mistakes a traveler can make unfolded one after another, before we even checked in. I didn't know for sure where the passports were, but after an exhaustive search through everything we had with us, I was sure we didn't have them. By this time, our flight to Hong Kong was getting ready to board. There was nothing left to do but go back to the house and search. If there was a fortunate element in all of this, it's that we had not yet checked our luggage. With bags in tow and tails tucked between our legs, we went back outside to the upper ramp where we had unloaded less than an hour earlier. Another taxi was just unloading, so we hailed him, loaded the luggage and headed silently off to our next disaster, waiting less than two minutes away.

We didn't know it, but arriving taxis aren't supposed to pick up passengers on the upper ramp. They're supposed to loop around, pay a fee, get a ticket voucher and wait in queue for pick-ups on the lower ramp. Our enterprising taxi hadn't done this.

Exiting the airport, there were those Discipline Police, a dozen of them flagging us over to check the taxi driver's ticket, which he obviously didn't have. *Great! Now what?* One policeman was asking the frantic driver something, another was trying to ask me something while still another was tapping for Arlita to open her window. Arlita was trying to explain to them but wasn't getting through. *How were we supposed to explain something like this?*

I offered to pay but there were too many police who collectively didn't want to be seen accepting cash while they were working the discipline squad. They made us get out and unload our luggage, then ordered the taxi to pull over onto the grass. At least they were nailing him for this *hideous crime* and not us.

Stranded there in the wet grass along the roadside, our trip to America wasn't going so well. We had been up for nearly four hours, left home without proper money, traveled 25 miles through chaotic Jakarta traffic to the airport and there we were, near flight time with no passports, standing in the grass with our luggage at our feet.

We flagged down another taxi who actually had his ticket voucher, reloaded the luggage, then continued once more, returning through the congested city to our home. Arlita was looking out her window and I was staring straight ahead. We weren't speaking. *Déjà vu!*

Far ahead of our speeding taxi, I could see a big dog walking around a pool of sea water which had poured into the road. I cautioned the driver to be careful. He grunted as if he understood. It didn't matter. The lumbering dog and the speeding taxi were trying to occupy the only section of dry pavement left and it was obvious the dog was going to lose. Despite hitting the driver on his shoulder, frantically pointing ahead and my loud, repeated cautions, the driver ran over the dog without slowing or the slightest attempt to avoid it. He didn't even flinch! The worst of it was that the horrified animal was so big it became entangled in the undercarriage of the taxi, howling endlessly as the car dragged him down the road for more than 10 seconds. With a last, ghastly thump jolting the left side of the taxi, the poor dog was finally ejected from the rear, skidding to a stop in a tangled mess on the pavement behind us.

The robotic-like driver showed no feeling whatsoever. Although we said nothing, I knew Arlita felt the same as me—angry and sick.

~ ~ ~

We arrived back at the house to a very surprised Winarto. Once more, we unloaded the luggage into the garage and sent the incredibly insensitive driver on his way with no tip.

The first order of business was to locate the passports. They were there, right where I should have looked four hours earlier.

For some reason, all electricity in the house was off. So, the second order of business was to get the electricity to the telephones working. It seemed both of our two circuits were off. In a hurried attempt to adjust the power transformer, I broke the switch. Only then did Winarto tell me there was nothing wrong with the transformer. He had turned off the electricity at the circuit breakers to save power while we were gone.

"Ma'af, mister," he said as he re-energized the circuits.

Now, I had to repair the transformer switch which wasn't broken until I tried to fix it a few minutes before!

We had passports. The next thing we needed was new reservations. For once today, something went right. I contacted the airline and got a flight to Hong Kong scheduled to depart at 2:50 p.m. We had about three hours before we needed to be back at the airport, so things were looking better.

With all that had happened that morning, we instinctively retreated to different rooms in the house to rest (and lick our wounds). Sitting still in my quiet room, my throbbing tongue wouldn't let me forget my string of missteps and how all this started. As the afternoon progressed, we made peace with one another and when it was time, we again loaded the luggage into yet another taxi.

On the second trip to the airport, I got the feeling that Arlita and I were in full synchronization. She was equally aware of all the requirements, documentation, whereabouts of everything and our overall plan. The pain in my tongue was a little better. We checked and re-checked with one another to make double-sure we weren't forgetting an important detail. We weren't. We looked proudly at one another as the taxi turned onto the approach to the upper ramp. Soon, we would unload the luggage for the last time in Asia and not see it again until we arrived in the States. Although we missed the opportunity for evening shopping in Hong Kong, we were thankful that we'd finally gotten underway.

As luck had it, our afternoon flight leaving Jakarta was delayed about an hour and a half. By this time, we were beat, so we went to an airport restaurant for some (soft) lunch. While eating, I put my proverbial foot in my already-sore mouth, commenting that such delays are unusual in America. I was feeling smug. Arlita was not impressed. We made it to Hong Kong that night and on to America the following day.

We hustled our luggage through Los Angeles customs and on to the United Airlines shuttle counter where we enjoyed standing in line 40-minutes while the incredibly independent counter crew toiled slowly away at receiving passengers. Where was Sing air when you need them?

We were heading to San Francisco to catch a non-stop flight to Kansas City and our connection there was extremely tight. I was concerned that we'd miss the plane to Kansas City, especially if we didn't leave Los Angeles right away. We had stood in line longer than the flight would take.

Our plane out of Los Angeles left 30 minutes late. We arrived in San Francisco and hit the walkway running to the U.S. Air counter which was naturally, on the other side of the airport.

I kept coaching Arlita to hurry. "Every second matters. Remember, these U.S. airlines leave right on schedule," I boasted.

She had already learned that wasn't true. Her very first flight in the U.S. was late!

We arrived at the counter breathless and explained to the gate agent that we were trying to catch a flight that should be boarding right now.

"You can relax; this flight has been delayed about 45 minutes so you have plenty of time."

I now wished I hadn't boasted about the airlines in America being prompt and efficient. I continued tasting those unfortunate words for a long time to come. It was going to get worse.

Passengers in the departure lounge were growing more volatile by the minute as the airline announced each subsequent delay. As one announcement piled on top of another, that 45-minute delay stretched into more than seven hours. Because of the holiday season, there were no alternative flights to Kansas City for the next 36 hours, so we were stuck. After the sixth hour, they moved us to another concourse for a promised flight that didn't happen for another hour.

Unbelievably, we flew on a borrowed plane back to Los Angeles to pick up a fresh crew for the flight to Kansas City. "Damn it, we could've just stayed in Los Angeles in the first place," I said.

During the confusion over the borrowed plane and changing the crew, the airline forgot to cater the three-and-a-half-hour flight from L.A. to Kansas City. There was no food on board except pretzels and a dozen day-old ham sandwiches. So far, Arlita was quite unimpressed with these U.S. airlines. The crew apologized and attempted to calm the hostile passengers by offering free headsets for viewing the movie, *The Bridges of Madison County*. Halfway into the movie, the video equipment broke and the movie was cancelled. The crew knew they were helpless and just tried to keep some distance between themselves and the exhausted, angry passengers, who cheered and sneered as we got off the plane in Kansas City at 2:00 a.m.!

The rental car office was supposed to have closed at 1:00 a.m. Lucky for us, they were still open, doing administrative work. I left Arlita with the luggage inside the airport terminal and took the shuttle to the Hertz facility about a mile away.

I presented my reservation information to a grouchy man who, after checking my number said, "Sorry mister, we ain't got no reservation for you."

We had come halfway around the world on the trip from Hell, it was 2:20 a.m., nine degrees outside and he *ain't got no fucking reservation for me! Really?*

I felt the buttons on my thin shirt start to pop. I guess I must have yelled diplomatically enough because after talking it over with another guy in the back, the two of them managed to find me a car, a dirty white Mazda sedan half-covered with ice. The interior smelled like someone had been chain-smoking cigars. But hey, it ran, I had the keys and in that moment that was all that mattered.

I scraped a peephole through the ice using the back of my pocket comb. I peered through the frozen windshield, making my way back to the terminal to pick up my new wife, introduce her to ice and once again load the freakin' luggage.

Ultimately, we arrived at our hotel in Kansas City. Yeah, we unloaded the luggage once more. We spent three days making introductions and showing Arlita around the frigid Kansas City area. *Whose bright idea was it to come to Kansas City in December?* Alas, nobody to blame but me.

Christmas Day was spent with friends in Kansas City, sharing gifts and watching their kids eagerly unwrap theirs. A few days later, we flew to Greenville, South Carolina, where my brother Garland and his wife, Joan, organized a last-minute gathering at their Piedmont home. About twenty people turned up to celebrate and ring in the New Year. The spread included plenty of Budweiser, RC Cola and white-bread sandwiches piled high with tomatoes and slathered in my favorite, Duke's mayonnaise. The air was thick with cigarette smoke—a reminder of how pervasive smoking was throughout the South.

Piedmont was much warmer than Kansas City, but we still donned heavier coats as we gathered on Garland's porch that night. We laughed and watched as teenage boys yelled and set off fireworks, their bursts of color lighting up the open schoolyard next door.

Arlita easily immersed herself in the new surroundings, unaware that she was something of a novelty to the southern locals. While most of them were welcoming and made her feel at home, I did overhear some young women making crude jokes. They giggled and whispered in their deep southern accents, speculating about Arlita's anatomy. "Does 'eeit go sideways, like 'er eyes?" Yeah, it pissed me off, but it wasn't worth fighting over.

Before we left the Greenville area, we met with my brothers, Johnny and Bobby, as well as my sister Charlene. Later, we drove southeast to the Atlantic coastal areas, spending a cool day around Charleston and Sullivan's Island. Arlita enjoyed meeting my family, seeing where I grew up and the sights she had heard about, especially the Atlantic Ocean and quaint, coastal cities.

From the east coast, we used airlines and rental cars to work our way across the country toward the west coast. We stopped in Flagstaff for a quick visit with my friend Dennis and his family, then onward to California. Arlita wanted to see Disneyland. She was impressed. I was bored and ready to go home to Indonesia.

~ ~ ~

On January 9, 1996, we left L.A. on still another flight departing an hour and a half late. Once we landed in Asia, the remaining flights to Jakarta went like clockwork. Of course they did!

In Jakarta, Winarto and Minarti greeted us at the gate to our home. With their help, we quickly unloaded the luggage for the last time and put everything away. I didn't want to see that damned luggage for the next decade. The house was pristine. As always, Winarto and Minarti had taken care of everything so well. There were fragrant flowers on the table, fresh linens on the bed and warm tea.

~ ~ ~

While we were traveling, the Jakarta design office had been relocated from its old, large house to another old, large house about three blocks away. Metaphorically, it was as though someone had backed a dump truck to the door of the old office, loaded everything with a front-end loader, then dumped all of it into the new building from a hole in the ceiling.

Things were a mess. Files had been needlessly removed from their drawers, tied in bundles and set on the wet, dirty floors. All labeling and filing locations had been displaced. It took more than a week to get things reorganized and functioning. Later, I learned that our reduced staff of engineers had assigned the relocation task to the drivers and house staff, leaving them without supervision while taking the weekend off. This was a recipe for disaster. Add to that, the new office was without phone and fax service for three more weeks. We were able to receive, but could not make local or international calls.

The year was off to a busy start as February gave way to March. The intensity of our support for the Western Java site was gradually winding down. The first units at site were being tested. Initial operation was not far behind. We were still at 10-hour workdays, but getting time off was less restrictive. We became more efficient at our work, although some things hadn't changed. We continued to face downtime while waiting for the partners to sign off on the next inclusion. That could take days, weeks or more.

Those delays usually originated whenever the partners requested private negotiations involving the competing contractors. Our company was never a party to those private discussions, we didn't want to be. That was not within our scope of services, nor in the best interest of our international reputation. Simply put, it was none of our business.

We still had other contracts to prepare. Much of the work on those had gone as far as we could take it without a sign-off. Our processes were in place and our business relationships were good, so when a sign-off was released, we could move quickly to prepare the next portion of a contract. The partner's people whom I interfaced with the most had become friends. And it was no secret that my primary interface was also my mother-in-law, Ibu Niniek. This was a respectable, transparent arrangement for our partners and our company.

That year, Ramadan started on January 19, 1996. Jakarta slowed down as once again, workers prepared to make this important pilgrimage to their families and homes. Winarto and Minarti were already gathering food and gifts to take to their village. Each year, hundreds of Indonesians get hurt or robbed trying to travel at the last moment so I was eager for them to get ahead of the dangerous crowds. They were thrilled to leave five days before the beginning of Ramadan. I sent them off with a bonus equivalent to one year's salary.

Around this time, I noticed something was definitely off. I had seen signs before, but Arlita's mood was catching my attention far more often. It was obvious that she was increasingly angry. She had a short fuse and it wasn't just toward me. I saw it in how she treated Winarto and Minarti. She mentioned that I paid them too much and that they favored me while disrespecting her. None of that was true. She was often unexplainably irritable and not the least bit affectionate. I saw it in how she spoke to her parents. They noticed it as well. There was no apparent reason, at least none that I could identify.

At times, Arlita was distant, but refused to talk about it. In fact, gently trying to talk about it invoked more anger. *Where did this come from? Was it the difficulty of fasting?* We confirmed she wasn't pregnant. I wondered if it might be related to her first Ramadan as a married woman, but it wasn't. It would come and go.

We went through to the end of Ramadan and Eid Al Fitr without our domestic help. Arlita spent a lot of that time with her family and friends. At home, there were some tense, hurtful times. I was unsure how to bridge the growing gap between us, but I kept trying.

27

FIRST BORN

AMID INCREASING CHAOS

In the early months of 1996, stories of clashes within Indonesian politics began to appear in the local and international news. The corrupt President Suharto was head of the government. He was opposed by Megawati, the daughter of the former and founding president—and equally corrupt—Sukarno. Despite the late Sukarno's horrible, well-deserved reputation, he was still a popular legend. Megawati was capitalizing on that popularity, building a powerful opposition to the Suharto family. Starting in May and into July, Indonesian print and broadcast media were filled with this rapidly developing political news. The issue was escalating daily.

All eyes were on the Indonesian government. Suharto again ordered steps to silence the media. In addition to the first three, two more news outlets were completely shut down. Suharto's supporters infiltrated Megawati's campaign offices and held an official conference to completely oust her from politics. That move resulted in deadly riots around the country, mostly in Jakarta. Nearly 150 were killed and that many more were missing, never to be heard from.

It was a scary time for the country, quite noticeable by the reactions of Indonesians working in our office. Our local staff members were educated people, capable of understanding national politics, national volatility and their nation's secretive, violent history. They also believed this was just the beginning of more political upheaval. They were right. Local people were becoming apprehensive. The coming months confirmed that Indonesia was escalating toward another extremely dangerous period in its history—a period that would jolt the very foundations of the country, upend its leadership, change its politics and over the coming years, claim tens of thousands of lives.

Around Jakarta, we noticed more military presence but it wasn't something we were directly concerned with at the time. The city seemed to be calm. Arlita and I made a three-day weekend trip back to Singapore just to get out of town. There was no sign of trouble going or coming.

We kept abreast of uneasiness back in the States as well. On the evening of July 19, there was another major plane crash—a gigantic 747 went down just after takeoff from JFK airport. People from many countries processed the loss of 230 family and friends aboard TWA's Flight 800, bound from New York to Paris.

In and around Atlanta, someone was setting off bombs at the Olympic venues.

Somewhere along this time, Minarti and Winarto told me they were going to have a child. They were over the moon but concerned that they wouldn't be allowed to continue working for us. I offered sincere congratulations and made sure they knew they and their child were welcome.

Out in East Java, our company was preparing to start a new project along the coast. It would be another large energy facility with a consortium of international participants. There was a good chance I would get involved with that project when I completed my work in Jakarta. My plan to remain in Indonesia for the foreseeable future was on course.

It was late July 1996 when we confirmed Arlita was six weeks pregnant. This was big, welcome news for us both. Her parents, siblings and friends all arrived at our house, bringing food and small gifts. The impromptu gatherings lasted late into the night.

Before long, we were attending prenatal appointments, ultrasounds and we began shopping for maternity clothing.

By the end of August, Arlita was already beginning to show. She was uncomfortable and not particularly pleasant. Still, we made a weeklong trip to Australia. We enjoyed wandering around Sidney and spent two days in Melbourne.

As additional portions of the Western Java project came online, the Jakarta office continued winding down. There was still plenty of work to do over the next year, but it required significantly less staff. We seldom brought in additional short-term staff like before. Some of our long-term expats moved on to other projects in Thailand and the Philippines.

This natural downturn created an apprehensive environment among the peripheral staff. Our house guys, drivers and security people had been with us for years and could see a time coming when they would no longer be needed. In Indonesia, this apprehension, this concern for livelihood can lead to corruption and theft. Even though we kept our files locked, we were still at risk.

At night, our drivers, house guys and rotating security guys slept in the office and in vehicles outside. In the dead of night, some of them would go through file drawers, looking for documents to copy and sell. We could check the counters on the copy machines and knew they were used almost every night. Those on the prowl received specific directions on what to look for by crooked suppliers or contractor operatives seeking an edge on negotiations or price. We tried not to leave anything sensitive or valuable in the files. But enterprising bad guys secretly made spare keys.

In November, one of our long-term drivers arrived for work wearing new clothes, designer sunglasses and gold chains. This created quite a stir among the Indonesian staff, gossiping about what this guy was up to. I brushed it off, thinking he likely saved a bit of money over the years and was getting ready to move on to another job. I was actually happy for him. Happy, until I realized my $1,500 in hidden emergency cash was missing.

My cash had been inside a sealed envelope, inside a sealed manila folder with other boring, non-negotiable personal paperwork. Since my first year in-country, that folder had been in my locked, fully loaded desk drawer, safe and secure from prying eyes. No one other than me knew it was there. To find it, someone would have had to unlock the drawer and take the time to go through dozens of folders, opening and resealing everything. With his livelihood ending, apparently, that's exactly what someone did.

I was confident our fancy-dan driver in his name brand clothes, gold necklace and expensive watch was the culprit. I was really pissed off and pondered bringing the police down on him. They would no doubt beat a confession out of him, put what was left of his sorry ass in jail and make sure he never got a decent job again. Knowing what would happen was the reason I didn't call the cops. My anger, my loss was disproportionate to what his arrest would do to him.

A couple of days later, I took the manilla folder out front where the culprit was leaning against a vehicle, cutting up with some of the other guys. I moved along side and leaned right there next to him. He got super-quiet. I didn't accuse him. I didn't mention the envelope or the missing cash. I didn't say a word, leaning on the vehicle beside him, holding the folder, tapping it in my hand where he could see it. He wouldn't even look at me. After a moment, this usually chatty driver slunk away. He knew he was busted and so did his coworkers. Before the week was out, he left without a trace.

~ ~ ~

As December ended, time seemed to drag on even more slowly. One of dad's favorite aphorisms came to mind, *a watched pot never boils*. It felt especially true when waiting for the arrival of a child. At 46, parenthood was a new experience for me. In Indonesia, clinics performed ultrasounds at nearly every prenatal visit, so we learned early on that we were expecting a boy.

As preparations continued, we set out to gather the things needed to welcome and care for this new child. We bought a new Lazy Boy recliner, which in Indonesia was about the price of a decent used car in the States. We bought a wicker bassinette and a used Simmons crib from a British family who was leaving the country. Before long, the nursery was furnished.

I kept a list of roughly 30 names we were considering. Each day, one or two names were eliminated, only to be reconsidered days later. My goal was to find a name that was religious-neutral. A name like Richard or David might cause difficulty if growing up in a Muslim environment. Whereas, something like Muhamad or Abdul might make life in a Western country more difficult. This child needed a name he could take with him to any country in the world: one that would not prejudge him.

While waiting on the right name to appear, we playfully referred to our child as *Mimpster*. It's funny how, without any formal acknowledgment or ceremony, simply giving him a name solidified him as a full-fledged member of our family. Using headphones, we played music to him in the womb. I wrote him a goofy little song that I often sang and played on the guitar.

Oh Mimpster, come on out and play, tomorrow's gonna be another day.

Your mommy and daddy have been waiting so long, for you to finally come along.

Oh Mimpster, come on out and play, we're sure you already know the way.

We've got a lot of things just waiting for you, so Mimpster, come on out and play.

I was as committed to this new family—as committed to this coming child as any father could be. The previous month, I had written him a letter:

To My Unborn Child,
01 November1996
Jakarta, Indonesia

Throughout the years, I've imagined your arrival. Now in a few months, you'll be here in person.

When you're born, I'll be 46 years old. I've had many pleasures and many pains, but it's been a normal balance. It's been a good life and now, I'm going to be part of something that extends beyond this grain of sand called, me. It feels really good.

Your Mom and I love one another strongly. We are presenting you with some interesting circumstances in which to grow. You will experience different cultures firsthand and have some pretty good relatives living on opposite sides of the planet. You'll have the freedom to think, speak, choose and work to achieve your dreams. As you mature, you'll find yourself gaining knowledge and insights which seemingly surpass those of your Parents. Don't feel bad about it; it's supposed to be that way. Your children will surpass you, as well.

I've never thought of myself as much of a teacher, but I guess that's going to be part of my new role. I hope we can help you be wise, compassionate and happy; to keep an open mind; to look at all truths during analyses. You'll find there are many. As a family, we're each going to make mistakes. We must each learn to work through them by communicating and compromising. We're determined to develop a family filled with warmth, understanding, encouragement, forgiveness and unconditional love.

When I think really hard about it, perhaps my biggest fear is that someday, you'll be in serious trouble, and I'll be unable to reach you and help. My biggest expectation is that you'll respect yourself, look after your Mom and exceed us both in your abilities, reasoning, understanding of, and responsibilities in the real world around you. My biggest hope is that you'll live a happy life and one day, know the joy and anticipation of this significant and powerful moment for yourself.

As you are human, there will be times in life when you feel incredibly burdened and alone. Just as I am with you now, before you are born, so shall I be with you throughout your life, even when you can no longer see me.

This is a pretty serious letter for such a little baby, so let's get to something more immediate. Your Mom and I have been playing music and talking to you in the womb. We hope we've been entertaining, because we've sure had a good time. We're impatiently waiting on you to get here so we can all start having some fun. We'll see you soon!

With Love and Anticipation,

William Steele Tollison, Your Dad ~

Meanwhile, Winarto and Minarti had delivered a beautiful, healthy little girl the month before. Minarti and the child were staying with relatives in central Java while Winarto came back to work at our house. I offered to give him more time off, but he said there was not much for him to do back home since the ladies in their village were all taking care of his wife and daughter.

"Good time to be here," he said.

I finally got around to taking care of my dental work. I needed a permanent fix for the tooth that had been damaged by the traffickers the year before. I also needed a wisdom tooth removed and some straightening. The day of my first appointment, I was in the chair leaning back, looking at the ceiling. My dentist had already administered the anesthetic and was ready to go for the wisdom tooth. It was stubborn but she was relentless. She brought forth an ominous-looking tool that resembled a reverse hammer. She latched onto the tooth and started hammering backward. That tooth was absolutely unyielding.

As she continued pulling, repositioning and hammering, I noticed the hanging lights from the ceiling were swaying. A moment later, they flickered. She was still into the task, her knee into my waist when things started to fall off the shelves.

Damn, this is surreal. This woman is either going to extract that tooth or she's going to tear the building down trying.

Only then did we realize we were experiencing an earthquake. They're common throughout Indonesia, and this one started out strong. The dentist quickly got me disconnected from the equipment. We bounced from wall to wall as we struggled to get outside, away from anything that might fall on us.

The tall buildings in the downtown area swayed heavily but weathered the quake. Crying, distraught people would not go back in them for days. Phone calls confirmed everything was OK with our families. Forty minutes later, after stepping around broken glass and a little cleanup, I was back in the dentist's chair for another round of anesthetic. This time, she succeeded.

Arlita was now eight months along and notably uncomfortable as Ramadan began on January 10. We had completed all the prerequisites and readied everything we could think of. The go bag was sitting by the door. Two times, I had practiced the 25-minute main route to the Pondok Indah Hospital. Since protests and riots were occurring randomly around the city, I also scouted out alternate routes in case the main roads were blocked.

On February 9, Ramadan ended and Arlita's family brought food to our house for the Eid al-Fitr celebration. Arlita spent her afternoon and early evening partaking in the feast. As the evening wrapped up and our relatives went home, she commented that she had likely eaten too much. She was feeling exceptionally uncomfortable. But it wasn't the food. It was the first sign of contractions.

The plan was activated. We called Arlita's parents and told them we were heading for the hospital. I loaded the to-go bag. I helped her into the Katana while Winarto manned the gate, then we were off, into the night. We were both calm. So was Mimpster. We arrived at the hospital just before midnight and a team of nurses immediately took Arlita inside.

Throughout the early morning hours, I waited in her room along with Arlita's parents. She was in a nice delivery room and doted over by the wonderfully attentive staff. They kept me involved with little tasks so I could be with her the whole time. Her contractions came and went like clockwork. She was tired, but calm and handling labor quite well.

While waiting, I narrowed down the list of names and focused on just one. I had created the name, Aldin. At least I thought I created it. I hadn't seen it anywhere before and I liked how it lent itself to nicknames. I wanted Mimpster to have options throughout his life. For a middle name, I planned to use Orion, after the cosmic constellation. I liked that the Orion constellation contained vast, 'young super-giant' stars. I thought that fitting for our son.

In essence, Mimpster accompanied Aldin, seeing him to the threshold of his new world at 6:00 a.m., February 10, 1997. I held him, cut the cord and immediately fell in love with this little person looking back at me. Mom was well taken care of and doing fine. There were lots of happy tears all around.

At the last moment before filling out the documents, I envisioned a slight change to his cosmic name. This child would be known as Aldin O'Ryan Tollison. Arlita was cool with this name. I later explained to people that this gave him an edge during St. Patrick's Day celebrations. He received an Indonesian birth certificate before leaving the hospital. I quickly applied for his American birth certificate and passport through the U.S. Embassy in Jakarta. From this point forward, my life became even more serious. I welcomed it. I loved it.

Aldin's American birth certificate was in the form of a U.S. Consular Report of Birth Abroad (*CRBA form FS-240*). It immediately acknowledged him as a U.S. citizen. That and his U.S. passport became his ticket to the world.

Although he was born in Indonesia, local regulations considered Aldin to be a foreign tourist. From his date of birth, he was granted 60 days to obtain an Indonesian permanent resident visa.

That meant we'd be making another visit to the notorious Indonesian Consulate in Singapore. There, our newborn would be photographed, finger-printed and documented, all for another $100. At 50 days old, we packed Aldin off for his first international flight.

28

MOVING TO SURABAYA

New Horizons against a Gathering Storm

B ack in December, before Aldin was born, I received a call from Carl
Crenshaw who was the site manager for the new energy facility
being built on the east coast of Java. This site was in a rural area
580 miles east of Jakarta. Carl confirmed the site was already gearing up.
He was actively involved with initial construction as well as completing the
man-camp just west of the jobsite. Carl asked if I would be interested in
helping them out once they got going.

That afternoon, I talked it over with Arlita. She was excited about the
opportunity to live in a different city. She and her parents were
enthusiastically supportive and encouraged me to pursue the assignment.

"If they offer it to you, I hope you will take it, she said." "I should be
ready to travel in a few months."

The next day, I called Carl. "Absolutely," I replied. "I still have work
to finish here in Jakarta and our child is due in February. But I should be
able to shake loose within a month or so."

"Sounds good. Let's stay in touch."

Over the next month, I learned that the new East Java project was
owned and managed by an international conglomerate assimilated under a

single business *consortium*. Participants included but were not limited to our current Indonesian partners, two Japanese partners, and two groups from Europe—one Swedish/Swiss Corporation, and one partner from Germany.

As engineers and construction managers, our company was retained by the consortium. Our work would be organized from the Missouri office with the part-time help of a guy from Chicago, Norm Dingler, and a team of engineering and support personnel.

The East Java project would eventually have more than 2,000 workers plus 300 staff and management from various international contractors. This same consortium had plans for additional power projects over the next decade. If I were lucky, I could be involved in these projects for years to come. Meanwhile, I continued to support our Jakarta office even as work there slowed.

Around the end of February 1997, a couple of weeks after Aldin was born, I met with Carl and some of the consortium leaders in Jakarta. The group wanted to talk with me about my logistics background and how it could be structured to support the especially complex logistics plan already in place for their new project. The Europeans and Japanese recognized the need to have an operational logistics representative stationed in Surabaya, Indonesia's second largest city. Quick access to the port, customs and financial institutions was an essential part of their plan.

During our discussions, the consortium provided details of their plan along with additional information. The Port of Surabaya was where most of the equipment from around the world would arrive, be cleared and processed to the jobsite, 95 miles further east of the city. Surabaya is home to the only deep-water port in the region where large cargo ships carrying our components could be offloaded. Larger ships would be offloaded a mile or more out in the harbor. The cargo would then be brought to port on smaller vessels. Depending on size and weight, our cargo would clear customs then continue to the site over the narrow roads or via shallow-draft barges hugging the northern coastline while moving east.

The person they envisioned for the role would coordinate clearances, carrier payments, equipment movements, inbound cargo ships, site deliveries, route planning and other related logistical matters. This person would find ways to keep the materials flowing. Monthly summary reporting would go to the consortium with direct reporting to the East Java site management. His services would be covered through our company with costs divided between members of the consortium. As such, they wanted this person to be autonomous and self-directed.

The consortium emphasized that an uninterrupted supply of specialized components from around the globe was critical to the success of the project. Construction and installation schedules were already established to coincide with the timely delivery of those components. Those deliveries were scheduled to occur over a two-year period. During that period, dozens of ships carrying hundreds of containers, bulk cargo and thousands of tons of components would arrive.

Many of the smaller components were already on site, but the first major shipments would start arriving in April and May. With manufacturing well underway at facilities around the world and ships already on the water, there was no room for error.

Talking among themselves, the consortium expressed concern about Indonesia's deepening political situation and the risks it could pose to the overall project, especially the financiers. Any lack of, or delay in deliveries could cause serious financial damage to all parties involved. They agreed to monitor that situation from a higher level. For the time being, it was full speed ahead.

The European members of the consortium planned to set up an office for this logistics operative within their suite at Surabaya. They would provide a local assistant.

"Steele will be coming off the Western Java project in March," Carl said. "Based on his logistics experience and success in Jakarta, I recommend we assign him."

The consortium agreed.

Their offer presented a significant shift in responsibilities—more than I had dealt with before. But with stateside and Indonesian experience, I believed I could handle it and agreed to take the assignment.

Arlita was thrilled with the news and if it weren't for her having recently delivered our child, she would have started packing.

~ ~ ~

Shortly after accepting the assignment, I put out feelers for rentals in and around Surabaya. Referrals and offers from independent owners and agents poured in. Renting to expatriates was a lucrative business. In March of 1997, I flew there early one morning on a weekend house-hunting trip. Of course, it was the rainy season!

I hailed a taxi. "I'm here to look around the city and find a place to live," I told the driver.

The driver offered to show me the city and its many neighborhoods. That worked fine because my appointment with an agent wasn't for a couple of hours. My helpful driver took me to communities within my required radius. It was important to be within a 20-minute drive from there, so I mapped out a general radius in which to search. Driving around pinpointing my locations on a paper map gave me a good feel for the areas.

Along the way, we drove to the BRI Tower, the building where my new office was located. The BRI Tower was completed back in 1991. At that time, it was Surabaya's tallest and most prestigious structure. Its 23 stories glimmered with darkened glass, copper and stone accents. The lobby was majestic with marble and granite reaching its tall ceiling, modern chandeliers and fragrant, fresh flowers throughout. It was the nicest building I'd worked in since arriving in-country.

After an hour, my driver insisted I see *Jalan Dolly* (Dolly Street). Jalan Dolly was Surabaya's notorious red-light community.

"You see in daytime, not at night. More safe," he said.

Entering Jalan Dolly, we were instantly surrounded by a sea of red and black *Bir Bintang* (Beer Bintang) signs attached to everything that could hold a sign. There were hundreds of placards, metal signs, paper signs, banners and flags making sure everyone passing through knew the dominant beer. There must have been 200 tiny houses sitting in rows and alleys, not more than a couple of feet apart. There were several beer halls and entertainment places. The wooden structures appeared to be built from flimsy material that could be blown away by a serious storm or quickly bulldozed by a change in the local government. Jalan Dolly covered around 10 acres. "How many girls worked here?" I asked.

"*Mungkin seribu, 'Pak.*" (Maybe 1,000)

As we drove through narrow earthen streets, many of the girls sat on tiny porches or steps in front of the houses, taking in the warm, morning sunshine. The place was quiet. The driver assured me that everything changes once the sun goes down and the men come. I couldn't help but remember the trafficking stories Tanya had shared back in 1994. I knew this was one of those places she had mentioned. Once again, I could see, even feel the plight, the pain of young, captive women on display; acres and acres of girls stripped of their hope, their freedom and even their children.

Where were the champions? Where were the saviors? Where were the gods?

By noon, the day had become exceptionally hot and muggy. Storm clouds were gathering in the southeast. The driver dropped me at the newly built French hotel, the Mercure, where I would overnight. But the first order of business was to meet an agent, Indah, who would show me some houses over the next two days.

Indah worked as the marketing manager for the Mercure Hotel and also had her own small businesses including retail marketing and real estate referrals. She was a busy young lady. After I checked in and had a quick lunch, Indah drove me in her car to the first community on the list where I viewed two houses. Before we could get to our third viewing, the clouds opened up.

When the rain came, it came with a vengeance. With wipers at full speed, we could barely see where we were going. Indah got ahead of it just enough for us to park, grab an umbrella and run to a street-side *warung* (small restaurant) that had a grass-covered porch. We were cold and wet, but safe on high ground. Indah borrowed a blanket from the proprietor as the sky continued hammering the earth with everything it had. The lower area of the main road out front quickly began flooding.

Sharing that blanket, we watched in awe as within minutes, the flash flood increased from a trickle to a torrential river three feet deep and 100 feet wide. It roared straight across the road and to our left, bringing with it mud, tree limbs and all kinds of debris. I saw two vehicles helplessly pushed off the roadway, their drivers scrambled to get out and on to higher ground. The heaviest rain lasted another 30 minutes. The flood waters didn't safely subside for two hours. Indah explained that like Jakarta, street flooding was common throughout Surabaya. The deluges in the area we had just witnessed were notorious. We sat on that porch, enjoyed hot tea and talked until it was safe to drive again. It was an exciting afternoon. Welcome to Surabaya!

We continued our search and the next day I selected yesterday's second house. Because of the political tensions and frequent break-ins, I selected this house that not only had the needed amenities but had a way to escape should trouble ever find us. Most homes had high walls with embedded glass shards and barbed wire atop. Most had only one way in and out through a front gate. This house was more modern and much nicer than our house in Jakarta. It was also around 20 percent less expensive. It had a concealed doorway that opened onto an adjacent street. Between the back of the house and the wall behind was a large, beautifully tiled courtyard, open to the sky and protected on all four sides.

Beyond the tall rear wall, a pathway led into the community behind. I planned to keep a thick quilt handy in case we ever faced trouble. If need be, we could climb a ladder, throw the quilt over the glass shards and get to the path on the back-side where we could escape on foot. That gave me a degree of comfort, even if we never needed to use it.

~ ~ ~

Indah and I would become good friends and business associates. We shared trust. She was an honest, compassionate person and offered deeply discounted rates at the Mercure to all our personnel coming through town. She introduced me to other local hoteliers who welcomed our business and provided safe and secure services to our people. She connected me with small manufacturers who made or sold quality products needed at our East Java site.

~ ~ ~

As April approached, it was time to leave Jakarta and head east to Surabaya. We were excited about the change and comforted that direct airfare between them was affordable. We wouldn't be far from friends and family. Arlita and I packed the key items to take with us and hired movers to bring the rest.

Winarto and Minarti had now been with me for two and a half years. I arranged for them and their child to come to Surabaya by bus.

Arlita, Aldin and I flew to Surabaya. Arlita's father, 'Pak Jonny, drove the Katana.

After visiting their family, Winarto and Minarti arrived in two days, helping us finish setting things up before working on their own quarters. With help from 'Pak Jonny, Winarto and Minarti, we had a smooth transition.

After we settled in, 'Pak Jonny took a train back to Jakarta. Over the next few weeks, I needed to establish internet service and cable TV, but first things first.

The responsibilities in my new Surabaya office were broad and more challenging; clearly a welcome change. Developing relationships within the consortium and with the local folks would prove invaluable. I went to work negotiating the acquisition of vehicles for the jobsite while developing logistics procedures for this specific project.

It was important to hire a company; an Indonesian counterpart to help me manage the movement of equipment from the ships, through customs and on to the jobsite. After three interviews, I made my selection. That company promptly assigned an operative, Sugianto (Su-ge-antoo), who would be dedicated to our project until completion. Sugianto would represent the land-based truckers, haulers and harbor barge providers in Indonesia.

Sugianto was a bright, resourceful young man. At 38, he was skinny as a rail and full of energy. With his long, unkempt hair, perhaps he didn't look the part but he knew what he was doing. His English was excellent. So were his connections in Surabaya and across all of Indonesia. He had a stellar reputation with the harbor, dock and customs people as well as rail, water and over-the-road providers. He knew the local roads and coastline well. He was an easy person to like and would become a valued friend.

If it was 5:00 p.m. and I needed a particular tractor to pull a heavy load to site the next morning, Sugianto would have it in place by 5:00 a.m. His company really valued our logistics business and was willing to go out of their way to keep it. I would never regret bringing them onboard.

On the ocean side of our logistics plan was my friend and associate based in Houston, Phillip Kaisharis. Phillip was a giant of a man; tall, learned, clever and compassionate. He was of Greek descent, an Australian living in the U.S.

Before I came to Indonesia, Phillip and I had worked on large logistics operations around the world, communicating from our offices in Texas and Kansas City. He knew his way around the global maritime and freight forwarding industries like the back of his hand. If there was a bridge collapse in Ghana, an inoperable crane in Manila, or a ship trans-loading cargo in the middle of the Pacific Ocean, Phillip knew about it.

In every large, global logistics operation spanning months or years, something inevitably goes wrong. It could be something as simple as a small mechanical breakdown, a ship losing power at sea or a greedy customs official needing his palm greased. Unexpected delays could happen anywhere in the world, at any time. The important thing was to get them quickly resolved.

Whenever logistics operations were in jeopardy, Phillip was especially effective at creating alternate plans and work-arounds. His methods of getting things back on track were at times unorthodox, but he was the resource needed when the going got tough. He had skills and connections around the world. His connections had connections. As we had done on past projects, Phillip established a code word for the two of us. If he or I needed to do something outside the established norm, outside the rules—something practical to get the logistics back on track, we would use the word, "Birdie" to let the other know we had gone off script. We seldom used the code, but sometimes there was no alternative.

From Texas, Phillip was paramount to the shipping and ocean voyage of equipment coming to our jobsite. He had backup, including a competent logistics staff based in our Missouri office. But make no mistake; Phillip was the man managing all the cargo heading my way.

My European hosts in Surabaya suggested I look for an assistant to manage the office while I was out. I prepared a flyer with the general scope of work along with hours, compensation and information on anticipated duration. I routed it to my hosts and to our team at the jobsite. I received responses from all across the country. Nonetheless, I preferred to hire someone local.

One of the responses came from a young woman who lived in a small, rural village about 10 miles south of the jobsite. Her writing was neat and brief, requesting an interview and leaving a contact number that would relay a message to her. Yeah, maybe I should have passed it by and focused on applicants with the skills listed in the scope of work. But this one piqued my interest. Here was someone from a rural area just needing that first break, that first chance at a rare, good job. I made the call and left a message for Siti.

The next morning, Siti called from a distant neighbor's house where she had walked at daybreak to use their phone. Her accent was thick, her English a bit unsure but she was enthusiastic about applying. She said she had experience with typing, filing and telephone and was a quick learner. I gave her my contact and address information and asked her to come by at 11:00 a.m. the following Monday.

Monday, right on time, the secretary knocked on my door to introduced Siti, a 20-something-year-old kid. She stood there looking like a deer in the headlights. She was waifish—perhaps five feet tall. I looked at her long, blue dress. *It must be as old as she is,* I thought. The fabric was heavy, perhaps a blend of rough cotton and rayon. Several safety pins around the sides and hem failed to fit the dress to her small frame. It was still a size or more too big. She awkwardly carried a black, `50s-era purse, well worn, scratched and patched.

Siti's black shoes were like her dress, a size too large. She walked on the balls of her feet to keep the shoes from falling off. Her long black hair was in a bun that had been tossed around by the wind along her journey. She was not a traditionally attractive girl. But a genuine, hopeful smile and her crooked, weathered face made her pretty in a more unusual way. In short, she was a mess. I recognized right away that this was all she had. She had done the best she could to get there for this interview and I vowed to make sure she was treated with respect.

Over the next hour, I discovered that Siti had never seen a computer. She had typed on a manual typewriter a few times, used a rotary phone and filed papers in a drawer here and there. But this cheerful, honest young girl had few skills to bring to the task. She humbly shared that her whole village had taken up a collection, helped her get some clothes and encouraged her to try out for this job. Well before dawn, she had walked paths across the rice paddies for hours to reach the bus route, then waited another hour for the first of three buses she would take before reaching the Surabaya terminal. From the terminal, she walked to our offices. This was her first time in such a big city.

Siti was disappointed but not upset when I told her I needed someone with more experience. I asked if she would mind sticking around while I helped her identify her attributes. I wanted to prepare a general CV (curriculum vitae or resume) she could use in her job search. I asked several questions and she told me that she was a good writer in the Indonesian language and basic English. She was top of her class in arithmetic. She was organized, helping the farmers keep track of their income, expenses, supplies, seeds and tools. She took care of what little money her family had at home. She was outgoing, friendly and got along well with everyone in her village. She loved animals, especially dogs. And she was accustomed to working long hours. I took this information and created a brief CV.

When it was time for her to go, I handed her a manilla envelope with a dozen copies of her general CV printed in English on one side, Indonesian on the other. I ensured she had ample money for food and bus fare back to her village. I also sent along an envelope with the rupiah equivalent of $100. She would be able to repay the villagers, help her family and have a bit left for herself.

Later that afternoon, I called Carl at the site and told him about Siti. By the next month, she had been hired to run the camp's new general store. It wasn't a big store, but she kept it clean and stocked with essentials and treats that the men and women working in the region would need. People from all walks of life, from different countries, would stop by just to talk to this perpetually friendly young woman with the crooked smile, wearing her new jeans, Bon Jovi T-shirt and sneakers that fit perfectly.

Whenever I went to the site, I never missed the chance to say hello. And she never missed the chance to point to the two copies of her CV pinned to the plywood wall of her store, one English, one Indonesian. She was happy and proud. So was I.

29

SETTLING IN

SORT OF

More than four years had passed since I first arrived in Indonesia. In Surabaya, I continued to expand my network of local folks and other expats within the sphere of our business. Being in the city provided a unique opportunity to become better acquainted with the region's industries and business potential. I identified and shared information on capable material and service providers in preparation to support current and future projects in the country's eastern regions.

Arlita and I, along with our son Aldin, were still learning our way around town and having fun in the process. Arlita felt at home, fearlessly making her way around Surabaya on her own. We became accustomed to sunnier skies, hotter temperatures, more fierce storms and even more frequent power outages. Aldin liked the prolonged outages because Mom would pack him off to one of the massive, air-conditioned malls where he was certain to get his cheeks tweaked by the local girls

I sensed Arlita was mostly content being a mom, but not always. That volatile unhappiness was always just below the surface. Before long, she began making trips back over to Jakarta once or twice a month. For the most part, I was OK with her and Aldin spending extended time with her family and friends in Jakarta. I was busy with work at the office, driving all over the city and out to the jobsite. I was comforted, knowing they were safe with family.

At the office, I built files on every shipment and every piece of equipment coming into the country. I knew precisely what was being loaded on vessels around the world. I knew when they sailed and when they would reach Surabaya. I tracked each piece, including the intended system, size, weight and importance. I followed the condition, clearance status and other administrative matters. Everything was timed to minimize handling while supporting the installation schedule.

When I first arrived in Surabaya, three weeks were required to unload our equipment, inspect it, process letters of credit and clear customs. This was normal for other importers also. There were few justifiable delays or incumbrances. But justifiable or not, delays often occurred at every level of Indonesian business. I wasn't upset by it. By now, I was prepared—I expected it. Whenever delays occurred, it was important to identify the reason and the agency or the person in a position to resolve it. This is where those relationships became essential. I kept files on what it might take to encourage those individuals to act. These incentives were always friendly, respectful and didn't cost me much. At my level, they understood I was not a high-roller. Neither were they.

These people in key positions and I sometimes shared lunch. We knew the names of each other's wives, kids and favorite restaurants. I discreetly and proactively applied *preventive maintenance* to head off delays. The occasional beer, movie tickets, perhaps a family voucher to one of the five-star hotel buffets helped keep delays to a minimum. The authorities and I treated one another as friends rather than adversaries. I followed the old saying, *you can catch more flies with honey than with vinegar*. All across the country, Indonesians subscribed to that same philosophy. Occasionally, a wife might send a special lunch or treat to my office. If a friend needed something, it felt good to help. These folks were professionals. They were not greedy, but they earned a tenth of what we expats earned. And even then, a portion of that tenth had to be pushed up to their boss. Understanding their plight was important. Our partners, site management and Missouri team understood what I had to do to keep the equipment moving. They all had my back.

In early May, I was still looking for an assistant. Meanwhile, our host's secretary was fielding my calls. One afternoon, I went upstairs to the eighth floor where IndoVision Cable had their regional office. I wanted to subscribe so that I could get better internet and TV options at home. The young woman assisting me was Annisa. She was 21, clearly tech-savvy and convincingly knowledgeable. She was dressed in sharp business slacks, a white shirt and a blue jacket. She wore a headset and seemed to be voicing acknowledgements to others while seamlessly attending to me. She was clearly in charge. She quickly brought up my records from Jakarta and my new Surabaya location on a large-screen computer that faced me. She identified their nearest connection points. My house was not on their main route, but she was confident they could install cable along the entire road and activate service within three days. That sounded overly optimistic to me.

She ordered the cable service and finished the documentation while I made small talk. I casually mentioned I was looking for an assistant to work in my fourth-floor office and would appreciate any referrals. She was focused on what she was doing and didn't seem to hear me. I was in and out of their office within 20 minutes. Two days later my internet and cable were fully operational.

On the third day, our host secretary told me I had a visitor. It was Annisa from IndoVision, upstairs. I invited her in and offered her a seat.

"Just checking that your service is OK, Mr. Tollison."

"Yes, it is. And that was fast. Thank you."

"Would it be acceptable if I applied for the assistant's position?" she asked while passing her CV across my desk.

I promptly agreed to talk with her. Annisa went by the nickname, Nisa. She lived with her family in Surabaya, not far from our office. Her father was a prominent doctor and she had been educated in English from an early age. She had graduated from high school, business and technical school. She was up to speed on computers, networking, proprietary programs and most commercial business applications. Technologically, she was over-qualified.

I was concerned about taking her away from a stable, long-term job. "This job will end in two or so years," I explained.

Nisa assured me that was not a concern. "I like my associates at IndoVision but I'm interested in opportunities that have a more international feel." She went on to explain that IndoVision and other tech start-ups were actually not that stable and as the technology advanced, they were prone to hiring one day and firing the next. "And," she added with a smile, "This job pays more than twice what I'm making now."

I took time to explain our projects, our partners and our team back in the States. I went over my role, her role and some of the many people she would be interfacing with. She asked good questions. I showed her the electronic file systems I had put into place. They were primitive compared to her capabilities. She understood the tasks and respectfully assured me that if she saw a better way of doing something, she'd bring it to my attention. I quickly realized she was also subtle and diplomatic.

Nisa gave her two-week's notice at IndoVision. At each day's end, she would come by my office for an hour to learn what we were doing. When it was time for her to start, she hit the ground running. Before long, she was coordinating with new counterparts across Indonesia, the jobsite and in the U.S. Nisa helped build rapport and earned the respect of everyone with whom she interacted. Within six weeks, our customs clearance and processing time improved from three weeks to one.

~ ~ ~

Each week the city showed more evidence of increasing tensions. A couple of times, I walked through platoons of troops with machine guns just to get to one of the local food courts.

Across the country, national legislative elections were taking place on May 29. Leading up to that, May 23 was the last legal day for political campaign rallies, which resembled controlled riots. For safety concerns, each rally was held on a different day. Although the government allowed each of the three sanctioned parties to hold these day-long events, the president's party, *GOLKAR* was as always, the shoe-in. *GOLKAR* and *Partai Buruh* had already held their rallies and now it was *Partai Persaturan Pembangunan* (PPP's) turn and in Surabaya, rally they did! Since they were the last of the three parties to rally, they naturally tried to outdo the other two. Everyone, every vehicle, every flag was decorated in green.

Early Friday morning on May 23, tens of thousands gathered at a large open area where they were worked up by fiery speeches. After their rally, they would inch across the city in wide, three-mile-long parades of green humanity so thick we could barely see the thousands of vehicles carrying them. Trucks, buses, cars, mopeds, bicycles and thousands of noisy 125cc motorcycles squeezed through the streets, each carrying as many passengers as could possibly pile onto them. Every other vehicle held someone with a bullhorn, screaming out their party's slogans. Neither party would speak on platform issues or what they wanted to accomplish for the country. They were mostly voicing nationalistic pride and high decibel noise.

The banks and businesses had rolled down their metal doors by 10:00 a.m. At first, I thought they might be overreacting but soon enough, I understood. The U.S. Embassy issued a precaution that by noon, the day would become especially risky. Nonetheless, I figured I could go out ahead of the march, grab some lunch and make it back to the office before they started down the streets.

On my way out, I phoned for a DHL envelope pick-up and the guy said, "Yeah, right."

I had just finished lunch and was driving back to my nearby office when the street turned green in an instant. I had miscalculated. Immediately after the noon mosque, the parades and rallies quickly spilled into the streets across the nervous city. Thousands of PPP revelers carrying green banners, flags and sticks seemed to appear out of nowhere on hundreds of motorcycles, trucks and practically anything that rolled. I had no choice but to slowly drive along with them as they quickly surrounded my Katana. Like it or not, I reluctantly became part of their parade.

They slapped the sides and windows of my vehicle as we crept up the main street. At the reveler's angry insistence, I exaggerated a big smile, repeatedly blew the Katana's tinny-sounding horn and waved an arm and extended index finger out the window. They saw my enthusiasm, my white face and suddenly, we were best friends. That bit of recognition allowed me to keep that one arm out the window and beg my way to an eventual exit. I snaked the (luckily-green) Katana through the mob, into an alley and back to the office before traffic stopped completely. If I hadn't made it to that exit, I would have been stuck there among them way into the night.

From my office on the fourth floor, I could see an estimated 3,000 participants, troops and local spectators in this one-block area that used to be a street. Outside my limited field of vision, it went on for miles in both directions. All afternoon, they choked off several roads including the main thoroughfare, Jl. Basuki Rakhmat. Even from four floors above, the crowd was exceedingly loud. Our spotters sent word that all major roads were cut off and that similar conditions existed east and west, all the way past East Java.

I saw four people fall off trucks and motorcycles. They all got up under their own power and limped away. There were ambulances inching their way along the sidewalks, likely with revelers injured by their own recklessness. Partiers were on top and hanging off the ambulances. From my vantage point I didn't see any violence, just reckless rowdies by the thousands.

At mid-afternoon I was on the phone with the owner of a local business located near the train station. A riot was breaking out. I could hear banging as people tried to break through his metal roll-up door. "I've got to go," he shouted before running out the back!

Via the internet, our contacts reported unconfirmed riots throughout the city and in Jakarta. By late afternoon, local TV reported sporadic violence in other cities but nothing too severe.

As darkness approached, truckloads of armed troops, water cannons, light armored vehicles and fire trucks passed by with lights and sirens. Tenants in my office building were advised to sit tight until at least 7:00 p.m. There was no argument from me. A little after 7:00 p.m. the melee seemed to be settling down. I could even hear a familiar Wall's Ice Cream vendor among the sirens.

From out at the jobsite, Crenshaw sent word he was taking his Indonesian staff to the man-camp compound until he was sure it was safe for them to travel to their homes in Kraksaan and Probolingo later that night.

When the dust settled after the election on May 29, once again President Suharto's *Golkar Party* had won. No one was surprised. The party's crooked, one-sided elections had dominated for 32 years.

Average Indonesians were disappointed, seeing no real change, just a recycling of chaos causing them to become more impatient week by week. Neither the country nor the world had any idea what was going to happen in less than two months.

I had been in Surabaya around three months and was really enjoying the city and my work. It seemed that each day held a different challenge, something to hold my interest and make me think.

In the weeks that followed, Crenshaw had his hands full trying to keep the site work on schedule while expanding the man-camp to accommodate more engineers and technicians. The site schedule was the more critical of those two tasks. That schedule was overly optimistic, therefore demanding, as they were not yet fully staffed. Carl and the few other guys there found themselves dividing their time between the two tasks, robbing Peter to pay Paul. More staff would arrive in the coming weeks, including a new construction manager. But right then, the guys were struggling.

With government tensions increasing by the day, the airport at Surabaya had become more difficult to navigate. Trigger-happy troops checked documents and searched travelers inside the terminal. Troops manned numerous checkpoints along the road leading to the airport. They randomly pulled vehicles over, coming and going. They searched passengers, drivers and vehicles, rifling through luggage and confiscating whatever they chose.

Whenever new staff members flew in, Crenshaw would notify me. If I was available, I'd drive out to meet them at their arrival gate and guide them through the maze. I had done this many times and knew my way around the airport. I had made friends with a few of the airport custom's guys and operation's personnel. My dad used to say, "You can't have too many friends."

Most times things went smoothly with new arrivals. Other times? Well, it didn't. Now that expats were flying around the world with powerful laptops, hard drives, miniature data storage cards and other electronic devices, the poorly trained airport customs people were overwhelmed. They weren't always sure what they were looking at, but they were certain it was important to the arriving passengers and that alone presented opportunities to score some cash.

Each time I went to pick someone up from the airport, I carried lots of rupiah. Airport customs had a habit of confiscating travelers' medications, eyeglasses, 2-way radios, computer equipment, cameras, machine parts and things I didn't even recognize. When that happened, I would meet with agents behind closed doors and discreetly negotiate the release of those items. All it took was my awesome personality—and some cash.

At times, I'd take heat from our own expats for caving to these airport customs shakedowns. But standing on American values, ethics and righteousness could result in never seeing their belongings again. More than once, I had to tell our own people to "Shut up."

Depending on the time of day, I'd connect the arriving member with a ride to the jobsite or an overnight stay at one of the hotels where I had negotiated discount rates for our people.

~ ~ ~

At home, there was a different kind of tension. There were periods when Arlita and I enjoyed wonderful times that brought weeks of joy. But in an instant, her mood could shift from content to condescending and angry. Arlita was clearly unhappy and it was not getting better. I asked for an explanation but she still wouldn't talk about it.

One afternoon, she suddenly raged at Winarto and Minarti because their child had played with one of Aldin's toys. She was vicious and humiliated them. I had to step in to get her to back off. Winarto and Minarti retreated to their quarters. Sometime during the night, they quietly left, walking into the heavy rain with their belongings and their young child. They didn't even collect their wages.

I never heard from Winarto and Minarti again. I tried, but couldn't find them. These kind, wonderful people had taken care of me for three years and this one, unnecessary display of rage and superiority had destroyed that forever. It broke my heart.

With work being my primary focus and with Arlita going back and forth to Jakarta, it took nearly three weeks to find, hire and train a new housekeeper. But I had learned the hard way, it's essential to have one. *A'an*, (ah-ahn) was clearly a village woman and spoke zero English. She did her best to stay out of view. I gave her a set of basic instructions and unless I needed to talk to her, I wouldn't even see her. She wasn't nearly as efficient or effective as Winarto and Minarti. I had to show her how to clean the dishes and counters. The pleasantness was gone. But I wasn't going to say another word about it. Bringing it up would set Arlita off and our little family simply didn't need that.

By mid-June 1997, the airways were inundated with news of the coming Hong Kong handover to China. CNN-Philippines carried segments of the planning and festivities being prepared along with China's countdown clock in the lower corner of the screen. Pundits across the world argued back and forth, endlessly debating whether China would abide by its promises to allow autonomy. *How will this handover affect the rest of Asia?* I wondered. A lot of the world believed it would be seamless, as if nothing happened—perhaps even forgotten after a week or so. Thinking in practical terms, something within me knew better.

Just after midnight on July 1, 1997, I, along with the world, watched on TV as the British yacht, HMY Britannia ceremoniously sailed away from Hong Kong toward what would be her final voyage. The next day Thailand's entire financial system collapsed and the country suffered a colossal currency devaluation.

Economists were quick to put distance between the two events. They went on to create reports detailing the instability of the Thai Bhat, saying that the collapse would have occurred anyway. I don't argue that point. But at the time, Hong Kong was the financial and banking capital for all of Asia. That's where the biggest deals were made: the solid and the shaky, the honest and the crooked. All of Asia's financial roads led to Hong Kong. To my reasoning, the slightest shiver in Hong Kong's financial system would send shock waves down those roads to neighboring countries. With China now in charge, that shiver was more like an earthquake.

Again, it was said the two events had nothing to do with one another but then and now, it didn't seem totally coincidental. I believe that perhaps inadvertently, the handover provided a catalyst—a trigger that set off an already-ticking bomb. Catastrophe loomed all across Southeast Asia as currency values tumbled. People were losing their money and were helpless to stop it.

Within days, the economic crisis spread to other Asian countries. Indonesia was hit fast and hard. The country was already struggling with crooked politics, high inflation, a teetering rupiah, an angry populace and a jittery military. *Now this? What more could possibly go wrong?*

In mid-July, I accepted a second position as a voluntary warden, this time to the U.S. Consulate at Surabaya. John Bernlohr was the consul general. Gradually, I became familiar with the staff there and exchanged mutually useful communications.

In late August, I had meetings with the consortium in Jakarta. I arranged for Arlita and Aldin to stay at the hotel while she spent time with her friends and family. On Sunday morning, we turned on the TV to the news that Princess Diana had died in a car accident while visiting friends in France. This tragic event filled the media for months to come.

In September 1997, I again took the family to Jakarta. All around the city, the effects of the Asian economic crisis were painfully visible. Throughout Jakarta, the extensive construction boom had completely halted. Hundreds of large buildings, malls and high-rises that had been under construction stood shuttered and abandoned. The tall construction cranes were disassembled and hauled away. Ghostly sheets of white plastic slowly waved from unfinished high-rises like a distraught widow bidding farewell to her lost love. At street level, many businesses were long boarded up while others struggled to sell products that were three times the price of last month.

~ ~ ~

October saw massive, mostly peaceful gatherings across Indonesia, but violence began to erupt. The Islamic leadership, including the nation's young people, tried to unite the population and stop the violence. They gathered by the hundreds of thousands in white robes and head coverings. Even the military tied white linen ribbons on the barrels of their rifles.

In late November, we took the rest of my accrued vacation time for a short trip to Thailand. My U.S. dollars went a long way there. Most of our time was spent in the Phi Phi Islands, relaxing, hopping from boat to boat with Aldin on my shoulders. Arlita surprised me when she wanted to try bungee jumping. Phi Phi had an exceptionally high platform over water. I didn't think she'd go through with it, but she did.

Back in Surabaya, the nation was preparing for Christmas and a rare second Ramadan of the year. With the annual chaos of multiple holidays and continuing tensions across the country, it would be January before the city returned to anything resembling normal.

~ ~ ~

Out at the East Java site, progress was lagging behind the projected schedule. A couple of manufacturers in the U.S. had missed their deadlines, resulting in equipment shortages at the site. Ships carrying that equipment were now on the ocean but they were two weeks away from landing at Surabaya. The site was also hit by shortages of manpower and qualified supervision.

30

A NATION ON EDGE

EVERYBODY LOOK WHAT'S GOING DOWN

round 4:00 p.m. on the afternoon of January 8, 1998, I received an email from the U.S. Consulate advising that chaotic, panic buying was taking place all across Indonesia. This was the result of that day's currency slide from Rp.3800 = 1 USD, all the way down to Rp.10,500 = 1 USD.

The message warned, "Due to the possibility of increased tension and criminal activity arising from today's economic uncertainty, American citizens may wish to exercise prudence, common sense and avoid demonstrations and other situations that could rapidly turn violent."

It was undeniable: Indonesia's currency was indeed in a freefall. As civil and political unrest increased, the population started to panic. People understood what devaluation of the rupiah would do to the price of everything.

Sporadic power outages occurred all across the region and this time, it wasn't only because of storms. After I heard from the U.S. Consulate, I was out until 10:30 p.m., scouting food markets around the city and looking for baby food. At the Makro store (a large, retail facility slightly akin to a Costco) vehicles in rows two and three wide lined up for a good half mile, just to turn into the feeder road leading to the store. I couldn't get near the place. One of the other drivers told me "There are thousands of people inside and thousands more who want to be!" Police in riot gear were deployed to keep other roads in the immediate area open. Indonesian marines with machine guns and tactical vehicles guarded the road to the nearby airport. At any moment, any misunderstanding, any wrong turn could spark a shooting— which in Indonesia, usually sparked another.

Amid fears that it was about to be looted, the local market near our house closed earlier that afternoon. A crew of private, make-shift security guys with ball bats guarded it that night. Many areas of the city were totally dark. Other areas I drove through had nothing more than battery-powered entrance and exit signs telling me there was a building there. In my inadequate headlights, I saw a bunch of police near markets, banks and all over the darkened downtown area.

At one point, I rounded a corner and encountered a military check-point. Waving their flashlights, the soldiers trained their rifles on me, telling me to get out of the vehicle with my hands up. I stood there facing their headlights for what felt like eternity. After an ID check and a half-hearted look inside the Katana, they waived me on. It was quick and easy enough and within minutes, I started to breathe normally again. I was accustomed to being stopped by the police, but this was the first time by the trigger-happy military.

I continued my quest for baby food. The Papaya, Topps and Fair Price markets in my area were similarly crowded. Fair Price and Makro were the only consistent sources for Gerber's. I parked about four blocks away from the usually empty Fair Price market and worked my way inside to see if they had any semblance of baby food. Their shelves had been stripped of non-perishables, including Gerber's and all other brands.

And so it was. By day, I made cargo move to the site. By night, I was a hunter/gatherer. That night, I went home empty handed.

At home, local television continued to broadcast the government's standard message that, "there's nothing to worry about." But Indonesians appeared to be making up their own minds. For months they had been told not to worry, their rupiah was solid. Now this? In a matter of hours, the banks had all closed, the rupiah had lost more than half of its value and no one had access to their money.

CNN International carried financial and political articles relating to that afternoon's events. Rioting, food shortages and deaths were again being reported in Jakarta. Across the country, other large cities were experiencing similar conditions. The news anchors and their guests that evening were especially bold in their reporting of what they referred to as the rapidly deteriorating economic and political conditions in Indonesia. Instead of President Suharto addressing the nation, he seemed to be staying away from the public eye. CNN was left to show video of Indonesian military leaders appealing for calm.

Food shortages became a problem for Indonesians and expats alike. At home, I planned to conserve our food stocks which could stretch for 10 days or so. Meanwhile, our family made use of the regional hotel restaurants a bit more. All the larger hotels had operable generators, gates and robust private security. The five-star Hotel Shangri-La was within walking distance of our home. I knew the management there and considered them an asset. I had developed a winding, one-mile suburban foot trail that kept us off the main road should we ever have to bug-out to get there.

By January 10, the rupiah was still highly unstable, but beginning to regain some of its losses. For the coming weeks it hovered between Rp.6,000 and Rp.8,000 to the dollar.

After the Eid Al-Fitr holidays, Surabaya gradually returned to normal. Many commercial businesses remained closed but smaller retailers were open; their metal roll-up doors propped and ready to be quickly closed if trouble started. Stocks of basic food commodities were still low. Markets remained stripped of the most commonly used staples such as rice, sugar, cooking oil, flour, instant noodles and canned soups. Searching for provisions required driving all over the city at night. There wasn't a lot to choose from but I could still find canned fish, fruits and vegetables. Canned mackerel? Yeah, a last resort. There was plenty of coffee, tea and sugar-laden soft drinks. When available, beer could be used to barter.

The military remained visible in the mornings but by noon, the soldiers usually pulled back from the main streets. They maintained fortified positions at all major intersections and near potential flash points throughout the city. Traffic was pleasantly light, although the environment was still tense and dangerous. I felt more comfortable than at the start of the month, but still apprehensive. I kept one eye on the sky, certain it wasn't over.

At the end of January, the American Embassy sent a bulletin advising expats that the Indonesian government had increased the Fiscal Tax (departure tax) from its current Rp.250,000 per person to Rp.1,000,000 per person: a 400 percent increase. Our company paid or reimbursed our employees for this tax. But expats leaving the country needed to be aware that this increase had taken place and be prepared with additional cash when going to the airport. There were similar increases in the tax for departures by land or sea.

It felt as though every business and government entity was jumping on the inflation bandwagon. Without notice, Indonesian customs increased our equipment clearance fees. There was no room for negotiation. For me, this involved creating dozens of replacement documents with the new fees, getting those independently notarized and into the hands of our banks. The banks then issued the mandatory letters of credit required to post for each of our incoming shipments.

Throughout the month, there were significant disturbances including one that occurred in Pasuruan, about halfway between Surabaya and the

East Java site. The road to the site was cut off for two days. There were fires, rocks thrown through windshields, buildings torched and traffic blocked. About 30 participants were detained but at least no one died. These disturbances resulted from demonstrations against the tremendous price increases. As usual, the ethnic Chinese merchants were unfairly targeted.

Dramatic price increases had heretofore been most obvious in the retail businesses. An example was the Florsheim shoes which I bought six months prior, paying Rp.130,000. For the same shoe, the store now charged Rp.1,100,000, more than an 800 percent increase. Increases like these far exceeded the currency differentials. The proprietor told me he hadn't sold a pair of shoes in a week and may face closing, displacing his employees. The increases were reaching widely into the general population. Not only did the local McDonald's triple their prices, they reduced the size of all their burgers by one-third. Cute little things, but by this time, I was avoiding them altogether.

Indonesia's economic meltdown continued to worsen. Not only had it crippled the finances of people at all levels of society, but also the drastic devaluation of the nation's currency had wrecked our consortium's ability to manage their own finances. Many downstream businesses, agencies and individuals were not being fully funded. Hence, they were reducing staff and slowing down. At any moment, Indonesia's inability to pay its bills could affect the consortium's ability to continue the project.

The economic situation also affected all handling, inspections and custom clearance. Slow-downs were occurring on every incoming shipment. I emailed the management teams on site and back in the States, alerting them to what I was seeing from my vantage point in Surabaya. The crisis had already begun to affect the jobsite, delaying inbound cargo still at sea, unloading at the port and everything else involved with getting equipment out to the field.

We were receiving more than a dozen major ocean shipments per month. There were no alternate ports. Surabaya was it. Ship captains had begun refusing to enter the harbor without written assurances that their vessels could promptly dock, unload and refuel.

During the day, I coordinated alternate financing and guaranteed letters of credit to port officials and customs in order to land and clear our equipment. At night, I coordinated via phone with Phillip Kaisharis, my freight-forwarding counterpart in Texas. Phil and I worked together to reassure and schedule the ocean carriers to keep that side of the work flowing. The responsibilities had become constant. Between tasks, I carved out time to play with Aldin or take the family to dinner, often fielding phone calls while dining. It was tense, at times troubling, but it was also exciting. I felt like I was managing it.

A big part of my job had shifted from logistics and administrative processing to include even more hands-on work. I shuffled tractors, containers and often used my Katana to drive disassembled or smaller parts out to the jobsite. Desperate times called for desperate measures. If no one was paying attention, local bargemen sometimes slipped in a cheaper, dilapidated barge that could sink while transporting our cargo. So I also inspected and approved the large flat barges that transported our heavier equipment to the site via shallow, coastal routes.

The Surabaya harbor had offshore holding areas where ships were assigned to wait at anchor. Most standard cargo ships waited about a half-mile out from the docks. Larger vessels, a bit further. Volatile oil, fertilizer and liquid natural gas ships were spread far apart between three to five miles out. Four small companies provided water taxi services between, to and from those waiting vessels.

The average water taxi was small and filthy, not much more than a wide, long canoe with an outboard motor. Water taxis worked great when the water was calm. On occasion, I took water taxis out into the harbor to inspect our larger cargo for damage before bringing it ashore.

One morning I set out with a backpack containing my cameras and clipboard. The little boat had six other passengers plus the driver. As usual, the men were dressed in oily coveralls that likely never were washed. There were no life preservers. The bottom of the flimsy boat was littered with crunched-up papers, soda cans and other debris that sloshed back and forth in the dark, grungy water around my feet. Along the way, we'd stop to drop off someone or pick up someone else to drop off at another vessel. This was my first experience boarding a ship during rough water.

That day was clear, but the winds were out of the northwest and the water was choppy with rolling swells. At times, we were so deep in a swell that for a moment, I'd lose sight of the shore and other ships. The edge of our taxi was only inches above the water. The driver pushed on like it was a pleasure cruise, picking up new passengers while dropping others off. I searched the silent, weathered faces of the other passengers, looking for any clue that they were worried. If they were, they didn't show it. I'm sure I did.

We were about 40 minutes into this precarious ride as we approached my vessel. It was a large mixed-cargo vessel. I guessed it to be at least 600ft. At this point, it was just the driver, the water taxi and me. As he brought us alongside, the swells were thrashing higher than three feet and the wind was kicking up a lot of spray. Next to us, the ship was slowly rolling back and forth against the winds. Whenever the swells pushed our little boat against the ship's hull, I felt like *Moby Dick* was going to roll us under. The angry sea, the drunken ship, our miniature toy boat—everything was colliding and tossing about in different directions.

The people on deck above knew we were down below but because of the ship's contour, they couldn't see us. My pulse picked up—again.

Our little taxi boat was unstable, moving sporadically and taking on water as it fought each deluge. As the massive ship rolled against the swells, the bottom of the ship's ladder varied from two to six feet above. Trying to stand, balance and grab it could instantly put me overboard. I wasn't the best swimmer, especially under these conditions and saddled with a backpack of gear.

The driver spoke no English. In language that crossed between Javanese and Indonesian, he tried to coach me on making it to the ladder. I struggled intently to understand, following his hand gestures, hoping I was getting the gist of his instructions. I had watched as other passengers made it look easy. *How many times did they have to fall in the water before they learned how to board during rough swells?*

As best I could understand, the driver's plan was to bring our boat within about one foot of the ship, parallel with its hull but not touching. He would use a paddle and the motor to try and hold that position. When the next swell lifted us close enough, he would yell and from a sitting position, I was to launch myself upward in one movement. I was to grab the third rung of the ladder with my hands while planting a foot on the bottom rung. This felt dangerous and I wasn't the least bit confident I could pull it off.

The first two attempts failed miserably. I crashed back into the little boat, minimizing my profile when I landed. I was soaked, filthy and considered telling him, "Just take me back." But on the third attempt, I snagged the ladder as the boat fell away below me—down into the retreating swell.

From the corner of my eye, I could tell the water taxi had pulled away, leaving nothing below me but churning water and a dangerous, rolling hull that could pull me under like a one-winged gnat in a whirlpool. Now, I had to climb 40 feet to that deck while holding onto a wet, slippery ladder with everything I could muster. I was scared and had never been so focused. Every rung, every step, every grip was mentally evaluated before making the next move. *Don't look down! Don't look down,* I told myself until I was firmly on the deck.

My arms and legs trembled when I finally made it. I looked around to see workers performing various tasks, paying no attention whatsoever to this stranger who, by himself, had just crawled onto their ship. For a tiny moment, my brave accomplishment felt second only to Armstrong landing on the moon. To the busy crew, I went unnoticed. *What's wrong with these people?*

Once I was secure, I looked back down that ladder into the chaotic waters below, allowing myself a deep, calming breath. My wrists and fingers were numb and still shaking. Part of me realized just how stupid I had been to do this. Another part was elated that I had met the challenge. A more appropriate word might be, "survived."

I made it through the inspection that day. Riding back to shore on the less-dramatic barge carrying our equipment I realized, *I could have gotten killed out there. And for what?*

From then on, I'd leave the offshore inspections to other professionals. I had plenty to do on dry land and a family to consider.

My little Suzuki Katana was all over Surabaya almost every day. I had frequent meetings with local freight forwarders, inland transportation carriers and other vendors supplying goods and services to the site. We met in offices, customs yards, field staging areas, manufacturing plants and at times, along the side of the road. Nisa took care of the office and stayed in close communication via cell phone.

Nearly every day, the road out to the East Java site was laden with some form of truck or heavy-load vehicle transporting our cargo. Sugianto had spotters all along the route watching for sporadic civil unrest, accidents and other circumstances that could stop their trucks. No truck would head out on the 95-mile journey unless all spotters gave the green light.

Anticipating a government declaration of default any day, the carriers were already beginning to limit the larger loads. They were carefully staging and scheduling deliveries according to their own priorities and not those of our jobsite. The carriers and other suppliers were nervously providing services at net 60, (receiving payment 60 days after delivery). With hundreds of new invoices being generated each month, their concerns were valid. If the government suddenly declared insolvency, they could instantly lose all their earnings for the last 60 days. On top of that, they likely wouldn't be paid for anything currently in transit. So the carrier's plan was to halt deliveries the first time a payment was missed. My goal was to keep the equipment moving, regardless of what it took.

In addition to keeping the carriers rolling, I also had to double down and put even more emphasis toward expediting and encouraging Indonesian customs to continue clearing our cargo. The unrest and political turmoil caused new slowdowns in their work, giving them reason to ask for more favors. I had to find out specifically what else they needed. I learned who was on duty each day and their preferred simple treat. American cigarettes or a six-pack of beer usually did the trick. There were times when someone might need something a bit more specific. If one of their children needed glasses for school, yeah, I'd make it happen. Responding to these additional little favors didn't cost me much and they went a long way toward building win-win relationships.

Sure, it was the twentieth century and people around the world were supposed to do their jobs honestly and above board, but they didn't. At my level, no one was asking me for much. Taking an ethical stand or raising the issue would be disastrous for them, my company and me. So I found ways to work within their systems. I nurtured and grew my Surabaya network. And when it came to keeping critical deliveries moving, I called in favors.

The jobsite notified me if they had a critical need for a particular part. If that did not fit with our carrier's schedule, I might have to provide a case of *Bir Bintang* (a brand of Indonesian beer) or another incentive to get the critical part moved to the front of the yard. Whenever I went to the staging yards, I took a couple dozen donuts. I did not smoke but when I went to customs, I took American cigarettes I had bought from a German expat in my network. The things I did to keep our equipment moving to the jobsite would have gotten me fired back home. Here, I received thanks from the site, the consortium, and our team back in the States.

The eastern, two-lane portion of Indonesian Highway One was a precarious roadway. There were no established shoulders or sidewalks. Under normal conditions, the narrow 95-mile stretch between Surabaya and East Java was congested with overloaded ox-drawn carts, bicycles, motorbikes, buses, pedestrians and farm animals. Even with all this, speeders threaded their way through the maze at more than 70 miles per hour. Accidents were frequent. Fatalities were common.

A regular automobile could make the drive in just over three hours. Pull time for a loaded flatbed or 40-foot trailer was around four. A heavy/wide load with escorts, armed security and facilitators often took 12 hours or more. Risky during the daytime, it became dangerous as night fell.

Flash points for protests and riots could break out anywhere along the route. Most often, they occurred at major intersections in the sizeable towns such as Probolingo or Pasuruan. Rioters planned their activities to shut down traffic everywhere. At times, they dragged people out, then set their vehicles on fire. If any fire departments were in the area, they kept their equipment inside the firehouse until the riot subsided.

By this time, I was making trips out to the East Java site a couple times a week. Sugianto created a rough, hand-drawn map that showed alternate roads, pathways, driveways and alleys that could be used in an emergency to get around a riot. I kept copies in the Katana, the office and at home. I checked with the spotters before traveling in either direction. If there were credible reports of impending trouble, I would stay overnight at the East Java man-camp.

All around Surabaya and the outlying towns, people were desperate. The price of food and food shortages were hitting the poor especially hard. Their despair generated a lot of petty theft, vandalism and break-ins. It was increasingly challenging to keep the equipment flowing, the household running and a young family safe. I often questioned if I was doing the right thing by being there. But with the understanding and support of my company and the U.S. consulate, I continued to feel confident they had my back.

Sometime during the night of February 5, the electricity in my Surabaya community went down. We were without power, water and the much-appreciated air conditioning for more than four days. The problem appeared to be a distribution error by the electric company, who accepted no responsibility for damage. When the problem first occurred, the household voltage spiked to a prolonged 420 volts, (normally 220). By the time I realized something was critically wrong, it was too late for many of my electrical appliances.

When the electricity was finally restored, it became obvious that the high voltage spike had damaged the surge protectors and virtually everything that operates from remote controls. I had to replace the burned-out adapters before determining if the equipment they served was still operable. Equipment affected included cordless phones, answering machine, baby monitor, televisions, radios, water dispenser, air conditioners, florescent lighting ballasts and multiple lamps. Even the toaster was toast. Frozen food loss was minimal, but there went our 10-day safety stock.

One evening, I was by myself at home when I got a call from Sugianto, my logistics counterpart.

"I got something for you from Phillip Kaisharis," he said with an air of secrecy.

"What is it?"

"Don't know, 'Pak. We find out soon."

He picked me up and drove to an off-road, isolated point where local fisherman launched their small, rickety boats. It was a dark, undeveloped area on the south end of the bay. There were no streetlights or signs anywhere in the area.

I could barely tell there was a turn off as Sugianto doused his headlights and inched the vehicle into the bushes. Using only the parking lights, the antiquated Land Rover growled and jerked side to side, navigating the narrow, muddy road and occasional tidal creek. The tight curves were lined with thick, high grasses and briars that brushed the sides of the vehicle making its way toward the water. When we reached the edge, Sugianto backed into the tall grasses and pointed the Rover out toward the dark waters. He flashed his headlights once, then turned everything off.

"What are we waiting on, 'Pak?" I asked. I was a little nervous, hoping we didn't attract the harbor police. We sat there in the dark, looking out toward the main harbor lights a mile or so up the bay.

"Not sure, but we know soon," Sugianto said.

Ten minutes passed before we saw a small boat approaching. We got out and walked to the water's edge to help secure the oars and pull the boat partially onto shore. Not a word was spoken. The lone man in the boat passed us two sealed, unmarked cardboard boxes. Sugianto handed the guy some rupiah. We shoved him off and he rowed back out into the night. Within two minutes of the boat landing, the boxes were in the Rover and we were heading out of there. I still didn't know what we had, but I knew it had bypassed customs.

When we got back to my place we opened the boxes. Turns out, Phillip had sent supplies for Aldin. Inside the boxes were solid and dry baby foods, powdered milk, advanced formula, a blanket and other essentials. We now had enough food to supplement our stock and last Aldin a month or two.

Also inside the box was a note on an index card that read, "Watching the news. Thought you might find a use for this." It was signed, "Birdie." I recognized Phillip's handwriting.

Phillip had apparently called in a favor from one of the sea captains who smuggled the boxes on board in L.A., then crossed the Pacific with them securely stashed in his voyage gear. I didn't know when or how at the time, but somehow Phillip had arranged coordinates for a large, Malaysian-bound cargo ship to stop just outside Indonesian territorial waters. Concurrently, he and Sugianto arranged for this lone man with a flashlight and little fishing boat to rendezvous and pick up the boxes, miles out at sea.

I would never again question Phillip's resources, his influence, his capabilities or for that matter, the size of his heart. Sugianto, as well. This effort took detailed planning from a lot of really busy people—good people who weren't sure everything would go as planned—but they didn't let that stop them. They all understood what they were doing and why. They all signed on to bring food to a little kid on the other side of the planet. They all sent word they would do it again. My kind of people.

31

OF RAGE TO COME

MADMEN AND SPECIALISTS

A new month was upon us, bringing Aldin's first birthday on February 10. His party was attended by Indonesian and expat friends along with their children. Aldin loved his cake. He loved eating it, throwing it, laughing and wearing it. He was a happy boy.

Aldin enjoyed his car seat in the Katana; it was one of his happy places. He always had three or four of his favorite things within reach. He also knew his way around the house. He was rapidly developing. Occasionally, I'd find him in my office chair, exploring the desktop computer for cartoons.

Arlita grew up on the outskirts of a major metropolitan city with two million more people than the City of New York. She was a city girl. I had been to most big cities in the world but was more of a small-town guy. She loved big events, glamour and the excitement big cities offered. I remembered how much Arlita had loved our elaborate three-day wedding. Sadly, she wasn't nearly as into the marriage. As best I could understand, it wasn't anything I did or didn't do. She had moments of joy. We had rare moments of intimacy, but they were not continuous. She was simply not happy. I didn't want to admit this to myself, but for some time I had made excuses for the situation. Perhaps my wife was weary from the stress of a one-year-old, tired from the housework and responsibility. Maybe all these things had come together to rob her of her affection for me. Trying to understand, to identify and repair whatever was wrong was the right thing to do for our marriage. But I found no cause and certainly no solution. I could only make excuses on her behalf.

Arlita had shown no romantic interest in months. Attempts to initiate and nurture intimacy were nearly always rejected, and rudely. If I had been looking at the situation from outer space, I'd clearly see a young woman with an abundance of physical and emotional energy to share with her friends in the city. I'd see that she had a housekeeper who took care of the laundry, cleaning, cooking, the car and even the biggest portion of the grocery shopping. I'd see that her parents and family were eagerly available to care for our son when I was working. I'd see the image of a girl who wanted to be free of serious responsibilities; to pursue leisure, travel and staying away from her husband at every opportunity. That hurt.

Something was wrong and I was trying hard to keep us on track. As our third Valentine's Day approached, I sincerely enjoyed being the romantic and caring husband. That's who I was. I arranged a dinner, flowers, a nice gift and a Valentine's card for a wife who simply tossed it in the junk drawer with last year's unopened card. More hurt. I was disheartened and beginning to function out of responsibility rather than joy.

As my work continued, I sat in on two crucial meetings at the East Java site. One was with our consortium's officials, another with our East Java staff. These were bad-news meetings, the kind no construction manager wants to face—ever. Having struggled to meet milestones since the beginning, the project was officially behind schedule. Reports prepared by the consortium and independently by our own team confirmed that expected quarterly progress had not been met. The site work under our control was off course from the critical path schedule. Describing it as *a big deal* would be a gross understatement. This could quickly turn into a multi-million-dollar liquidated damage claim where one party has not met their commitment to the other.

Building every large energy facility required around 3,500 *critical activities* that had to be performed accurately, in sequence and on time. Any expert in the field of scheduling would have quickly recognized that in East Java's case, hundreds of critical activities were not properly budgeted (time, manpower, financial resources), and would take longer to complete than the schedule showed.

Everyone involved with creating this early schedule knew from the beginning that it was too optimistic. The consortium, financiers and project leadership in the States all knew it was a long shot, doable under ideal conditions, but still a long shot. With all the variables of building such a complex project halfway around the world, a stroke of luck and genius would be required to meet such a risky schedule. Back then, however, all those big players agreed to go forward with this ticking time-bomb, leaving it to the site team to find a way to make it work.

The site team had done the best they could to bring the project this far along, but the best they could hope for was to simply kick the can a little further down the road. At the two-year mark, reality could no longer be denied. The doomed schedule blew up and suddenly our contracting director and the consortium acted surprised and angry.

During the initial planning years before, these participants, including our own contracting director, all knew the schedule was perilous. I guess they forgot because it shouldn't have been a surprise. Back then at the project development levels, they all decided to ignore the risks and move forward.

This matter quickly reached the highest levels of our company, who wasted no time. They promptly fortified the management team in the States. They took steps to ensure any riffs between the entities were identified and addressed; they sent more direct employees and hired more independent contract engineers to support the site. Whatever the site needed to regain schedule, the company approved it.

Our site staff increased working hours and added Sunday as a mandatory workday. Tensions among the staff were stretched to their breaking point but the project could not afford or allow any disruption. This level of professional attention was highly effective, but the overall problem could likely have been completely averted with a quarter of this attention expended a year earlier.

The top tier of our company included white-collar board members, a CEO, president, attorneys, marketing, HR and other high-level executive positions. The second tier consisted of seasoned construction and engineering professionals. They were usually directors and people who knew firsthand how to build from the ground up. They were experienced, they were the teachers, the folks who organized large projects—who presided over the project managers, levels below. Their role was to delegate, direct and monitor rather than supervise the day-to-day management of a project. It was a good structure.

In early March 1998, Norm Dingler arrived from Chicago to personally take charge of all site activities. He had been given the title of Contracting Director. Dingler was a white-collar, suit and tie guy; somewhere between a top and second-tier level. His role was unique in that he was a contracting director and not a full-time, direct employee. He provided services and direction to various companies with business similar to ours. Although he was a contractor, he still commanded a lot of clout and had a tarnished reputation for wielding it. Regardless of that reputation, he was said to be unusually well-connected with executives at the pinnacles of the companies he supported.

Sending a contracting director halfway around the planet to reside and recover an ailing project was previously unheard of. This was a big deal. I knew what Dingler looked like but I had never met him. I knew very little about him, but word around the site was, Dingler was a big fish being sent to a jobsite pond to clean up his own mess.

About a week after his arrival on site, Dingler called me at my Surabaya office. After a quick, gruff introduction, he said, "Crenshaw tells me you're our guy to get things done. I need to get some large photographs professionally framed. Is that something you can handle for me?"

"Yes sir."

"Well, get out here and pick them up and I'll show you what I want done with them. And we ought to see about getting you out here to help me get this thing back on track. I need people that can get things done," he demanded.

I told Dingler that I was up to my ears keeping materials flowing from the ships, through customs and onward to the site.

"Well, you can do that from out here, can't you?"

"No sir," I said. "The consortium is paying for two-thirds of my overall costs. They need me in Surabaya where I can effectively take care of the administration, customs and logistics involved in keeping you supplied with materials."

Certainly, he can see my logic, I thought.

"I need to be in Surabaya nearly every day and the site is 95 miles away." *From the site, it would take me three hours to get to Surabaya*, I thought but didn't say. *Three hours I could be spending on "getting things done".*

My answer seemed to anger Dingler, especially when I mentioned the consortium.

"Well, we'll see about that. Just get out here and see me when you get here."

"I'll see you tomorrow morning," I replied.

Well before dawn the next morning, I left Surabaya to drive to the jobsite. The Katana was weighed down with four large hydraulic cylinders. The site had been waiting on this equipment, but they had just cleared customs the day before. The staff was starting their morning briefing when I arrived. When they dispersed, I introduced myself to Dingler.

"Let's talk in my office," he barked.

We went in and he closed the door. Dingler showed me the eight photos and etchings he wanted framed. He specified in detail the matting, colors and settings he expected. The work included various scenes from downtown Chicago and two 12" x 16" glossies of himself. I took notes. "I'll locate a shop to get them done."

Dingler went on to tell me that he didn't like the arrangement our company had with the consortium regarding my work and where I was based.

"I'm going to do something about that," he said with unnecessary vehemence.

I was quickly developing a sense for this unexpected, volatile personality. I would have to adjust. He clearly wouldn't.

Sure, any perceptive logistics manager could have filled my shoes but someone who knew how to work this particular system actually needed to be in Surabaya doing it. With an out-of-control site schedule, it was no time to be recruiting and training someone else. To demand the role be eliminated would be like shooting himself and the project in the foot. That would have devastated the established supply chain and put the project even further behind.

To me, Dingler was clearly angry about something—something corporate between him and the consortium. Because of my close association with consortium leaders, he seemed to target me with his anger. Somehow, I had to help him understand the importance of the logistics arrangement. But he didn't seem interested in listening. His focus was on something other than the work, perhaps a squabble he had brought with him to the site, a fight he intended to win, even if he had to burn the house down to do it.

I chose my words carefully and respectfully. I did not argue. Again, I explained to Dingler that the consortium was paying two-thirds of my cost in country. The agreement was serving the project well, that it was an essential, effective link keeping the materials flowing, particularly in light of the national chaos. I volunteered to provide him with a detailed scope of my responsibilities and recommended he talk with Carl Crenshaw, and perhaps the site material manager, to get a better feel for the system we had in place. Changing the system at this critical time would cause more harm than good.

Dingler suddenly blew up.

"You don't give me shit and you don't talk back to me. I'm running this goddamned show and you'll do what the fuck I tell you to do. Missouri needs to get somebody out of that lazy-assed Jakarta office to come out here and take care of that goddamned Surabaya shit," he raged.

I smoothly picked up the photo materials. "Understood," I said. "I'll get these taken care of."

Dingler walked me to the door.

Once we entered the crowded hallway, he put his hand on my shoulder and said in a loud, friendly, fatherly manner that others would be sure to hear, "It's great to meet you, Steele. Thanks for doing this and please let me know when they're ready."

"Sure thing, Norm," I said. But I was thinking to myself, *What the fuck just happened?*

Visiting with my counterparts around the field office, I realized just how tense everyone else was. *It's not just me.* There were rumors of infighting between the European partners, the consortium and Dingler. But no one at our field level had a clear picture of what was causing the strain in relations. We would find out that back in the States, Dingler had a reputation for being angry and vindictive regardless of the company he was supporting. Unchecked by company executives, it affected partners and associates alike.

My German associates in Surabaya had been reluctant to escalate the issue within the consortium. They discreetly told me that Dingler's behavior was at the heart of the disputes with the other consortium entities stationed in Germany, Switzerland, the U.S. and here in Indonesia. It had gone on since the initiation of this project.

They shared with me their understanding that my company had told Dingler, "You screwed up the schedule; you get out there and fix it. But instead, he brought all the disputes with him to Indonesia."

The strain created by this powerful lunatic as well as my wife's unhappiness at home was hard to ignore. But as times grew tougher, I understood my responsibility was my family and the assignment. I couldn't drop the ball on either one.

Back in Surabaya, Dingler called my cell every day, asking about the framing. I expedited the shop and got the photos back to him. It wasn't long before he started asking me for confidential, personal favors. Each request started out nice and friendly.

He went on to explain the favor, then came a warning, a demand for loyalty and my silence, "or else."

Over the next couple of months, Dingler had me call in favors from suppliers and contractors to locate and procure his favorite foods. These included wines, American beer, Australian steaks and Kobe beef. The suppliers and contractors also covered his green fees and female caddies at regional golf courses. My contacts told me they were accustomed to this kind of graft, but rarely from Americans.

Three times, Dingler had me arrange complimentary, deluxe rooms with a full weekend buffet at the Hotel Shangri-La in Surabaya. He paid for none of this. He didn't even pay for his framing. That was more than $200 out of my pocket.

Many times, Dingler warned me not to mention his name in relation to any of this. His behavior and demands were crooked, evil and conniving. He reminded me of General Dreedle in the film, *Catch 22*. Sure, company executives needed to know what he was doing, but the cost of reporting it would be my career. Dingler would see to that. He held that kind of power, and not just over me.

Regarding my autonomous role, he was infuriated by the arrangement between our company and other consortium partners. No matter how effective my role was, he attacked it at every opportunity.

All I could do was keep the jobsite advised, try to stay out of his way and figure out how to roll with his punches. Oh, and I did take notes, lots of notes.

With the political issues continuing to deteriorate across Indonesia, our people were becoming increasingly concerned with having so many direct employees in harm's way. In Missouri, a crisis team of specialists was set up to monitor up-to-the-minute status on the ever-changing situation. That team in the States relied on me and other key employees across Indonesia for information. I provided the crisis team with daily bulletins from Southeast Asian reporting agencies, establishing direct communication among the team, the American Embassy in Jakarta and the American Consulate in Surabaya. The team was tasked with preparing complex contingency plans to shut the site down and evacuate our employees if it became necessary. Those plans were tentative and nowhere near complete.

The jobsite and man-camps at East Java were relatively safe. They had their own independent security and because they were in remote areas, they were not an easy target for rioters. By now, there were only five company families remaining in East Java. Additionally, we still had six full-time engineers on single-status. These engineers had been on site for a couple of years. Any new direct employees being sent to the site were short-term, single-status. They agreed to come for assignments of six months or less. The company was quickly shifting to outside contractors who were more mobile and traveled light. More and more, they were relying on specialized agencies to supply those independent, short-term contractors who could be there one day and gone the next.

Being a long-term, direct employee based in Surabaya put me in a different situation than my associates at the site. If I had to leave in a hurry, I was not nearly as mobile. I faced personal matters which the guys on site didn't have to consider. At that time, I had lived in-country well over five years, had an Indonesian wife and an American child.

My long-term plans were to remain in Indonesia and work for other projects after East Java. But with Dingler's attacks, that might not happen. He understood my goal and reveled in holding it over me, constantly reminding me that careerwise, he could send me away tomorrow, and my wife and child would be left behind.

If Dingler fired me, I'd be between that proverbial rock and a hard place. Getting the proper visa for Arlita would become critical. Timing would become a moving target. The visa application would have to be submitted months in advance. Then once it was issued, Arlita would have to move to the U.S. within three months. In addition, our furniture and car would have to be liquidated, which might take a month. Every day, I lived with that hanging over me.

I had always accepted that in Indonesia, one cannot take too much for granted. The country doesn't have the infrastructure, security or safety nets we have in the States. There was no FDIC, no protection for account holders whatsoever. To me, that meant I needed to pay close attention to my finances. Daily planning was crucial. No one wanted to get caught holding too much rupiah because of inflation and daily currency fluctuations. Life here was manageable, but it required much more personal diligence.

As national tensions increased, even the average Indonesians were drawing down on their bank funds. Each week, small and large banks all over the country collapsed. My receiving bank in Indonesia could collapse and close at any moment, so it was not a good idea to keep much cash there. I gradually upped the amount of U.S. *bug-out* cash kept on hand. To operate the household and cover family expenses each week, I transferred additional smaller amounts of U.S. dollars from my bank in the States to my bank in Surabaya. When the transfers arrived, I quickly converted them to rupiah and withdrew the whole amount. In-person dealing with the bank twice every week was inconvenient but necessary.

I was reminded of my priorities when one morning, Arlita called me at the office. Aldin was crying and his face was red. She had given him his first peanut butter sandwich for breakfast, but we had no reason to suspect that he could be allergic. I left the office and drove straight home. What I saw scared me to my core. I couldn't recognize my son; his face and body had rapidly turned red and swollen. He was struggling to breathe and seemed too stunned to cry. I grabbed him and got into the Katana. I don't remember why, but Arlita stayed behind. I remembered there was a Catholic hospital along the route between home and my office, so that was my destination. I was angry with myself for not scoping out emergency medical facilities before.

There was a sign at the hospital pointing to an emergency area and within minutes, we were inside. I told the nurses about the peanut butter sandwich. They examined him and quickly administered a shot of epinephrine. Along with the nurses, I stayed by his side, holding him while calling Arlita. The epinephrine worked immediately. His color started returning and I could feel the tension leaving his body. The staff watched him closely and within the hour, gave him a green light to go home. From then forward, I read all about peanut allergies and carried an EpiPen that travelled everywhere with us.

32

INTENTIONS

A DARKER SIDE OF MYSELF

In April 1998, the year's rainy season had produced more frequent and heavy storms than usual. I had just come from a custom's inspection during one of the many torrential downpours and stopped in the Surabaya office to dry off and catch up with business matters, giving the storm time to subside.

When the afternoon sun appeared, the streets below my office again rang out with sporadic protests. At times, the protestors stopped traffic and yelled slogans through blaring bullhorns. I couldn't understand a thing they said and neither could Nisa, even though she lived there!

For 40 of the last 60 days, Arlita, along with Aldin, had been in Jakarta, 500 miles west. They flew there a lot and stayed at her parents' home in Maura Karang.

Because my wife and son were gone so often, I sometimes stayed over in one of the spare rooms at the man-camp instead of driving back to Surabaya. It wasn't often, but if I worked late, if weather was bad or if there was rioting along my route, it was a safer option.

Most nights when they were away, I stayed by myself at home in Surabaya. Given the social chaos, I would double-check to make sure all the doors were locked and battery-powered security devices were armed. Twice, desperate crooks breached my tall walls, only to be chased away by the motion lights and sirens.

At home in the evenings, if atmospheric conditions were right and the electricity was on, I was able to watch day-old re-broadcasts of the Tonight Show. The monologue usually started with Jay Leno ripping hard into Clinton and Lewinsky. With this new scandal, Jay had enough comedic material to last for years.

I seldom saw my new housekeeper, A'an. She was kind of ghostly, but I knew she was somewhere in the house. It was always clean, my clothes were tended and there was always coffee, toast, papaya and peanut butter waiting each morning.

One afternoon, Nisa told me, "Mr. Steele, you have phone call, but connection not so good."

She transferred the call and out of the blue I heard, "Hi, it's me, Susan."

I was surprised. Nearly three years had passed since I'd last heard from Susan. I'd finished the Susan chapter of my life in Indonesia and never expected to open the book to that page again. Yet here she was, on the other end of the line. She said that in about two weeks, she was going to come through Surabaya to talk with a company about a manufacturing job. I gave her my cell number and told her it would be good to see her; she should call me when she got to town and had a moment. A lot can and usually does change in a couple of weeks, so I didn't expect to hear from her again.

Sure enough, two weeks later, Susan called from a pay phone. "I'm here and finish my interview." Once again, I was surprised to actually hear from her. I still had to finish some business, so I gave her directions to the Surabaya Mall and told her to wait inside the McDonald's for about an hour. Right after we hung up, I received a call from customs that another batch of equipment was ready for sign-off. If I could get that sign-off done today, the four flatbeds of equipment could make it out to the jobsite before the weekend. I decided I could briefly meet Susan but afterwards, would have to come back to wrap things up with customs.

At about 5:00 p.m., I approached the mall and was caught off guard by the armed troops stationed at every entrance. The military had just closed the mall and all fast-food places within a block of either side. Therefore, meeting at McDonald's was out of the question. I had a cell phone but Susan didn't. Nor did she know what I was driving. I started circling the perimeter of the mall and there she was on the opposite side of the street. I pulled in as close as I could, honked once and waved.

We drove around until we found a little refreshment kiosk that was open. We had a soft drink and briefly talked. She told me she didn't hold out much hope for a job after today's interview. In the short time she had been there, more than 30 people came through applying for the one opening. The employer told her to check back in a couple of weeks but their instruction sounded more mechanical than encouraging. She would continue to try elsewhere around the country. Through our brief conversation I learned she had a train ticket back to Bandung early the next morning but she hadn't found a place to stay overnight.

I contacted Nisa, who had just finished work and left the office. Nisa agreed to arrange accommodation for Susan at the Hotel Equator. This would be on my private account. I had placed incoming expats there before and the management knew I was good for the cost. I gave Susan some cash for the taxi and expenses.

"Listen, I have to go back to work, but if you're OK with it, we can have dinner and catch up on everything that's happened over the last few years."

We agreed I would pick her up at 7:00 p.m. I drove back out to the customs yard to finish the sign-offs.

Later, I swung by my house just long enough to shave and shower before heading over to the hotel. Susan was waiting in the lobby. We drove to my favorite, traditional Indonesian restaurant five miles away. Along the drive, those dreaded evening clouds were once more gathering. A light mist fell from the darkening sky around us.

As we pulled into the restaurant parking lot, the rain was coming down hard and it wouldn't stop for hours. The restaurant had an open-air design with a wide, long foyer. The authentic, thatched roof extended far out over the walls, allowing guests to enjoy the rain without getting wet.

Inside the foyer stood a rustic, old upright piano that looked as though it might have fallen off a ship generations ago. It was there just for decoration and clearly never used.

I placed my oversized umbrella against the foyer wall with dozens of others.

Susan joked, "They can talk to each other."

After being seated, we talked about her interview, her other jobs and my family.

"I am very happy for you and your new family," she said. "You deserve to be happy and I wish the best for you."

"After all you've been through, I wish the same for you, Susan."

We talked about the situation at the compound where she was held years before. She repeatedly told me how grateful she and her family were. After the traffickers had taken her to the compound, she realized she had made a mistake, but the perpetrators kept adding debt and would have never let her go.

"Today, I still am free, because you help me," she said. "Since then I only search for jobs in business or manufacturing. If job sounds too good to be true, it is."

Susan described one of the jobs she had taken just over a year before but hadn't held very long. It was at a 24-hour towel factory in Bandung. The Chinese-run company made a variety of high-quality towels for overseas customers, including the U.S. She usually worked 10 hours a day, six days a week. All of the supervisors were Chinese expat men. All of the 70 or so shift workers were young Indonesian women.

What could possibly go wrong with that, I thought.

Susan enjoyed her association with the girls she worked with. But to keep their jobs, the Chinese bosses insisted that after hours and on weekends, select groups of various female employees accompany them to bars and karaoke clubs. Sometimes, the girls might be offered or slipped drugs. A boss often went back to his room accompanied by two or three of the girls, which was not exactly voluntary.

One night, Susan was "asked" to join one of the bosses in his room. After understanding what was expected, she and another girl slipped away from that group, heading out into a dark night and heavy rain. Her coworker shared a small, rented shanty with two other girls next to the Cikapundung River that flows through Bandung. They sheltered in that shanty that night.

Both girls were soaked, but they had a couple of factory-rejected towels to help with the chill. There was only one incandescent light hanging in the middle of the tiny, single room. A mattress lay across two wooden shipping pallets to keep it off the dirt floor. The bedding was still dry, no thanks to the torrential rain and leaking roof. It was a little better than being outside on the streets.

During the night, Susan was looking for a drink of water when she opened the back door of the shanty. In the darkness, she lost her balance, grabbed hold of the doorframe and nearly fell into the swollen river that had silently reached the top of the back steps. She lurched back into the shanty, then stood in the doorway, her heart pounding as she gaped at the gulping water rushing past her feet. Until the rain stopped and morning came, one of them remained on *river watch* while the other tried to sleep. Neither of them ever went back to the factory, not even for their paychecks.

I told Susan I wasn't sure how much longer I would be in Indonesia. I explained that the country's troubles and increasing problems at our jobsite were changing the way we were staffing the work. As our direct employees completed their assignments, independent contractors were replacing them. Given the circumstances across the country, that was the right approach.

"Our company has never, nor will ever abandon a partner," I said. "As long as our partner is able to continue, we will do whatever it takes to complete the job. But I may not be a part of that completion."

I told her I wanted to go to a different country but many of those opportunities that were there just a year ago were drying up as the Asian economic crisis spread across the globe. Susan seemed to understand what I was facing. We had a meaningful conversation and a really enjoyable meal. It was a good reunion.

The relentless, east Java rain continued as we stood to find our way out of the restaurant. Back in the foyer, I dug through the piles of umbrellas while Susan lingered by the old rustic piano. Picking over the cracked, broken keys, she tapped around the distorted keyboard, gradually finding most of the notes to an old tune that sounded something like...*wherever you are, wherever you go...* Nestled under the umbrella, we made our way from the restaurant out to the Katana.

As usual, the storm had knocked out sections of electricity throughout the city, including streetlights. The Katana's basic headlights could only penetrate 50 feet into the deluge. Those beams and the headlights from the few other vehicles we encountered were all we had for navigation. I knew those commercial areas quite well but it was so eerily dark. All the buildings and other landmarks I depended on might as well have been swept away by the current. Relying on the nearly invisible power poles as a guide, I could see just enough to keep the vehicle in what I hoped was the center of the road. I counted six sedans that had stalled out in low areas where the streets had flooded. The Katana had a wee bit more ground clearance, so it could maneuver through the high water and around the stalled vehicles. Still, the dark flooded streets of Surabaya that night were a bit of an adventure.

We finally made our way back to Susan's hotel. What should have been an easy 10-minute drive took 30 minutes of white knuckles. I went to her side of the car and held the umbrella for her as she got out. We huddled close under it, walking through water that was over our shoes as we made our way to her bungalow. With the rain blowing sideways, there was no way to stay completely dry.

Reaching the door, we stood under an elongated crescent canopy that offered a brief shelter from the storm. She unlocked the door as I put the umbrella down to say goodbye.

As natural as any moment can evolve, she reached to offer a thank-you and goodbye hug. She didn't let go, nor did I. The hug became an unintended embrace. The embrace led to an unintended kiss. Reason, right and wrong, lost all value as we held one another, falling into the warm, darkened room.... closing the door behind us.

The bright morning came early as chickens and other free-range critters began their shenanigans in the tall grasses outside the bungalow. We were both still awake, if that's what you could call it. We had been all night. The train to Bandung would leave early so we had to get going.

It was a quiet drive to the station. We were both exhausted and stunned from lack of sleep. Neither knew quite what to say. Susan pushed back tears as she reached across the console, holding my arm as if she were clinging to our night together.

Again, she told me, "I wish the best for you and your family. I will be forever grateful." We both knew it was our last goodbye. Indonesian girls had seen it a million times.

Looking straight ahead, she kept her hand on my arm as we neared the station. She smiled and said, "Our second meeting was much nicer than the first."

I reached across, touching her face.

A moment later, I parked the Katana and we made our way through the military check point, onto the train. I walked her through the narrow isles to her seat, near the front of the last passenger car. Many people were already on board.

We really needed to sit and talk for a moment. But just as she placed her bag in the overhead, the train jerked forward, catching us both by surprise. Any chance of a lingering goodbye instantly vanished as the train quickly accelerated. There was no time for even a word as she stood in the isle, waving while I scrambled for the exit. I bailed off the moving train, running alongside it, nearly tumbling into the dirty, splintered gravel as I watched it rapidly pull away from the station. Then she was gone.

The image of that last moment was haunting: Susan standing in the isle of the train car, surprised, her face with so much to say, both of us robbed of that opportunity by an unforgiving railway schedule.

As I drove to my office, the crooked notes from that old piano bounced around in my head. I felt as though the music was torturing me because of what I allowed to happen last night. I suppose I could have justified the intimacy as unexpected and unintentional; but no, not all of it.

Somewhere last night, something had changed for both of us. We had selfishly taken that one moment for ourselves. Susan was a bright, warm and caring young woman. Neither of us were looking back nor looking for any justification. I knew perfectly well what I was doing. Equally, I understood what I had done.

33

THE VERGE OF COLLAPSE

THE STORM UPON US

Everything you'll read in these next two chapters took place in the 12 extraordinary days beginning May 10 through May 21, 1998.

Fueled by continuing political and financial instability, the nation's troubles hit the proverbial fan at all levels within the Indonesian government and all across the country. Massive protests involving thousands as well as deadly rioting broke out and became an everyday occurrence. In some instances, factions of the disjointed military spilled into the streets and people were killed.

Initially around Surabaya, things didn't seem as dangerous as they did over in Jakarta. The Surabaya airport remained heavily guarded but operating. Marines were still set up along the roads with machine guns mounted behind sandbags. The week before, a mobile demonstration lasting eight hours locked up most of the primary streets, disrupting traffic and commerce throughout the downtown area. The Surabaya disturbances were inconvenient and intimidating but largely non-violent. Conditions were more dangerous in other large cities.

Thankfully, Arlita and Aldin were back in Surabaya with me.

Around the city, there were groups—hundreds of young men and boys—squatting along the roadsides, waiting idly to join whatever melee took place. The military kept a close watch. I called one of my contacts at the U.S. Consulate in Surabaya. I could sense his concern when he confided in me, "We expect a more dangerous demonstration to start after tomorrow's noon prayers."

I remember thinking, *it's going to be a long night.*

Across the country, stability deteriorated by the hour. Throughout these events I continued my work with customs and banks and proceeded to route equipment to the jobsite. I still went to my Surabaya office, but improved my computer, internet and phone capabilities at home.

I was in frequent contact with the consulate. I exchanged daily, sometimes hourly information with two international reporting agencies my company had engaged to help monitor the situation. There were frequent communications with our security liaison and management teams back in Missouri. A cellphone and charger were my constant companions.

From my office and home, we continuously monitored television news from CNN-Philippines, who had reporters and boots on the ground throughout Indonesia. Whenever I was moving around Surabaya or traveling out to the site, I could observe local conditions for myself. I usually managed to stay away from the violence and fortunately, did not witness any deaths. I did see buildings burned, mobs with bonfires at several intersections and retail stores looted. Random roadblocks could pop up anywhere, anytime. If it was a mob-related barricade, I learned how to quickly drive the Katana backwards and get myself away from danger. If it was a military roadblock, I obviously didn't do that. Sugianto's network of spotters helped me navigate my way around trouble spots. If I couldn't get to or from the office by driving, I could walk or more often, catch a ride with an *ojek*, (motorbike taxi).

Looking back, I think being so involved with all the agencies and activities gave me a sort of adrenalin high, perhaps to a point where I sometimes downplayed the danger.

On the afternoon of May 12, snipers deliberately killed four young students at Jakarta's Trisakti University. These innocent children were not directly involved in the protests or rioting, but merely walking near a peaceful sit-in on campus. They were shot in the back of the head from hundreds of yards away, simply easy targets for a military trying to show its force and make a point. Dozens of other students were shot but survived. The attack on the students became known as The Indonesian Tragedy. To me, this brought back painful memories of the Kent State Massacre in Ohio on May 4, 1970. Decades later and worlds apart, these senseless shootings in Jakarta caused even more violent unrest and riots that went on for three days, then simmered, then erupted again. In another incident, 12 people were burned to death when someone set fire to the bar where they had gathered.

Even though President Suharto was away at a conference in Cairo, Indonesians believed his government was behind all of these killings, trying to frighten people into submission and quell the protests. That's what authoritarians do.

These latest events sent shockwaves across an already angry, disappointed nation. The senseless murder of these young university students was the catalyst that fostered unity among the protestors and the average Indonesians. Anger and violence quickly magnified 10-fold, spilling into the streets, cities, towns and villages. The cities most affected were Medan, Jakarta and Surakarta but all across the country, the fight was on.

Indonesia was coming apart. Eye-for-eye riots targeting the Suharto government, his family, his oligarchs and ethnic Indo-Chinese continued all across the country. Reports of beatings, arson, rape and murder were appearing in the media as well as in bulletins issued by the U.S. Embassy in

Jakarta. Events were happening quickly. Dangerous occurrences once measured in days, were now measured in minutes. Events that used to occur in other cities were now happening in my own backyard. I didn't want to but I was becoming numb to all the reports bombarding me.

Overnight, all modes of travel became extremely precarious. The military took control of the major roads and began collecting tolls. Travel by car was especially risky. All across the country, there were makeshift roadblocks with no way around them. Even our spotters found it difficult to keep up with the changing conditions. Four-wheeled and larger vehicles were at times stopped, delayed and in extreme cases, burned: left smoldering in the streets. During this time, if I needed to go to the harbor, staging yards or customs, Sugianto would pick me up on a small motorcycle and we'd make the trip using back streets and alleys.

Most commercial businesses were boarded up. Store shelves had been stripped. The man-camp had enough supplies for a week or two but beyond that, they were not being resupplied. This directly affected expatriates from all countries, including our people. All across Indonesia, foreigners, as well as ethnic Indo-Chinese were fleeing by the thousands. Some were trying to leave via the airport. Others were holed up, trying to ride out the danger in the relative safety of the larger hotels. The hotels could buy some time but were not a long-term solution. For expats, the danger was increasing by the hour.

From the jobsite, Norm Dingler seemed oblivious to the rioting and chaos. He continued his personal vendetta against the consortium and hounding me to relocate to the site. I wasn't the only one who understood the construction delays this would cause at such a critical time. With specific instructions from the Missouri office and consortium, I was doing my best to delay his dangerous demands in order to keep the equipment moving to the site.

Before this week-long turmoil was brought under control, more than 1,000 citizens across Indonesia had been killed. Thousands more were injured. As often happens in Indonesia, hundreds more went missing, never to be accounted for—and it wasn't over.

Following that turbulent week, the fighting slowed in areas where there was concentrated military presence. In other areas around the country, it was still simmering. Our Missouri team closely watched the volatile situation around the clock, engaging with private monitoring services based in Singapore. Like the major news agencies, these services had people on the ground in Indonesia, gathering security information from trusted sources including me. We continued receiving at least three bulletins each day. This provided our company with the most current of frequently changing conditions.

On Thursday May 14, the U.S. Embassy sent out a series of warnings and alerts detailing new lawlessness, sporadic violence and killings again breaking out across the country. Our government advised against further travel to Indonesia and announced that select embassy personnel and families were being evacuated. Shortly thereafter, a subsequent bulletin confirmed the U.S. Department of State had ordered all non-essential government employees to leave Indonesia immediately. That was our trigger. Although we were a private company, our management would not ignore the State Department's directive. I wasn't sure what our company's next step would be or what I should do. The next 58 hours were a blur.

Jakarta, a city of 12 million people, seemed to be suffering most of the wrath. Riots would develop in one area then be put down by the military, only to erupt in another part of the city. The military was struggling to control the violence, focusing on what they considered the most strategic institutions and the important downtown area. Other large swaths of the city were left unprotected and volatile.

On May 15, President Suharto returned from Cairo to a country and its capital in chaos. A rampage of looting, rioting and carnage just the day before had left a portion of the city on fire. Hundreds of charred bodies were pulled from the wreckage of businesses and burned-out shopping malls outside the military's reach.

In the city of Semarang on the north Java coast, demonstrators had taken over the governor's palace. Similar incidents were taking place in other major cities. In Jakarta, thousands—mostly students—converged at the Parliament gates, clamored to be let in and have their demands heard. The outnumbered soldiers gave way and opened the gates, powerless to restrain the flag-waving demonstrators who marched to Speaker Harmoko's office.

President Suharto's initial public reaction was to get tough. His foremost priority was to demonstrate that he was back and in control. He issued stern warnings and alluded to the possibility of invoking emergency powers or imposing martial law. All the while demands for his resignation and political reform grew louder.

Indonesia was dangerously close to martial law. The president made televised attempts to reconcile with the citizens, his entourage and the two differing factions of his military. A split military could easily push the country into civil war. Around the clock, a steady stream of advisors, scholars and military officials held court with him. Journalists and those with knowledge of the events described it as a story of maneuvering, palace intrigue, wheeling and dealing, deceit and betrayal.

I was at home early Friday evening, May 15, when a Missouri office representative called. He told me orders had just come down from the U.S. Embassy in Jakarta that all our expatriate personnel should prepare to evacuate.

"That's all the info I have for now,' he said. "You'll need to coordinate with the embassy."

Within the next 15 minutes, I received my first ever *Warden Activation Request* from the U.S. Surabaya Consulate, asking me to engage and assist with assimilating names of Americans and Canadians needing evacuation. I immediately reached out to our people, making inquiries and notes.

I first called the East Java site and learned that most of the expats were already heading east that night in a caravan of vehicles. They planned to cross the strait by ferry into Bali before morning. That's a five-hour drive just to the strait, but that road was safer than driving west, into Surabaya.

I soon found out we had other American employees as well as Brits and Canadians sheltered in hotels or temporary quarters in the region. I planned to have this information ready for the consulate by morning.

As the night went on, I received fresh reports via email every 30 minutes or so. One report said that access to the national Sukarno-Hatta Airport in Jakarta had been cut off. Expats were urged to stay away from that facility until further notice. Flights out of Jakarta were fully booked but leaving mostly empty because roads leading to the airport were blocked by angry mobs.

For months, Arlita and I had anticipated this might happen and were somewhat prepared. This was the first time I had seen her scared. She and I were both tense. She was focused, making lists and setting priorities. She set out backpacks and luggage that could be easily carried onto a plane. Higher priority items were designated for the backpacks. With my adrenaline peaking, I could feel my pulse rushing through my ears. I knew it was wise to evacuate, but as best I could, wanted to do so in a controlled manner.

Our phones and email were lit up from incoming queries. Arlita and I were both trying to respond to messages from family, friends, the Missouri office and other expatriates. In between, we were making plans for our own safety. She and I were in sync.

Our residential neighborhood was quiet and I didn't sense any immediate danger. We were much safer at home than out on the roads. Even if we wanted to, we couldn't go anywhere for a while. Over the coming hours, we gathered our most important papers, film negatives and essentials for Aldin. Sadly, most of our belongings would be left behind.

Our Plan A was to get to the Surabaya airport and fly to Bali. Bali is a peaceful, Hindu Island and not as prone to the violence that was sweeping the rest of the country. From Bali, we'd decide if we needed to completely leave the country. So far, all reports indicated the Surabaya airport was still operational but overwhelmed. All departing flights were fully booked. I knew if we went there during the night, we would just be caught up in a lawless crowd.

Plan B was to make our way to one of the more secure local hotels. I contacted my friends at the Hotel Shangri-La. They said they were near capacity but they had room for Arlita, the baby and me. They told me to let them know and they would notify security to watch out for us. I was somewhat comforted knowing I had scouted out the secluded footpath that would keep us off the roads if we had to walk the five blocks to the hotel. My years of developing relationships with the Shangri-La staff were paying off at a time when it could possibly be the difference between life and death.

Plan C was simply to lower the lights and hunker down at home until a better option was available.

Other preparations included sending email messages to my family and friends in the U.S. My father-in-law, 'Pak Johnny Hermin, was en route via train from Jakarta. He would babysit our house, vehicle and the company vehicle. I gave my housekeeper, A'an, enough money to pay her salary and the utilities for three months. I advised anyone accessing the premises to be familiar with both of these names. The house phone was operable, but neither my father-in-law nor A'an spoke English.

We were ready to go in one direction or the other at a moment's notice. Meanwhile, I monitored airport status and continued to share situational information with the consulate and our Missouri team.

Around 2:00 a.m., a call came in from Bob Zern, one of our expatriates. He and his family's passports were being processed in Jakarta, so they had no documents to get themselves out of the country. There was no safe way to travel the 500 miles to Jakarta and back and still get to an airport, especially on a weekend. I could hear the fear in his voice as he asked for my help. "Hang on." I said, "I'll pick you up first thing in the morning."

For hours, I continued working on the phone and computer. These devices were our lifeline and would travel with us. Because I was 12 hours ahead of Missouri, most of the communications during my nighttime involved status on who was where, and what were our situations. When I looked at the clock it was 5:00 a.m., Saturday the 16th. I was running out of energy, having worked most of the night.

Outside, the immediate area around our neighborhood remained calm. A dozen or more marines guarded businesses and the main road through the area. They were particularly visible around the larger hotels.

Dawn seemed the safest time to drive, so I left the house and picked up Bob and his infant son, Luke. As the sun came up, we drove four miles on the abandoned roadway toward the U.S. Consulate. Along the way, we saw the remnants of bonfires and hollowed out shops, some still burning. We maneuvered around a Timor automobile dealership where overnight seven or eight new cars had been dragged from the showroom into the street and burned. Timor was a brand of cars owned by President Suharto's family. They were still smoldering in the early, hot morning air. It was far too risky for fire departments to respond to these types of scenes, so they just stayed in the firehouses.

When we arrived at the consulate, their staff had been keeping a vigil. They went to work on Bob's new passports right away. They told us the earliest they could have the passports ready was noon. Bob remained at the consulate while I drove to my office a couple of miles away.

From the office, I was able to let our consortium affiliates know we hoped to evacuate and that the office was reasonably secured. Both of those companies said they were getting out of the city prior to the 20th, but not out of the country.

I called Nisa with instructions for her to manage the office. She had a key and would attempt to monitor our incoming equipment with the local agents during my absence. She would work from her home and if the situation clearly stabilized, might go briefly to the office to exchange electronic data. She and I would remain in contact from wherever I was until we all received further directions.

Before heading back to the consulate, I stashed $400 under a carpet tile at the office and let Nisa know where it was located. I arranged to wire her additional funds if needed to clear equipment through customs.

Back at the consulate, I went over my list of 17 Canadian, U.K. and U.S. expatriates with Consulate General John Bernlohr. I included locations, contact information and what I knew of their plans. I was relieved when he said he might arrange a charter flight, as there were numerous Americans unable to safely travel or make it to local airlines. "I'll contact you if that happens," he said.

I drove Bob and his son back to their place, then headed home to work on my own arrangements. Accommodations in Bali were filling fast and they were naming their prices. I managed to get a reservation at the Grand

Hyatt compound, one of the most secure in the region. It was Saturday afternoon and so far, Surabaya's airport was still open. The earliest I could get standby air tickets was for Monday morning, the 18th. I bought these, hung up the phone and said to Arlita, "It's a long shot."

Saturday evening, our team back in Missouri asked if I was able to stay in the country and monitor conditions at the jobsite. They also wanted me to intercept an important DHL package in route to the site. I told them my first priority was to get my family out. If I could get Arlita and Aldin settled safely and transportation could be safely arranged, I may return to the site. But, first things first. We were being warned that conditions were going to get a lot worse before they got better. President Suharto was planning to deliver a critical address to the nation on May 19-20, four days from now. The government anticipated even stronger potential for widespread unrest.

～　～　～

Early Sunday morning, the 17th, I emailed the final report to the Surabaya Consulate detailing the latest evacuation plans for the 17 expats. Eleven of those would fly out that afternoon on an international SOS charter. The remaining six, including Arlita, Aldin, the Zern family and I would fly to Bali early Monday morning, the 18th. Meanwhile, all we could do was hunker down overnight and hope we could get a taxi the next morning.

The rest of Sunday and into the night was spent monitoring reports, local conditions and exchanging information with a string of concerned contacts. My father-in law had made it to the house and was up to speed on what he needed to do. Lack of sleep made it feel like we were all moving in slow motion.

34

EVACUATION

Luck and The Best Laid Plans

Before dawn Monday morning, I walked to the main road. After several minutes, I was able to flag a taxi. He drove me back to the house where we loaded our essentials, then headed for the Surabaya airport. It was an unsettling feeling, not knowing if the country would survive or if we would ever return to this place that had become my home. It was also unnerving having marines along the route track our vehicle with their weapons. They were on critically high alert and not taking chances.

As the taxi pulled to the curb, I saw the mayhem through the windows of the terminal and was thankful that I knew my way around this airport.

We gathered our gear; two backpacks, two carry-ons and one child, smiling and hi-fiving everyone he met. Long lines started outside and threaded through the barricades and turnstiles inside the terminal. Frantic people were lined up at the local and international desks, trying to book outgoing seats on any incoming planes—planes that may not arrive for hours. People slept on the floors and against the walls. The food kiosks were long sold out, as were soft drinks and bottled water. The restrooms…, let's not go there. Most of these people wanted to get completely out of the country. That worked to our advantage. I managed to get help at a domestic desk from a gate agent who recognized me. She took our standby tickets then went to an office behind the wall. We waited anxiously, hoping for the best. A long ten minutes passed before she returned with our converted boarding passes. For the second time since arriving in Indonesia, I felt as though I had won the lottery! By 8:30 a.m., we were squeezing our way through the mayhem, people waiving papers, some crying, the gauntlet of edgy, armed troops shoving back the distraught crowds. We walked out of the terminal, crossing the hot tarmac, hoping no one would stop us as we made our way toward a small, Merpati prop plane that would take us to Bali.

Just after takeoff, authorities closed the Surabaya airport to domestic air traffic. People were lined up, encircling the building in hopes of an international flight, but we had made it onto one of the last domestic flights.

As we taxied to the runway, I received a message from the consulate that the Jakarta embassy was arranging international charter flights to Jakarta and Surabaya. These would take expatriates and families to Singapore and Bangkok. Other countries were also sending planes. Sadly, two British citizens were killed in Jakarta overnight.

In just over an hour, our little plane was on the ground in Bali. The sun was high in a clear, blue sky. As gentle winds blew in from the south, I could see other volcanic islands in the distance. It was a completely different world. Our relief was overwhelming.

We got to the Bali Hyatt and checked in. This was definitely a luxury five-star place—five outdoor swimming pools and a private beach! If you had to evacuate to some place, this was it. We'd long make jokes about the hardship of being an evacuee in Bali.

I took some time to contact most of the other expats that had made their way to Bali. In all, there were 22 of us including our family members. We were scattered at hotels around the island. I forwarded that information to the Surabaya Consulate and let them know we were OK for the time being.

I felt safer in Bali but there was still a chance that violence could erupt there. During the brutal, Suharto-led massacres of 1965-1966, there was no safe place in the entire country. Back then, Bali saw thousands of deaths so this was neither the time nor place to take security for granted.

~ ~ ~

After some breakfast, I walked to one of the ferry ports and discussed the availability of their boats, if needed. My goal was to buy our small group of expats a little extra insurance—another option to completely leave the country—just in case. After some haggling back and forth, I gave the operator a small retainer and told him he would be paid well if his services were actually used. I left with a promise of passage. How good that promise actually was, I didn't know, but at least we had a back-up plan if all else failed.

Arlita, Aldin and I settled in and planned to get some rest. I opened my email and found the message below from my friend, Phillip, in Texas.

18 May 1998, Monday 8:34am, From: Phillip Kaisharis, Houston:

Steele: Sorry, didn't realize the situation is so tense... Is Bali really safe if things escalate? Understand it is closer. We looked at using one of IMC's vessels which are going by Surabaya to your north as sea lift possibilities for jobsite which has anchorage pick-ups. They have agreed in principle to talk to their vessel masters if situation is critical. Diverting one of these ships would need to be quick with tight coordination as vessel would be bending territorial regulations. Sea Lift 'cargo' would be called specific names to clear immigration regs. I understand you have resources including Embassy. If assistance is required contact me immediately, all hours. Advise number in your party. Stand by to receive secure satphone device, contact info and instructions to operate. Delivery to your hotel there. Have made arrangements with several vessels passing your area from May 20 thru June 15, 1998. If requested, they will hold at sea but will not approach harbor or coastline. You will need nighttime passage from shore to anchorage at no less than 20 miles. Sugianto can assist. Stay prepared for moment's notice. Passage will be small craft, rustic and under local radar, not leaving from dock. Scout out shoreline marsh area with Sugianto or his agent for rendezvous and departure under darkness. If you can get life preservers, do so. We have other connections if needed. Could get risky. If this becomes necessary, use extreme caution. Standing by. If you can't get out, we'll get you.

Phillip's message was reassuring. We were on the same page but I hoped it wouldn't come to any of us actually getting on the water. Getting from the shore, 20 miles out into the Indian Ocean to rendezvous with a cargo ship in the dead of night was a complex and dangerous plan. But Phillip had already surprised me more than once. He had good connections and friends who owned ships. I had every reason to believe that if it became necessary, he was serious and capable of diverting a large, ocean vessel to just outside of Indonesian territorial waters to pick up our people.

If we had to move beyond Bali, a flight to safety would be the best and most likely option. But if flights were cut off and all Hell was coming our way, I felt like we had some possible, albeit risky alternatives. There was comfort in knowing that. After reading Phillip's email, I wrote back:

From: Tollison, W. Steele To: Phillip Kaisharis, Houston:

Thanks, Phillip. Communicated with Sugianto's guy and know where the Surabaya marsh point is. I'm monitoring carefully while laying low at the Bali Grand Hyatt, seemingly secure. Limited number of commercial flights out of Denpasar are available thru Friday. Watching to see if it's safe to return to the projects, or go to next phase of evac. Appreciate your offer of evac. Satphone info and equipment received. How did you do that? A birdie? Please pass along to vessel operators our deep appreciation. Be advised that our evac group has shifted from Surabaya to Bali. Hoping that your/their services will still be available here. If it reaches that point, I have shore-to-sea on retainer as long as my connections hold out—a couple of small 20-pax ferries normally used between islands. $$$ is high, but hey, can't take it with you!

We have names and ID info on approx. 22 employees and dependents here. Some may leave quickly. Wednesday and Thursday are politically pivotal days, Hold your breath! Thanks again, Birdie.

~ ~ ~

After a good nap, Aldin and I went to the hotel's nearly secluded, white sand beach while Arlita chilled in the room. I sat under an umbrella as Aldin raced back and forth between the water and my spot. A beach waiter brought me a cold Beer Bintang and at least for the moment, our little world was at peace.

The next morning, May 19, the public and government expected President Suharto to broach the topic of resignation. Instead, he went before a national television audience and announced a compromise—a gradual *reform-now* plan he thought would end the months of rioting and demonstrations. Under this plan, he would remain in office while setting up a new reform council, eventually holding elections for a new parliament, then stepping down once that parliament chose a new president and vice president. The problem was that this was 1998 and his plan called for those elections to take place in 2002. Indonesians knew it was likely such promised elections would never take place.

The nation saw through this crooked plan and wanted no part of it. Suharto's ministers began handing in their resignations while the riots and killings escalated. The government and the people began calls for the president, his family and oligarchs to surrender their personal wealth to the state. It was estimated to be in the range of $40 billion U.S.

In the past, President Suharto could always count on the support of his loyal, two-tiered armed forces. General Wiranto was Suharto's more powerful, primary military leader who was focused on the good of the country. The other general was Suharto's son-in-law, Lt. General Prabowo Subianto (Prabowo), who was head of the army's strategic command. There were signs that high-ranking military commanders under Prabowo were starting to lean toward President Suharto's *reform-now* camp. Of course they were, they were family. A dangerous division between those two military leaders began taking shape.

Wiranto understood that if President Suharto's plan was adopted, that would leave the future of the nation and his own future in doubt.

Meanwhile, Prabowo, the son-in-law, had already moved thousands of his troops into Jakarta. The stage was being set.

Wiranto met once more with the president, firmly telling him that for the good of the nation, the time had come to step down. President Suharto knew Wiranto was right. Suharto also knew that General Wiranto was more powerful than his son-in-law and a civil war would likely evaporate his vast presidential wealth. If Suharto persisted, many members of the first family would likely be imprisoned, including himself. The world was bracing for a civil war that seemed inevitable, two well-trained armies in theater and only moments away.

But it didn't happen. A bloodless military standoff took place and General Wiranto prevailed. In the end, President Suharto chose to remain head of one of the richest families in the world, letting someone else run the country. Greedy and selfish as this was, Suharto's decision to step down saved countless lives.

With the majority of his support diminished, President Suharto resigned on May 21, 1998. He named his long-time friend and business associate, B.J. Habibie as interim president. The day after Habibie was sworn in, General Wiranto fired his chief military rival, Lt. General Prabowo, consolidating a single hold over the armed forces. Then he sent out soldiers with orders to peacefully remove students and protesters still occupying parliament and other government institutions. Asia's longest serving leader had been toppled and consolidation of a new regime had begun. The nation breathed a huge sigh of relief.

President Habibie himself was surrounded by corruption and nepotism but would ultimately be remembered for stabilizing the nation immediately after President Suharto's resignation.

Indonesia had surprised the world by pulling off a traumatic presidential transition and avoiding a prolonged, violent massacre like the one that took place during their only other transfer of power back in 1966. No one knows for sure how many were killed back then, but global reports say it was as many as a million.

~ ~ ~

After a couple of days in Bali, Aldin got sick and ran a high fever. We flew with him to Singapore for treatment and a couple of days later he was fine.

We returned to Surabaya, picking up where we left off. 'Pak Jonny and A'an had taken good care of the home.

Within 10 days, all of our expatriate employees who wanted to return to Indonesia had done so. A few chose not to return.

~ ~ ~

As June arrived, Indonesia remained a dangerous place. Expats were still under State Department advisories and told to use extreme caution at all times. Political tension, riots and violence still occurred but were far less intense and no longer as widespread. The Indonesian people were beginning to have meaningful communications with their government.

The country was trying to adjust to a new president who, only a couple of weeks ago had no idea he would be holding the office. Within the next three years, there would be two more presidents. The country was wounded and recovery was slow.

The danger to this fragile country would continue well beyond 1998 and years into the future. Along Indonesia's roadways, highwaymen were still randomly stopping people and stealing their belongings and vehicles. Organized gangs robbed trucks carrying essentials. Trucks, especially those carrying rice and other foods, were forced to travel in armed convoys. Home break-ins, looting and other forms of opportunistic crime flourished. This and other debauchery went on for years following Suharto's resignation.

Back at the jobsite, things were also tense. There was confusion and disorder as expats returned to a troubled jobsite. I was up to my eyeballs getting the cargo moving again while the site team struggled to recover the construction schedule.

The psychotic contracting director, Dingler, was still in place. He had returned from the evacuation with a new list of restrictions and mandates he wanted to enforce at the site. These included increased working hours, decreased time away from site including lunch breaks, zero tolerance for his definition of insubordination, limits on alcohol, and a ban on non-employee females in the man-camp. The presence of females in the camp had never caused any of Dingler's problems. He was just looking for any way to exert his power, decreeing there would be no exceptions without his personal approval. He seemed to be looking for a fight. In addition to the professional women working on site, some of the men had families and female partners with them in the camp.

It was obvious this wasn't going to sit well with many of the staff, especially the seasoned construction engineers. They preferred Dingler to mind his own business.

35

ANY REASON TO RAGE

TOXIC FALLOUT

Since its beginning, the man-camp had been a peaceful place. There had never been any trouble in more than two years. But with Dingler's continuing tensions, new restrictions and mandates, all of that was about to change. One Saturday night a bloody altercation broke out between two of the guys at the man-camp.

My role in this hot mess started early Sunday morning when the site administrator called, telling me about the situation.

"One of them is in the hospital. The other is missing and I need your help finding him," he said. "Best I know, he was headed your way toward Surabaya."

"I'll work on it." I began making calls and putting together pieces of the puzzle. At every call I made, Dingler's name came up.

Afterward, another call came in from Tad Pine, one of the international manpower contractors back in the States. It would have been around 8:00 p.m. Saturday night, his time. Pine was a big, heavy man. His grey hair and unkempt salt and pepper beard hid the face of a guy who drank a lot. I knew that directly. I first encountered him when routing equipment to a jobsite in the Philippines years ago. Over the years, I found reasons to personally question his honesty. He had a talent for recruiting and assigning field personnel and after decades on projects around the world, had recently worked himself into a weighty second-tier contractor position. I neither liked nor disliked Pine, but respected the position.

"Steele, what the hell happened out there? Where's our missing guy?"

"I'm working on details," I said. I've been in communication with the site since sunrise, trying to find the guy."

I made sure Pine understood that what I was telling him was what I had been told. It was second-hand and might not be the whole story.

"I've talked to a couple of our crew on site. They tell me that after the event was contained, Dingler went ballistic and started raging at the guy. He fired him; maybe even threw him out of the camp on the spot and told him to get out of the country on his own."

As I talked with Pine, I tried to imagine the missing guy barely able to walk, broken and bleeding.

"Our staff indicated the guy was in pretty bad shape and not fully coherent," I said. "Some locals had helped him stuff his belongings in whatever bags were available and he left. As far as I know, he did not receive any first aid and no one is sure where he went."

"Do you have any idea how all this shit started?" Pine asked.

"Not for sure, but according to the site staff, tensions at the site have been exacerbated by Dingler."

"Well, finding this guy needs to be your priority. Dingler's certainly not helping things, but I can't tell him what to do and I don't want that son of a bitch after me."

After I talked with Pine, another sensitive situation developed for me. Just before noon, Dingler called me at home. He opened the conversation and immediately lit in to me.

"If you lift one fucking finger to help that son of a bitch, I'll have your piece of shit ass. You let somebody else track that fucker down"

I could almost see his face getting red.

"I'm warning you, you'll by God wish you didn't. You don't want to make me any madder than I already am. You ignore instructions from anyone other than me, and report only to me...*or else!*" he yelled.

Dingler's instructions put me in an unusually difficult spot. Pine directed me to help. Dingler warned me not to. I knew his angry instructions were dangerous to both the injured man and the company. Moreover, they were not in accordance with what Pine had asked me to do on behalf of the company.

Regardless of what Dingler said, we had a missing, injured employee in a foreign country who was in need of medical attention. Whatever happened at site, including the fact that Dingler fired the guy, did not relieve the company of some level of responsibility. Pine understood that. The right thing, the legal thing to do was for the company to ensure the guy was OK. I was going to try to do that. Afterward, administrators could proceed with a proper demobilization, ensuring he had what he needed to leave the country in an organized manner.

I emailed Pine, telling him details of Dingler's phone conversation and the conundrum it created for everyone, especially me. "I'm on this now. Unless I hear differently from you, I'm going to try to locate the guy," I said. "Do I have the company's support?"

Pine replied, "Yes, absolutely. Stay on this. Whatever it takes. The lawyers have been alerted and we've got you covered from here," he assured me. "We need you to be our eyes and ears on this and see it through. Your top-down instructions are to find him and see if he needs any help. Keep me posted on what you find and have him contact me if he is able. Don't let Dingler distract you. Just stay out of his way."

Stay out of his way? How was I supposed to do that? None of this made me feel much better. I could only hope that in Missouri, others besides Pine were aware of what I was asked to do. I knew Pine was shady, but Dingler's behavior was psychopathic. It was clear to me that even those in high places were scared of his clout.

On the strength of Pine's assurances, I started contacting my network of friends and hotel managers throughout the region. On Monday morning the 8th, one of those connections located the missing guy at a small hotel in Gresik, just outside of Surabaya. I immediately headed out.

When I got to his room, I could see he was sober, although he didn't sound like it. He was in a lot of pain, slurring his words, complaining of an incredible headache, neck and facial pain. He had been taking OTC pain relievers but they were having little or no effect. His exterior injuries looked like nasty lacerations and scrapes: head, face, arms, elbows, but not deep. He was notably bruised and beaten.

"Damn dude, you look like hell," I told him.

He could barely stand and was nearly incoherent. He was bent over, shaking and holding his head, nearly screaming. I got him out to the Katana and took him to the nearest hospital emergency room, told them what I knew and translated for them. They stabilized him and ran several panels of tests. They suspected tetanus.

When I got a break from translating and filling out forms, I messaged Pine and Dingler, letting them both know the latest information. The guy remained in the hospital, receiving sedatives, pain meds and antibiotics. He was in good hands.

While he received treatment, I went back to his hotel, settled his account and took his belongings to my house.

Overnight, I received an acknowledgement from Pine in Missouri along with a handful of voicemails from Dingler. Arlita had regretfully answered Dingler's first call.

"You tell Steele I said to call me right away," he yelled, obviously enraged. "He's not supposed to be doing anything for anybody except me, do you understand me?" Dingler railed.

She had to cut him off, telling him she would give me the message. We didn't answer his other more-threatening calls that night, letting them go to the answering machine.

The next afternoon, I messaged all concerned parties with an update. The doctors confirmed the guy had Tetanus but was stable.

Later, I messaged Pine again. "Listen, Tad, I really need you to run interference with Dingler, please. He's at it again, angrily threatening me with immediate dismissal and he's made several rude calls to my wife at home. I'm a sitting duck if he decides to fire me. My wife does not have a visa and if I apply now, we're committed to leave the country within three months. Backup requested!"

Dingler had a style of playing the good guy in public as well as in emails directed to company officials. He made himself sound like a wise, compassionate leader whose every intention was in the best interest of the company and our staff. I knew better. He was just the opposite. By Wednesday, he was proving me right.

Early Wednesday morning, Dingler messaged, "Goddammit Steele, I did not hear anything from you yesterday. What the fuck is going on with the hospital? Remember our conversation? Apparently not. You should have done only what I told you to do. This is private. Call me, and don't talk to anybody else!"

He didn't copy anyone but me in *that* message.

I immediately wrote back, politely informing him that I had sent a detailed update to all concerned parties the day before and it should be in his inbox.

Within the hour, Dingler sent the following flowery message to me, making sure to copy Pine and several officials in the Missouri office.

"Let's all thank Steele for his good work involving this matter. But I need him here at the site helping me. We need to get someone from the Jakarta office to coordinate with the consortium and manage all the extracurricular activities such as the embassy, logistics and these things with wayward employees. That work taking care of the injured man has taken a lot of my own time that I need to devote toward construction activities here on the site," he wrote.

Not 15 minutes later, he sent me another message, careful not to copy anyone else.

"Steele, you need to report to the site ASAP after somebody else takes control of the hospital deal. And I will personally handle the goddamned embassy from here on. This shit is above your pay grade and more in my wheelhouse. You do remember our conversation, right? We're going to talk about that when you get here."

I had been pulled into this mess to ensure an injured man received the help he needed. That was the right thing to do for him and for our company. The company confirmed this was my priority. But by following company instructions, I had drawn the wrath of an angry, powerful contractor who privately swore he was going to destroy my reputation, accomplishments and my career, all because I followed company instructions instead of his.

On Sunday morning June 14, Dingler called, saying he needed to see me on site the next morning. I knew it wasn't going to be pleasant, but I headed out before dawn. When I arrived at the jobsite, we went into his office and he closed the door.

He wasted no time tearing into me. "I told you motherfucker. I told you I was going to have your ass if you didn't do exactly what I said. And what the fuck were you doing talking to the goddamned embassy again? I told you I'd handle all that. I'm inches from sending you and your family out of here to find your own goddamned way back to the States."

I was firm but as calm as a Sunday morning sunrise when I explained, "Norm, Tad Pine sent me a directive from the company's upper management to stay on this missing man thing until he was safe."

I could tell he was itching for a reason to escalate, maybe even fire me on the spot. I believe he would have if I had not documented so much of this incident in emails and voice messages left on my answering machine. I bit my tongue. I was not going to raise my voice to this madman.

"I don't give a goddamn what kind of message you got or who the fuck sent it," he raged. "Your fucking career is toast. Everything about you is fucking toast. Now, get the fuck outside and pick up cigarette butts by the front door until I figure out what the fuck I'm going to do with you."

~ ~ ~

The whole site staff was on edge. In the two months leading up to that day, we had witnessed Dingler fire 13 technicians over minor disagreements—valid scheduling points they were trying to get across that he didn't want to hear. We all knew he was vindictive and malicious. He seemed to derive pleasure from humiliating and pushing people around, daring them to speak up so he could *swing his sword.*

Dingler had free rein to wage his own personal war with zero accountability. Apparently, his actions were not challenged by our executives regardless of how badly he abused employees. Although he was a contractor, the company apparently had a lot invested in him and they were not about to let these issues take priority over any of that. I knew Dingler held all the cards and if I didn't handle this right, if I didn't submit, he had the power to wreak havoc on my family. For the time being, there was nothing I could do but keep my head down, keep my mouth shut and pick up cigarette butts while he glared at me from his office window.

~ ~ ~

A week after the injured man was safely back in the States I sent one more message back to Pine, explaining what I was up against: still taking serious abuse from Dingler. Pine's disappointing reply convinced me that in spite of telling me they had my back, there would actually be no further support. Their crisis was over and I was on my own to deal with the toxic fallout it generated.

Pine wrote, "Steele – Do your best to get along with him and stay out of his way. He's got some issues and is under a lot of pressure. We will get someone out there to evaluate the situation and maybe take a load off him. We got your back and he's not going to do you harm there. We want you to stay in place, but do what you have to do with the visa matter. Keep in mind it's not in the best interest of any party to report this any further. I'll take this from here."

At about this time, we confirmed that Arlita was newly pregnant with our second child. This was wonderful news, but with the Asian economic meltdown affecting so many countries, Indonesia's continuing turmoil and a contracting director hell-bent on destroying me, my one-time goal of retiring overseas was no longer practical. I was up for fighting for my own rights and my position in-country, but this new reality told me this would be no way to safely educate and care for two children. I reluctantly began letting go of that dream.

Toward the end of July, I began the initial application for Arlita's U.S. visa.

And by the way, no one ever came out to *evaluate the situation.*

36

LEAVING INDONESIA

THAT REARVIEW MIRROR THING

It was tough for me to accept that our time in Indonesia would end. But it was inevitable and to make the best of it required a smooth transition. Similar to moving here from the Midwest, there were many things to do. The first was to establish a target date. Barring any unpleasant surprises, that would be in five months, near the end of December. The second was to notify the tenants renting my house in the States. They already knew my return was possible, they just didn't know when.

At the end of July, Arlita, Aldin and I drove to Japara to buy Indonesian furniture for my house in Pleasant Valley, Missouri. We bought unique beds, chests, carvings, benches and other décor. I had these purchases packaged and shipped to my home in Surabaya where I kept them in the garage. I would later buy a 20-foot shipping container from Sugianto. It was beat up but still water-tight enough to make the trip to the States. At $400, it was a bargain.

Months later, 'Pak Johnny and I would separate the essentials, then pack the house, loading our belongings and the new furniture into the container. It was a tight fit. I bought $30,000 of insurance from my associates at Alliance Asia, then sealed the container with two padlocks. Sugianto held it for me in his staging yard until I was ready to ship it.

I bought a used Mitsubishi sedan and gave it to Arlita's parents. Though both of them could drive, they had never owned a car and I thought this would help the family in the future.

Our house in Surabaya was under lease through the end of 1998. We maintained the house as a primary residence, keeping our housekeeper on board to keep things clean and safe. Over the coming months, we would gradually move out of the house and turn it back over to the owner.

By late July, I began to comply with Dingler's directive that I relocate and work from the site. He said he wanted me there under his control so I could manage the site's *claims*. But everyone knew this site had no claims to manage. My actual role was the same as before; keep the materials and equipment coming to site on time and keep my head down. Managing the process was no longer as convenient or as efficient, but I would communicate with my associates in Surabaya and we'd quietly get the work done.

At the man-camp, nights were far easier to tolerate than the muggy, 94-degree days we were experiencing. Being outside during the heat of the day felt like standing in front of a blow dryer. During this period of transition, there were no vacant apartments. With Arlita spending most of her time in Jakarta, I would finish my day at the site, then work nights on building out one of the unfinished units at the camp. First priorities were electricity, lighting and air conditioning. That allowed me to sleep there while completing the work.

Over many nights, I installed the kitchen and bath plumbing fixtures, shower, windows, two doors and finished the painting. I added rolled-reed panels to the main room and brought in enough wicker-style furniture and camp bedding to make it homey. As a bonus, there were two productive banana trees just outside the back window. Building this by myself was a bit worrisome at the time, but when I finished, it looked really good. Looking back, I actually enjoyed that little project.

On the last day of July 1998, from Surabaya, Nisa forwarded a letter via one of the drivers, delivered to me at the site. I stepped outside, found a sliver of shade and opened it. It was from Susan. She was pregnant with a son. The dated ultrasound photo was there in the envelope. The timing was spot-on. The child would be born around year's end.

I was utterly stunned. I went through long moments where I hated myself. Here I was the guy who talked a good game about always doing the right thing. Suddenly, I was in a situation of my own making where there seemed to be no right choice. I stepped out into the oppressive heat, out through the dusty laydown yards and walked aimlessly. I was shaken, trying to grasp the implications of Susan's letter. I ran 'how to fix this' scenarios over and over in my head. All the while, I knew there was no fix. This was the lowest point I could imagine. I could not think less of myself. All self-worth had instantly been destroyed when I learned the consequences of my own actions. I needed time to think. But there was no time, no easy outs, no place where this complication would not follow.

After an hour of feeling sorry for myself, I lifted my head and picked up my pace. I had to resuscitate the part of me that knew how to be practical. If I couldn't make this right, then what was the next best thing to do? My thoughts went to those orphaned children with Western faces, hustling for food and shelter along that dusty road to Merak. With that image haunting me, I knew I would not walk away from this child. Regardless of the circumstances, this was a child I helped create and if he was going to live on this planet, he was going to have a father who loved and cared for him, even if I couldn't be there with him. I embraced my commitment to this child. It became my direction—one of my directions.

Within a week, I opened a bank account in Susan's name at a branch in Bandung. I could wire or transfer to that account from anywhere in the world. Over the years, I had stashed idle funds in several Asian accounts including HSBC in Jakarta. I would draw financial assistance for Susan from those dormant accounts.

I arranged funds to meet Susan's and the baby's immediate needs: medical support, food, transportation and a place to live. I set up an email account that we could both access, allowing her to keep me informed. I knew it wasn't everything this child would need but for now, it was all I could do. My *next best thing* gave me no real comfort or forgiveness.

I wrote to Susan, telling her about the provisions I had put in place, asking for forgiveness and letting her know I would not abandon them. We corresponded via email, although not very often.

Until I could think this through and consider all the intricacies and consequences, I would keep this my secret.

~ ~ ~

At the jobsite, the months inched forward. I was carrying nearly three weeks of excess vacation time and would lose it when I transferred back to the States. We decided to spend that vacation time visiting Europe while Arlita was still early in her pregnancy. In the two weeks between September 6 and 20, we traveled to the U.K., France, Italy, Germany, Switzerland, Belgium and the Netherlands.

Traveling around Europe with a toddler and a pregnant wife had its moments, but Arlita was happier whenever we were traveling. In the Netherlands, she sought out many of the authentic Indonesian restaurants. Often, these were owned by descendants from the centuries of Dutch colonial rule over the East Indies.

In the afternoons, ladies of the evening came out onto the sidewalks dressed in almost nothing. They'd set up booming speakers and dance as part of their advertisement. Their risqué solicitations drew quite a crowd. At just over a year and a half old, Aldin joined right in, flashing a big smile and wowing the girls as he bounced along with the beat right there among them.

In Switzerland, we retraced some of the places I had visited before. Aldin enjoyed watching the fish swimming along the bottom of the crystal-clear rivers. I bought three Champ Swiss Army Knives, stashing them away for years later when I'd give them to my children.

When we returned from vacation, we officially lived full-time at the camp apartment. It was pleasant enough, but it was boring for wives stuck there day in and day out. I was still paying the utilities and housekeeping at the Surabaya house, so Arlita took Aldin and unofficially spent time there. For the remaining months, Arlita and Aldin would alternate between the Surabaya house, Jakarta and the man-camp. This was convenient whenever we had pre-natal appointments in Surabaya. I would drive there in the afternoon and the doctor would see us in the evening. Our ultrasound indicated we were having a girl. I was cool with it either way, but having a son and a daughter? Yeah, I suppose that was a little extra cool. As I had done for Aldin, I wrote a little pre-birth song and stashed it away for March.

When Arlita was at the camp, she and I would walk with Aldin to have dinner at the mess hall. The food was usually good, albeit a bit heavy. One evening, we were having dessert when Dingler came by.

He stopped and patted Aldin on the head saying, "You're going to grow up to be a fine man, just like your dad."

I thought I might have to tackle Arlita to keep her from pouncing on him. She had seen Dingler's emails and tolerated his nasty, irate phone calls. She knew he was bullshitting.

"Please don't touch my child," she said firmly.

Surprised, Dingler moved on.

This memory is unique for a couple of reasons. First was the way Arlita shut Dingler down. Second, when we went outside to walk back to our place, I saw Mars for the first time in my 47 years. It was an exceptionally clear night with beautiful stars above, and right there in front of us was the unmistakable orange planet during one of its closest passes to Earth. I've felt more at home with the Cosmos ever since.

One late night at the camp, a strong, offshore earthquake rattled the countryside all around us. The shoreline was less than a quarter mile away. We were less than two feet above sea level. The vibrations went on for a minute or so, breaking a few windows, knocking out the electricity. The night became pitch black except for an occasional flashlight. Residents started vehicles and turned on the headlights. We couldn't run further inland because of the cliffs. We didn't know if it was wise to drive east or west. Either way could lead to even more danger. Instead, we waited there in silence, hoping we were not in the path of a tsunami. Luck was with us.

~ ~ ~

It was mid-November when Norm Dingler abruptly left the site, unexpectedly returning to his home in Chicago. A new general manager, Rick Baylor, was assigned to take his place. Rick was a calm, soft-spoken guy with a strong background in construction and the management of related activities. Our entire staff drew an immediate sigh of relief when he came on board.

I often wondered, *if I had known Dingler was leaving, would I have tried to reverse course and stay in Indonesia?* I did think about it. I had a deep affection for the country and wonderful experiences it had given me. But I was no longer that carefree, single expat with no one but himself to think about. I had become the head of a family that needed roots to flourish. That consideration came first.

As November ended, I wrapped up the last of our things at the Surabaya house. We turned it back over to the owner a month early. I gave Sugianto the green light to ship my container. And that was the last of our logistical preparations.

From Chicago, Dingler still found ways to torment the site staff. He'd send fax messages, reminding me about cigarette butts. I wouldn't respond or play any more of his power games. Other men would get messages that they had been seen having a girl in the camp.

The Friday before I left, Rick Baylor called me into his office. "I haven't been here long enough to understand this thing between Dingler and you, but I can tell you he has it in for you and is doing his best to gain support to have you fired. I don't know what you're going back into, but you seem like a good guy and you should know you're facing something big."

I thanked Rick for letting me know. I had heard rumors about Dingler's efforts back in Missouri but didn't have anything concrete until then. Whatever was coming, I'd have to deal with it back in the States. Our time to leave had come.

On December 19, 1998, Arlita, Aldin and I departed Surabaya in route to an overnight in Singapore. Indonesia was in the rear-view mirror. When we arrived in Singapore, Arlita was unexpectedly hassled by immigrations because she was pregnant. She was clearly showing and authorities were afraid she might be coming there to have the child and gain citizenship. Apparently, that was a problem in Singapore.

We had to show we were in possession of tickets and her visa, onward to the U.S. Although our documents were in order, they didn't want to let go of the issue. For 20 minutes, they kept coming back at us from different angles, trying to find any crack in our story or paperwork. It took quite a while before we convinced them and they backed off. Aldin took it all in stride. At nearly two years old, he was already a seasoned traveler.

The next day was spent getting to and waiting around the Tokyo airport for the next leg of the journey. There were no pregnancy hassles that time, but we weren't going through any immigration checkpoints. By mid-afternoon, we were on board a Northwest Airlines 747 heading to

Minneapolis. The flight was staffed with older, grumpy Americans who didn't seem overly concerned for the comfort of the passengers. I got a sense of how they felt by the way they looked at us. We were just cargo they had to deal with until they reached retirement—they were too short to care. There was nothing enthusiastic about their service or anything pleasant about that flight. They could have taken a lesson from Sing Air.

Into the vast celestial darkness, I carried the weight of my actions on my shoulders. My wife was sleeping beneath a blanket against the window. Aldin slept comfortably in my lap. The drone of the enormous General Electric engines was the only sound. Most passengers had closed their blinds and were sleeping. The crew had dimmed the interior lights and had settled in for the long trans-Pacific journey.

A moment later, I felt a gentle shift in pitch as the big jet tilted slightly to the left and climbed further into the long, dark night. It was then my tears of stress and sadness privately showed themselves. Within me dwelled an accumulation of all events the last six years had given me. With my family sleeping safely beside me, I knew that most of these years had been beautiful, positive experiences to share with the world where we were heading. But much of this weight I would continue to carry inside—no one else would know. It was mine to protect, respect and somehow find a way to reconcile as it would certainly affect me for decades to come.

Arlita's unhappiness was saddening but I was still hopeful for our marriage. I didn't know how I would manage our future, but understood the importance of remaining positive. I had to. And so it was during the calm, quietness of that flight, I wrote the following letter to our child Arlita was carrying.

To My Unborn Child, December 20, 1998

I'm writing to you from a Boeing 747 jet, about 40,000-Ft. somewhere over the Pacific Ocean. It's pretty quiet here on board. The meals have been served and the cabin lights dimmed so the passengers can rest. I can hear the soft hum from the engines and every once in a while, feel a slight shift in the planes position, reminding me that we're flying, and fast!

It's just before Christmas. After six years, my assignment in Indonesia is complete. Your Mom, Brother, You and I are moving from Indonesia to live in America. You're here with us. You just haven't been born yet. That's fine, stay right where you are for the duration of this trip, OK?

The last eight or so months have been especially turbulent times for your family. Indonesia has been in severe economic and political trouble and living there has become increasingly difficult. We've seen times when the stores are stripped of food and drinking water. Going shopping, even to places like McDonald's, requires walking through troops carrying machine guns and barbed wire barricades. And you never know if the crowd blocking the dark, narrow roadway ahead is friendly or will drag us out of the car. It's sad to see this happening to such a warm, gentle country. Most recently, I've been assigned to a project in East Java. It has been plagued with its own politics and mismanaged from on high by people who exemplify the term, Ugly Americans.

Without a doubt, the highlight of this period occurred last July, when we first learned that you were on your way. The joy and wonder of your anticipated arrival have overcome whatever turmoil we've encountered. If all goes according to predictions, we'll be face-to-face with you around 17 March 1999, about three months from now.

I feel it's important to communicate these thoughts to you well before your birthday; before the next stage of your being. Partly, because you're so much on my mind, but also to illustrate something I hope you'll come to understand and always remember. Right now we can't see one another. Yet, we're close here; within inches of one another on this plane. So shall we be close when one day again, we can no longer see one another. I will always be by your side, just as I *am now. And you will always live within me. I hope you'll share this concept with your mother and brother, as I have told them the same thing.*

Your Mom and I grow more and more in love as we share time, life's inevitable struggles and its adventures together. I worry for her as she leaves her home country to follow me in my pursuit of growth and security for our family. She's filled with hope, but will face some major emotional adjustments as she deals with raising two children in a country foreign to her. She'll always need your help and encouragement. Please stay close with your brother, as well. Trust me, he's a great kid and you're going to love him! I hope to provide you all with an environment where you're safe, smart, happy and have the skills to manage the difficulties and rewards of everyday life.

You are a wonderful, welcome addition to our family and we're so happy you decided to join us. My expectations for you are that you grow to be a compassionate, self-reliant and happy person who recognizes the love, strength and security within your family; that you draw on that foundation to someday experience this wonderful feeling of welcoming your own into this world.

Rest now, sleeping there inside your mom. I'll see you in March of next year and we'll have some fun!

Love, Your Dad, Wm. Steele Tollison

Our flight landed in Kansas City the evening of December 20. Regretfully, we soon learned that one of our four oversized, hardshell suitcases carrying cameras and electronics as well as important, undeveloped film and negatives had been stolen. It happened somewhere between the time we put it on the conveyor belt in Minneapolis and the time things were unloaded in Kansas City. The bag was extremely well marked with ID, destination and phone number. The signage and ID information was outside and in three places inside the large, green suitcase. I had photos of all the bags and the big white information tags. There's simply no way this well-marked, well-protected suitcase could have been lost. I was and still am devastated to lose the film and negatives.

Although I had purchased $5,000 insurance on each of the four bags before leaving Asia, Northwest Airlines was determined to pay only $75 in compensation. It would be five months before they were legally forced to honor the policy they themselves had sold me in Tokyo. After this and their snobby treatment during the flight, I would forever avoid Northwest Airlines.

A week after we landed in the States, Alby Reynaldy was born to Susan back in Bandung, Indonesia. Obviously, I wasn't there for his birth on December 28, 1998. I was the only one in the States who knew. Right or wrong, it would remain my secret.

A quick visit to the Missouri office confirmed that the people who had sent me to Indonesia were now retired, moved on or passed away. Few people even knew who I was. But I had been through this kind of thing before. This was something I could actually fix.

~ ~ ~

Between the office and family, there was a flurry of arrangements to coordinate as we prepared to move from a temporary apartment into my house in Pleasant Valley.

One of the first things we did on arrival was to find pre-natal care for Arlita. She was now around seven months. During the first doctor's visit, we provided the medical staff with our documentation while they prepared a baseline ultrasound. In Indonesia, they performed ultrasounds every other time we had an appointment. They cost around five dollars and we must have had four or five before leaving for the States. In the States, ultrasounds were apparently made of gold, as I had to pay $350 before they would start.

We were just minutes into the test when it seemed the staff was getting nervous. They brought in a doctor. Now, I was getting nervous. The doctor examined the equipment and the work done so far, then went in for a closer look at the screens.

A moment later, she turned to me and asked, "Did you say you were expecting a girl?"

"Yeah, a girl. That's what we've been told throughout this adventure," I assured her.

"I think you guys need to take a look at this. You're definitely having a boy."

So here we were, seven months in, finding out we were having another son. No problema! We would easily shift mindsets, go blue and plan for him to arrive in a couple of months. Having a second boy was every bit as cool as having a girl.

Just before midnight on March 7, 1999, Raymond Delano Tollison was born in North Kansas City. I was there and able to help him into the world.

~ ~ ~

And so it was. This unexpected journey along with my time in Indonesia had ended. Fate had given this reluctant traveler enough observations, adventure and experiences to last a lifetime. I would now devote myself to my young family, working to build a happy life for us in the States.

In another way, part of me was still there, disappointed, disillusioned—still searching for a way to correct an unbalanced Cosmos that I had created. I had never given up on things that really matter. I would find a way. ~

EPILOGUE

LOOKING BACK, LOOKING FORWARD

When I returned to the Missouri office in early 1999, Norm Dingler continued his campaign of hate, lobbying for months in his crusade to have me fired. I'll never understand why he focused his rage on me. Ultimately, he failed and from my perspective, faded into the woodwork and happily out of my life.

Over the next couple of years, I made short trips back to Indonesia transporting small, critical components to the jobsites, but I never resided there again. I spent 13 more productive years with my company, nearly 25 in all. I served three different divisions on a wide variety of interesting projects. But none of my work would ever compare to the responsibilities I successfully managed in Indonesia.

The unhappiness that engulfed Arlita shortly after our marriage never subsided. In fact, it grew worse. She was miserable, acknowledging our age difference was a factor. In essence, I was alone in this relationship, nowhere to turn, no comfort to find, and crushing responsibilities I was determined to get right. Family came first.

In the States, Arlita made new, younger friends, pursued higher education and started working outside the home. But she didn't want to be married or held back by the weight of parental responsibilities. She wanted; she needed freedom with no strings. After 10 years of trying to make our marriage work and Arlita asking me for a divorce three times, I filed in

2005, amiably stepping aside so she could pursue the freedom and happiness she wanted and deserved. Raymond and Aldin were six and eight years old at the time and stayed with me. For the next five years, I raised them as a single dad. It was the best gig I've ever had.

Throughout the years, the arrangements I set in place continued to financially support Alby and his mom back in Indonesia. I followed his happiness, health and his education. I had no way of knowing back then, but a month after sending me the letter and ultrasound photo, Susan married a man in their village. I didn't find out she was married until three years later. She kept it secret, writing occasionally that it was just her and Alby. She was doing what she felt was necessary to survive, protecting the lifeline I provided. If I were in her shoes, I'm certain I would have done the same. As more time passed, I learned that Susan had two additional children and had divorced her husband. I was surprised, she was embarrassed but neither of us bore any hard feelings.

In 2007 after much consultation, I started the delicate process of bringing Alby and potentially Susan to America. We were considering making a life together. They were enthusiastic and supportive of the plan, a process that would take more than two years. Alby was eight years old at the time. While this loose plan was developing, I met Chris. Chris was a source of strength while I worked through complex decisions that only I could make relating to Alby and his mother. Chris pulled back for months while I dealt with the 2010 arrival of Susan, Alby and Dias, her youngest son. Susan stayed three months but ultimately decided to return to Indonesia with Dias. Shortly thereafter, she married again, this time to an Australian gentleman.

"Alby is yours to raise and care for now," she said. She knew I would.

I had a lot of explaining to do with my family and friends, but my secret finally saw the light of day and that massive burden was lifted. Going forward, I made sure there would be no shame, no hiding, only transparency and love. Alby would join us as an equal, his father and brothers by his side.

Chris and I reconnected and together with Aldin, Raymond and Alby, we built a strong, happy family. We saw the boys through middle school, high school and on to college. All three went on to thrive. Each had a substantial musical background and many school achievements to their credit. Aldin and Raymond both graduated with honors from the University of Kansas in Lawrence. Alby graduated with honors from Kansas State University in Manhattan. Before their graduations were final, all three had accepted employment with well-respected companies and immediately chose to set out on their own.

By 2020, Chris and I had become empty-nesters, accompanied only by our loyal dogs, Gucci and Prada. Our household is smaller but the rare, special love we've nurtured fills it with an amazing warmth. We cherish our time together, seizing opportunities to explore the world: Bhutan, Thailand, Croatia, Bosnia, France, Ireland, Northern Ireland, Czech Republic, Hawaii, Portugal and even Indonesia.

In the years since we first met, we often gaze into the stunning night sky; in awe at the moon, the planets and the astonishing depth of space. It's those sentimental moments, void of any spoken words when she and I know that for both of us, the Cosmos found its balance. ~

ACKNOWLEDGEMENTS

Sincere thanks to the following folks who contributed their time, advice and professional services.

Sarah Donahoe, Consulting Editor, Author and Columnist

Jackie Macgirvin/Maresco, Consulting Editor and Author
   ChristianBookDoctor.com

Lauren Miller, Consultant

Emily Lam, Cover Design and Layout
   hlam93@gmail.com

Gary Tindale, Nature Photographer,
   Christmas Island Photos